Dennis Sheppard
Christopher Miller
AJ Liptak

Sams **Teach Yourself**

AngularJS for .NET Developers

in **24 Hours**

 800 East 96th Street, Indianapolis, Indiana, 46240 USA

Sams Teach Yourself AngularJS for .NET Developers in 24 Hours

ISBN-13: 978-0-672-33757-4

ISBN-10: 0-672-33757-6

Library of Congress Control Number: 2015910923

Printed in the United States of America

First Printing October 2015

Trademarks

All terms mentioned in this book that are known to be trademarks or service marks have been appropriately capitalized. Sams Publishing cannot attest to the accuracy of this information. Use of a term in this book should not be regarded as affecting the validity of any trademark or service mark.

Warning and Disclaimer

Every effort has been made to make this book as complete and as accurate as possible, but no warranty or fitness is implied. The information provided is on an "as is" basis. The author(s) and the publisher shall have neither liability nor responsibility to any person or entity with respect to any loss or damages arising from the information contained in this book or from the use of the CD or programs accompanying it.

Special Sales

For information about buying this title in bulk quantities, or for special sales opportunities (which may include electronic versions; custom cover designs; and content particular to your business, training goals, marketing focus, or branding interests), please contact our corporate sales department at corpsales@pearsoned.com or (800) 382-3419.

For government sales inquiries, please contact governmentsales@pearsoned.com.

For questions about sales outside the U.S., please contact international@pearsoned.com.

Editor-in-Chief
Greg Wiegand

Acquisitions Editor
Joan Murray

Development Editor
Keith Cline

Managing Editor
Sandra Schroeder

Project Editor
Seth Kerney

Copy Editor
Keith Cline

Indexer
Ken Johnson

Proofreader
Chuck Hutchinson

Technical Editor
Jesse Smith

Publishing Coordinator
Cindy Teeters

Book Designer
Mark Shirar

Compositor
codeMantra

Contents at a Glance

Table of Contents

About the Authors

Dennis Sheppard began his development career more than 20 years ago on an Apple IIe writing BASIC programs that printed "Hello!" an infinite number of times. It wasn't quite love at first sight, but it was close enough. Several years later, after graduating from Louisiana Tech University with a computer science degree, Dennis got all professional with front-end development using ExtJS and .NET. Since then, he's worked with a plethora of technologies, including a handful of JavaScript frameworks. He's quite smitten with AngularJS and the roller coaster ride that is being a front-end developer. Dennis is a Microsoft Certified Solutions Developer and has delivered enterprise solutions for the private equity, insurance, healthcare, education, and distribution industries. Dennis is now the Front-End Architect at NextTier Education in Chicago, and lives in the suburbs with his wife, two kiddos, and a golden retriever.

Christopher Miller is an Architect in West Monroe Partners' Technology practice. He received a B.S. with Highest Distinction in computer and information technology from Purdue University and started full-time at West Monroe Partners shortly thereafter. Beginning his career in the private equity space, he helped transform his client's aging applications into modern web applications with the help of newer UI technologies such as HTML5 and jQuery.

He has moved on from investment management applications and is currently working on a Software-as-a-Service solution in the renewable energy space at West Monroe Partners. A Microsoft Certified Solutions Developer in Web Applications, his interests include multi-tenancy, RESTful API development, message-based architecture, Microsoft Azure, and of course, AngularJS and other front-end web technologies. Chris lives with his new wife, Hatlyn, in Chicago's West Loop neighborhood.

AJ Liptak is a Senior Consultant at West Monroe Partners in the Technology practice, focusing on modern web applications. After earning his degree in computer information systems from Bradley University, he started at West Monroe Partners working in the banking, private equity, and distribution industries. He is a Microsoft Certified Solutions Developer and has recently provided transformative solutions for the telecom and healthcare industries. AJ lives in Chicago's West Loop neighborhood, where he spends most of his free time riding his bike, trying new restaurants, and exploring cutting-edge technology.

Dedications

*For my family, who inspires me to do crazy
things like writing a book. –DS*

*To my new wife, Hatlyn, for putting up with me writing
this book while planning our wedding. –CM*

*To my mom and dad for teaching me that hard work and
perseverance are the keys to success. –AL*

Acknowledgments

I'd like to thank my co-authors for helping me do something I never could have done alone in such a short amount of time. Thank you to Joan Murray at Pearson. Thank you to my former co-workers at WMP for making me a better developer or just supporting me (and in a lot of cases both!), particularly Kailin Johnson, Emily Bichler, Sarah Granger, Letteer Lewis, Ted Nubel, James Kinney, Rick Williams, Adam Kerr, Drew Leffelman, Andy Atteberry, Pamela Macario, Cory Chaplin, Ted Mazza, and Verite Pitts. Thank you Ryan Jones, Nate Tovo, Chris Jones, Jim Frantzen, and Karl Jackson for getting me started with front-end development in our ComScore days. Thank you for your support and/or teaching me things: Jim Lyman, Tom Dunlop, Alla Radunsky, Laura Foster, Fred Westrom, Clayton Chandler, William Bridges, John Smith, Mike O'Neal, and Chris Cunningham. Thank you Rundblades, Camerons, Hopkinses, and Velasquezes for your encouragement. Thank you to my mom and dad for instilling in me a love of learning very early in my life. And finally, I want to thank Betsy, Violet, and Cameron Sheppard—for everything. —DS

Thanks to my co-authors and to Pearson for giving me this opportunity. Also, thanks to my friend and former co-worker, Brett Davis, for introducing me to front-end development while we were at Purdue. Also, thanks to other friends and former co-workers who helped me develop front-end training materials and who attended front-end conferences with me: Jared Jenkins, Kailin Johnson, Kevin Kinnebrew, and Letteer Lewis. Finally, thanks to Hatlyn, Mom, Dad, Kyle, and Kayla, who always inspire me, support me, and motivate me. —CM

A huge thanks goes out to my co-authors, without whom this book wouldn't have been finished. I'd like to thank all those who have made me the developer I am today, especially Kevin Kinnebrew, Letteer Lewis, and Umair Rashid for not letting me drown on my first web project. Finally, a special thanks goes out to Dan and Megan for being the best roommates anyone could ever have. —AL

We Want to Hear from You!

As the reader of this book, *you* are our most important critic and commentator. We value your opinion and want to know what we're doing right, what we could do better, what areas you'd like to see us publish in, and any other words of wisdom you're willing to pass our way.

We welcome your comments. You can email or write to let us know what you did or didn't like about this book—as well as what we can do to make our books better.

Please note that we cannot help you with technical problems related to the topic of this book.

When you write, please be sure to include this book's title and author as well as your name and email address. We will carefully review your comments and share them with the author and editors who worked on the book.

Email: consumer@samspublishing.com

Mail: Sams Publishing
          ATTN: Reader Feedback
          800 East 96th Street
          Indianapolis, IN 46240 USA

Reader Services

Visit our website and register this book at informit.com/register for convenient access to any updates, downloads, or errata that might be available for this book.

Introduction

Congratulations! You're about to embark on an epic journey in front-end web development! Since its original release in 2009, AngularJS has become the most widely adopted JavaScript framework for building dynamic web applications. Angular empowers developers to organize, reuse, and test JavaScript code in ways few other JS frameworks have. The creators of Angular say that it is what HTML would have been, had it been designed for applications. You'll find out exactly what that means, and what the best ways are to use Angular to organize, reuse, and test JavaScript code.

Throughout this book, you will use your .NET background as a baseline to understanding new Angular concepts. There are a lot of parallels between Angular and .NET, and drawing on those comparisons should expedite your understanding of the framework. From models to modules and factories to filters, there are all sorts of new terms in the Angular world; this book will help you understand it all.

Audience and Organization

The title of this book says it's specifically for .NET developers. That's not entirely a lie, and if you've gotten past the title and are reading this, you're probably at least a little familiar with .NET. If you promise to tell all your non-.NET friends, here's a secret: You don't have to know .NET to get a lot out of this book. The goal of this book is to leverage a .NET developer's existing knowledge to more easily explain AngularJS concepts. If you don't have any existing .NET knowledge, however, just ignore the .NET parts. Other than Hours 20 through 23, which cover specific .NET topics, you'll be just fine.

It'd be great if you had some basic JavaScript knowledge. Hour 2, "Presenting JavaScript Patterns," is a refresher on some topics, but if you're completely new to JavaScript, you might want to check out a beginner's tutorial on it and then come back and try again.

How This Book Is Organized

This book is organized in a way that facilitates the gradual introduction of topics. AngularJS is known for having a steep learning curve, but the way this book builds on itself helps flatten that curve. Once in a while, you might come across a concept that isn't fully explained until a later hour. In these cases, a callout (more on conventions in the next section) will point you to the hour where that topic is discussed in depth. Due to the gradual introduction of topics, you should absolutely read this book front to back, and do the exercises at the end of every hour. By the time you've finished with this book, you'll have a fully working application and a solid grasp on AngularJS. Enjoy the experience!

Conventions Used in This Book

This book uses several design elements and conventions to help you prioritize and reference the information it contains:

- ▶ **By the Way** boxes provide useful sidebar information that you can read immediately or circle back to without losing the flow of the topic at hand.

- ▶ **Did You Know?** boxes highlight information that can make your programming more effective.

- ▶ **Watch Out!** boxes focus your attention on problems or side effects that can occur in specific situations.

- ▶ **Go To** boxes call out other places in the book where we refer to the topic you're currently learning about.

- ▶ New terms appear in an italic typeface for emphasis.

- ▶ In addition, this book uses various typefaces to help you distinguish code from regular English. Code is presented in a monospace font.

Exercises

Each hour in this book ends with an exercise that tests your mastery of the skills learned in the hour. Most of these hours build upon one another toward developing a full front-end application. If you complete all these exercises by the end of the book, you will have built a reading list management application that enables users to save books to a reading list, remove books from their reading list, mark books as read, leave personal notes on books, and view book reviews for books on their reading list. Books saved to the application have these properties: author, title, description, genre, publication date, publisher, number of pages, average rating, price, and ISBN. To check your work from hour to hour, we have published the source code for the application at each point during development. Please see the book website to download this source code.

Onward and Upward!

Whether or not you're a .NET developer, you're going to have a lot of fun working through this book. By the time you complete it, you'll be able to develop, debug, and deploy Angular apps. You will have gained foundational knowledge on the motivations for "thick-client" front-end web development, and you will have learned countless Angular best practices. We love using Angular on our consulting projects, products, and side projects, and we hope you will as well.

Introducing Modern Front-End Development

What You'll Learn in This Hour:

▶ Why front-end development has changed so much

▶ What's different about the front end versus 5 years ago

▶ What options there are for front-end development

▶ Why AngularJS could be the right choice for you

▶ Why AngularJS 1.x is still relevant

Welcome to AngularJS for .NET developers. You've made an excellent choice to further your web development studies.

Let's start your journey toward becoming an expert in AngularJS with a discussion about modern front-end web development. The landscape has changed drastically over the past several years, and it continues to change at a rapid pace.

This first hour explains why everything has changed on the front end. In this hour, you learn exactly what has changed and what your various options are for front-end development. The focus then turns to why one of those options, AngularJS, could be the right choice for your next web project.

The hour concludes with a discussion about why Angular 1.x is still relevant. Angular 2 is on the horizon, so is it worth reading a book about 1.x? Yes, and you learn why in this chapter.

The two main goals of this book are to leverage your existing .NET knowledge to help explain the concepts of AngularJS and to have fun. Front-end development hasn't been this fun in a long time. You should enjoy it, so let's get started.

Why Does Everything Look So Different?

Modern web development now, more than ever, has a clear delineation between the front end and back end. Browsers have made incredible strides over the past few years, leading to more and more code living on the client side. That's because browsers can handle it, and front-end frameworks can manage it. With the rise in popularity of single-page applications (SPAs), and hence the rise of the seemingly infinite number of JavaScript frameworks, the current web dev sweet spot is a JavaScript front end that hits a back-end application programming interface (API).

This is the programming model that is currently the most popular in the software development community, arguably in large part due to the meteoric rise of mobile devices.

Mobile is king, and apps are its instrument of conquest. The native feel of apps is ultra-important to users. Everything the user does in a (good) mobile app feels snappy and fluid. Users have become accustomed to this; and the web, with its ubiquitous postbacks and slow rendering, found itself left in the dust.

But, as Dr. Ian Malcom said how life "uh, finds a way," so, too, does the web. The user experience that results from an SPA is far better than traditional web applications (so much so that now you're starting to see applications moving from the desktop back to the web). This is partially a nod to platform agnosticism, partially as a nod to the omnipotent "cloud," but also a nod to how far the user experience on the web has come.

The web as a modern software platform is made possible thanks to SPAs driving the better user experience and thus the push to a thicker front end that needs less hand holding from a server. As more code moves to the front end, developers find themselves needing to pay more attention to the front end of their applications. No longer is the front of a web application a sprinkle of some DOM manipulation or a spaghetti salad of jQuery functions.

The front end is now a total workhorse, with tools ranging from front-front-end frameworks like Bootstrap and Foundation (not to mention preprocessors like LESS and SASS), to back-front-end frameworks like AngularJS and Ember.js (not to mention compile-to-JavaScript languages like CoffeeScript and TypeScript). Then comes the barrage of front-end workflow tools such as Gulp.js, Bower, npm, Plato, Grunt, and Yeoman. And not to be left out, unit testing has its own list of tools, such as Karma, Protractor, Jasmine, Buster.js, and QUnit.

Then pile on an equal number of tools, APIs, and languages for the back end.

Building your applications with a back-end API that a front-end can consume makes sense even outside the realm of SPAs. You can reuse that API for your mobile apps as well. Building a robust API that your web apps, mobile web apps, desktop apps, and native mobile apps can all use saves a lot of time and money.

How Is the Code Different?

You'll find many code examples throughout this book, and you'll get a good feeling of how the code you're used to writing in .NET or with jQuery has changed. To kick things off, though, let's look at a short example of how things differ now for the front end.

If you want to make something awesome happen when a user clicks a button, you could've done that in jQuery as shown in Listing 1.1.

LISTING 1.1 Antiquated Front-End Code: jQuery

```
 1:  <-- old.html -->
 2:  <div>
 3:    <input type='button' id='myAwesomeButton'></input>
 4:  </div>
 5:
 6:  // old.js
 7:  $(document).ready(function() {
 8:    $('#myAwesomeButton').click(function() {
 9:      //something cool!
10:    });
11:  });
```

"Well, that's not so bad," you might be saying. And you're right. If your application needs only a couple of button event bindings and you'll be all set, this isn't too bad. For most applications nowadays, however, you have a lot more going on than just binding a couple of buttons. Imagine trying to maintain hundreds of lines of code that looks like this. And then imagine trying to write tests for it. Oh, the horror!

So, what's a better alternative? Separating DOM logic from application logic makes testing much easier. Separation of these concerns eases maintenance and extensibility as well.

DID YOU KNOW?

What Is Extensibility?

Have you ever written an application and needed to add something to it much later on? That can be tricky, because often when we write software, we don't think about how easy it will be to add features or components to it in the future. The ease with which you can add on to your application is its *extensibility*.

AngularJS best practices call for separating your logic into services and your DOM manipulation into directives. You'll learn much more about those topics later; for now, though, Listing 1.2 shows how the jQuery example earlier can be written in a more maintainable, testable manner.

LISTING 1.2 Modern Front-End Code: AngularJS

```
 1:  <-- new.html -->
 2:  <div ng-app='app'>
 3:    <div ng-controller='myController as vm'>
```

```
 4:       <input type='button' ng-click='vm.doSomethingAwesome()'></input>
 5:     </div>
 6:   </div>
 7:
 8:   // new.js
 9:   angular.module('app', [])
10:     .controller('myController', function(){
11:       var vm = this;
12:       vm.doSomethingAwesome = function(){
13:         //something awesome!
14:       }
15:     });
```

Well, now wait a minute. We have more code here. How's this better?

Take a look at the JavaScript file. Do you notice there's no mention of the DOM in there? Factoring out DOM querying and manipulation when and wherever possible will greatly simplify your applications. Because the code doesn't reference the DOM, you can write unit tests that execute just the JavaScript code without any need for a browser, making your code much more testable. It's more maintainable because your code is encapsulated in modules and controllers, meaning that you can more easily find parts of your application you're looking for when tracking down bugs. One of the most important keys to building good software is to write code with structure. JavaScript frameworks provide your code with this structure.

Options for Front-End Development

We are in kind of a golden age of front-end development. It seems as though a new JavaScript framework pops up every week. When you're just getting started, it's easy to become over-whelmed with everything. But don't worry; you don't need to know them all. In fact, you really only need to know that a few exist, and play around with those. This section briefly covers the current three major JavaScript frameworks: Backbone.js, Ember.js, and AngularJS.

Backbone.js

Backbone.js is one of the most mature JavaScript frameworks that is still widely used. One of the biggest selling points of Backbone is that it is very lightweight. It only has one dependency (underscore.js). In fact, it's so light that the Backbone community likes to think of it as a library rather than as a framework. It focuses on providing developers with methods to manipulate data, but it isn't opinionated. Backbone allows developers to structure an application however they see fit.

Backbone provides developers with models, collections, views, and a router. Models are a representation of data. Collections are ordered groups of models. Views are how the data is represented to the user of the application. The router manages the state of the application in conjunction with URLs.

BY THE WAY

Backbone Is Lightweight, Except...

Backbone does tend to be a lightweight framework, but this is because it provides you with only what is absolutely necessary to structure your application. When you begin adding other tools to it (such as templating engines like handlebars.js), the size of the Backbone library quickly begins to grow.

Ember.js

Compared to Backbone, Ember.js is at the opposite end of the spectrum as far as having a defined way to develop your applications. Ember is very opinionated and tries to do the architectural heavy lifting for you. Whereas Backbone focuses on providing you tools that enable you to structure your application, leading to a lot of boilerplate code that you'll find yourself reusing, Ember focuses on helping you to write less code.

Ember consists of models, controllers, templates, views, routes, and components. The concept of models and routes is similar to that of Backbone. Ember uses controllers to add display logic to models. Templates describe the user interface, and views add reusable behavior to a template. Finally, components are reusable, encapsulated widgets you can use in templates.

AngularJS

Most of the rest of this book is about Angular, so let's not steal our own thunder in this brief synopsis. Suffice it to say that Angular also provides developers with a way to structure applications that falls somewhere between the rigorous, rigid architecture of Ember and the much lighter touch of Backbone.

At a very high level, Angular consists of controllers, views, directives, modules, and services. Controllers manage the application code and tie data to views, which display data. Directives are similar to the components that Ember uses, in that they're reusable widget-like pieces of functionality. Modules are entire containers for different parts of your application (the controllers, directives, and so on). Angular services are where most of your application logic should live. They do all the heavy lifting as far as fetching and manipulating data.

Why Angular?

Angular isn't a magic bullet. Sometimes a different tool is necessary to get your job done. However, you'll most likely find that Angular is the right tool more often than not.

Angular has vast community support. It's far and away the most popular JavaScript framework at this point and has a very wide variety of resources at your disposal.

In addition to the community support, Google created Angular, so there will be support for it for a very long time.

Angular focuses on testability and separation of concerns. The DOM is slow, and the less you have to interact with it, the faster and more maintainable your applications are. Angular encapsulates any DOM interaction into directives and allows you to more easily test your controllers and services.

Angular's dependency injection system makes using various components incredibly easy. You'll learn about dependency injection more in depth later.

There are lots of other reasons to like Angular, and by the end of this book you'll likely agree that it's a fantastic way to build software.

Why Is Angular 1 Still Relevant?

The second major release of Angular is right around the corner. So why is the first major release still relevant?

Angular 2 is a complete rewrite of the framework. No part of Angular is going to be untouched in the second version. Because there are a very large number of applications written in the first version of Angular, the Angular 2 team is working on a migration path. But it's unclear whether that path is ever going to exist at all.

The last hour of this book covers what some of the major differences in Angular 2 are going to be. But until Angular 2 is a much more mature platform, you should absolutely write your next web application in the latest version of AngularJS 1. It's a mature, stable framework with an immense number of resources. Google has pledged 2 years of support for Angular 1 even after Angular 2 is released.

Finally, if you inherit a front-end-heavy application in the next year or two, chances are that it's an Angular 1 app. It's a great framework, and although looking ahead to the future is great, you should learn the best technology available today. For now, that's definitely Angular 1.

Summary

In this first hour, you learned how and why front-end web development has changed so much over the past several years. You saw an example of how code has changed and what the benefits of using a JavaScript framework are. You also learned about the three biggest frameworks today: Backbone.js, Ember.js, and AngularJS. This hour concluded with a discussion about why the first major release of Angular is still relevant even though Angular 2 is expected to be released very soon.

Q&A

Q. Can I gradually start to use Angular in my .NET projects?

A. Definitely! The last few hours of this book delve into how you can use Angular and .NET together.

Q. Is AngularJS free?

A. Angular is open source and free to use under the MIT License. You can take a look at the source code on GitHub: https://github.com/angular/angular.js.

Q. Can I use AngularJS to write mobile applications, too?

A. AngularJS is a JavaScript framework you use to write code that executes in a browser. That said, there are ways to write mobile apps with AngularJS. Mobile web app performance has come a long way in the past few years. Ionic is a front-end framework that provides an SDK to help developers write mobile applications. Check out more here: http://ionicframework.com/. In addition, you can write applications with AngularJS that utilize other frameworks, like PhoneGap.

Workshop

Quiz

1. What is a benefit of separating application logic and DOM manipulation?

2. What are the three most widely used JavaScript frameworks?

3. True or False: All web development requires a JavaScript framework.

Answers

1. Code that doesn't reference the DOM is easier to test and maintain.

2. Backbone.js, Ember.js, and AngularJS.

3. False. You never have to use a JavaScript framework. Frameworks are tools that help you develop software in a structured manner. As your applications grow, you might find yourself needing a framework to help manage your code.

Exercise

Find examples of small applications written in Backbone, Ember, and Angular. What do you like about each? (Hint: Take a look at http://todomvc.com/.)

HOUR 2
Presenting JavaScript Patterns

What You'll Learn in This Hour:

▶ Five JavaScript tips and tricks for AngularJS development

▶ Useful JavaScript patterns to know for AngularJS development

▶ What closures are and why they're important

▶ How to take advantage of IIFEs to avoid global scope pollution

▶ How the Revealing Module pattern allows you to have public and private properties and methods

▶ Promises and how to use them to keep your async calls in order

▶ The Pub/Sub pattern and how it helps you to communicate

▶ Why all the fuss about MV* patterns

JavaScript has morphed into much more than just a scripting language developers use to manipulate the DOM. With the rising popularity of single-page apps, a great deal of application logic is moving to the front end of web apps. This has caused headaches, though, for a lot of developers trying to manage all of this code. Design patterns to the rescue!

If you're not familiar with JavaScript or the concept of software design patterns, don't let the term scare you. You've very likely been developing with design patterns for a long time and just never realized it.

This hour covers commonly used JavaScript patterns and how they compare to similar .NET constructs.

Design patterns can be intimidating, so let's ease into them with some important JavaScript refreshers.

This discussion assumes that you're at least a little bit familiar with JavaScript if you've reached this point, but the following may prove helpful anyway. If you're already intimately familiar with JavaScript, though, feel free to skip the tips and head straight to the patterns.

Surely Someone's Run into This Before

It's always nice when you run across a problem that lots of people have seen, too. That's the point of design patterns. They're a tried-and-true approach to solving commonly occurring problems. Often they're language-agnostic, because a lot of software engineering problems are universal. Design patterns are a huge software engineering topic, and you can read more about them in *Design Patterns: Elements of Reusable Object-Oriented Software*.

Five JavaScript Tips and Tricks

Before diving right into JavaScript design patterns, .NET devs should first know a few things about JavaScript. So, this section covers five important JavaScript tips and tricks you need to know for a seamless transition to AngularJS development:

1. JavaScript is loosely typed.

2. Functions are just objects.

3. JavaScript uses function scoping instead of block scoping.

4. Equality and ===.

5. Function overloading isn't really a thing.

JavaScript Is Loosely Typed

C# is a strongly typed language, meaning that once you assign a variable to a value, such as an integer, that variable remains an integer. You can't just suddenly assign it to a string. And if you try to do such a silly thing, the C# compiler is going to yell at you. When you create a method with parameters, you get a compile time error if you try to pass arguments of a different type to that method. The following example will result in a compile time error:

```
private void Lunch()
{
        var numOfPeople = "five";
        makeReservation(numOfPeople);
}
private void MakeReservation(int numOfPeople)
{
        //method to make a restaurant reservation
}
```

JavaScript, however, really doesn't care whether you set a variable to be a number and then make it a string. Function parameters aren't tied to a particular type and are more flexible. The preceding method in the C# example that is expecting an integer for `numOfPeople` wouldn't have a type in JavaScript. You can pass in a number or a string or anything at all. Of course, when it comes time to perform an action on that variable, you will get a runtime error (or some very unexpected results) if you don't pass in what the function needs.

```javascript
function lunch()
{
  var numOfPeople = "five";
  makeReservation(numOfPeople);
}
function makeReservation(numOfPeople)
{
  //method to make a restaurant reservation
  //numOfPeople can be anything
}
```

Functions Are Just Objects

Just as with a .NET `delegate`, you can pass around functions in JavaScript and execute them. In JavaScript, functions are just like any other object, with the exception that they can be invoked. Functions can have properties and methods just like other objects. They can be passed into other functions. They can have other functions inside of them, just as objects can have other nested objects.

In the following example, you'll see that we're passing one function into another. The function passed in as an argument is later invoked by the receiving function. In addition, the `OrderLunch` function has an inner function that is accessible only from inside `OrderLunch`:

```javascript
function orderLunch(cleanFn)
{
  function eatLunch(){
    alert('eating!');
  }
  eatLunch();
  cleanFn();
};
function cleanUp()
{
  alert('cleaning!');
}
orderLunch(cleanUp);
```

JavaScript Uses Function Scoping Instead of Block Scoping

In C#, variables declared inside of a block are scoped to that block. That means that any variable you create between a set of curly braces can't be used outside of those braces:

```
public void eat(bool isHungry)
{
  if(isHungry)
  {
    var lunchChoice = 'pizza';
    eat(lunchChoice);
  }
  Console.Write(lunchChoice); //Compiler Error!!!
}
```

JavaScript, however, uses function scope, meaning that any variable you create in a function can be used anywhere in that function, even if it was created inside an `if` statement as in the C# example earlier. Combining this with the information about nested functions discussed previously means that nested functions have access to variables declared in parent functions. This is a really important thing to remember going forward.

Equality and ===

Because JavaScript is weakly typed, you get some strange results when you use double equals (==) for equality comparisons:

```
if(0 == '0'){ // evaluates as true!
  // do something
}
if(0 === '0'){ // evaluates as false!
  // do something else
}
```

Double equals converts types on the fly to see whether they're equal. Triple equals, however, uses strict equality comparison.

Really, you should probably just forget that double equals even exists. There are very few, if any, cases when you would ever need to use it instead of triple equals. And even in those very few cases, you'd probably be better off finding a way to avoid using it, because it just leads to confusion.

Function Overloading Isn't Really a Thing

Function overloading in C# is a common way to reuse the same function with different parameters.

```
private void makeReservation(string restaurantName){
  makeReservation(restaurantName, 2);
}
private void makeReservation(restaurantName, numOfPeople)
{
  //make reservation in here
}
```

In this example, you can call the `makeReservation` method with or without the number of people on the reservation. If you don't pass in an integer along with a string, it just defaults that number to 2, because the method on line 1 gets called and passes a 2 along to the method on line 6.

C# also has optional parameters in which case you specify a default value for a parameter if an argument isn't passed in:

```
private void makeReservation(string restaurantName, int numOfPeople = 2){
  //make reservation in here
}
```

JavaScript is a little closer to the optional parameters example because in JavaScript, all parameters are optional. You don't have to pass anything into `makeReservation`, and the parameters will be undefined. If you pass in more arguments than the function is expecting, they're just ignored.

To give yourself the flexibility of a default parameter or overloaded function, just check whether the parameter is undefined, and if so, assign it to your default value:

```
function makeReservation(restaurantName, numOfPeople){
  if(!numOfPeople){
    numOfPeople = 2;
  }
  //make reservation in here
}
```

JavaScript Patterns

Everything so far in this hour was a brief intro to a few basic JavaScript concepts. This section more closely examines JavaScript using patterns. Remember, even though patterns can seem intimidating, they're really just tried-and-true solutions to common problems that other developers have run into before you. You don't have to memorize patterns, but the more you work with them, the more comfortable you'll become. In fact, as you get more into AngularJS in an hour, these patterns will start to feel completely natural to you.

Closures

One of the more difficult and slippery concepts in programming is that of a closure. It's really a fairly straightforward concept, though: An inner function has access to variables declared in an outer function, even after the outer function has returned. As you'll see in a bit, this is what allows JavaScript to use the concepts of private and public member variables that you know and love in C#.

First, though, let's take a look at an example of a closure in Listing 2.1.

LISTING 2.1   Closure

```
 1:  function makeReservation(name){
 2:    var restaurantName = name;
 3:    function displayRestaurantName(){
 4:      alert(restaurantName);
 5:    }
 6:    return displayRestaurantName;
 7:  }
 8:
 9:  var reserve = makeReservation('Blackwood');
10:  reserve();
11:
```

Let's start on line 9. We're setting this `reserve` variable equal to the return value of this `makeReservation` function, and also passing in a string. Fine. Next, you'll need to see what that `makeReservation` function is returning. That happens on line 6. And it turns out that it is another function, called `displayRestaurantName`, that's created on line 3. A function returning another function might feel a little weird, but remember that functions are just objects. So, now the reserve variable is set to the `displayRestaurantName` function. But what happens to the string passed in? It got assigned to a local variable in `makeReservation` called `restaurantName` and that local variable is being used by the `displayRestaurantName` function. That's normally okay, except that the outer function `makeReservation` here has returned, and because `restaurantName` is a local variable, it should now be out of scope and dead and gone and forgotten, right? Nope. Thanks to closures, that variable is still accessible to the inner function that our `reserve` variable on line 9 represents. So, when `reserve` gets called on line 10, it will still show the string that we passed in. Kind of crazy, huh?

Closures also exist in C#, but instead of inner functions, you have anonymous methods. Other than that, though, the idea is similar. The anonymous method has access to variables defined in the parent method.

Revealing Module Pattern

Just like C#, you can use private and public methods and properties in JavaScript. They aren't native features of the language, but using closures, we can emulate these features.

The example in Listing 2.2 is a little long, so let's step through it together.

LISTING 2.2   Revealing Module Pattern

```
1:  var orderLunch = function(){
2:    return{
3:        readMenu: readMenu,
4:        giveOrderToServer: giveOrder
5:    }
6:
7:    function readMenu(){
8:        console.log('reading menu...');
9:    }
10:
11:    function giveOrder(){
12:        if(determineHungerLevel() === 'super hungry'){
13:            alert('give me one of everything!');
14:        } else{
15:            alert('just one large pizza.');
16:        }
17:    }
20:
21:    function determineHungerLevel(){
22:        console.log('how hungry am i...');
23:        return 'super hungry';
24:    }
25: }();
26:
27: orderLunch.readMenu();
28: orderLunch.giveOrderToServer();
```

Starting at the top, you see a variable set to a function. Let's ignore what's in that function for a second. If you head down to the closing brace of that function, you'll see two parentheses, invoking that function. This is what's known as a *self-invoking function*. The value of orderLunch is set to the return value of the function. orderLunch is now essentially a singleton. There is only one instance of orderLunch. You could also remove those parentheses at the end of the function, use the new keyword to create a new instance of orderLunch, and assign it to another variable. You could do that as many times as you wanted to create multiple instances of that object. This mechanism allows orderLunch to behave a lot like the classes you're familiar with in .NET.

WATCH OUT!

The new Keyword in JavaScript

Douglas Crockford (a renowned developer in the JavaScript community) recommends against the use of the new keyword in JavaScript to create objects. The reasoning being that if you accidentally omit new when creating an object, you don't get any syntax or compiler errors (JavaScript isn't compiled), but instead you end up polluting the global scope.

Instead, he recommends using object literals

```
var newObject = {};
```

Or Object.create(prototypeObject).

This is certainly a matter of preference, and so long as you're diligent about using the new keyword when you need it, you should have no problem with any of these methods of object creation.

Next, let's see what the function is returning so that you know what orderLunch actually is. At the top of the outer function, you see that it's returning an object with a couple of properties: readMenu and giveOrderToServer. Those properties are pointing to inner functions with the same names. Below those two functions is a third called determineHungerLevel. The return statement at the top of the outer function is effectively exposing those two object properties as public methods. At the bottom of the example, we're calling readMenu and giveOrderToServer on the orderLunch object. You would not be able to call that third inner function determineHungerLevel from outside the outer function due to JavaScript's function scoping. It's not on the return object, so the orderLunch object doesn't know it exists, effectively making it a private method that you can only use inside of the function.

Notice the role closures play in this. Even though the outer function has returned, the orderLunch object still has access to objects and properties inside of it. Pretty cool.

IIFE

One of the biggest atrocities a developer can commit is global scope pollution. You've heard your entire development career that global variables are bad. And they're particularly bad in JavaScript. Why is that? JavaScript isn't compiled, so naming collisions aren't detected until runtime. If you declare a variable in the global scope, there's nothing keeping a variable with the same name in the global scope from overwriting your original variable. The ample use of third-party libraries in JavaScript makes this a dangerous proposition.

Recall, though, that variables in JavaScript are scoped to the function in which they were created. So, as long as you can stuff all of your variables inside of a function, you can avoid global scope pollution. That function still needs to be called, though, to run your code. You can accomplish this by using an IIFE, or an immediately invoked function expression.

As mentioned earlier, functions are just objects that can also be invoked. One of the ways in which a function can be invoked is with the use of parentheses.

You can't just plop parentheses at the end of a function declaration, though, because a function declaration is a statement, not an expression. You can turn a function declaration into an expression by wrapping the entire function in parentheses.

IIFEs are seen all over the place in JavaScript, and are the method you should use in Angular to prevent having variables in the global scope. In fact, every controller, directive, service, and anything else you read about in this book should be wrapped in an IIFE. To reduce repetition, this text does not do so in trivial examples, but they're definitely there in spirit.

```
(function(){
  //put your code in here
  //to avoid pollution!
})();
```

Promises

JavaScript is a synchronous language, which means that when you make a service call to an application programming interface (API), the execution of code isn't going to wait around for that call to finish before moving to the next line. It'll just keep moving right along (see Listing 2.3).

LISTING 2.3 **Synchronous Calls Without Promises**

```
 1:    function haveLunch(){
 2:      walkToRestaurant();
 3:      placeOrder();
 4:      waitForFood();
 5:      // this function call is going to take a while,
 6:      // because the order went to a back end
 7:      // service for the food to be cooked.  Since that code
 8:      //isn't executing in the browser,
 9:      // the browser kicks off that function and moves right
10:      // along to the next function.
11:      // The next function, though, is probably expecting
         // some food,
12:      //so it will throw an error.
13:      // We need the eat() function to wait for the
14:      // waitForFood()function to be finished before
15:      // it executes.
16:      eat();
17:    }
```

The solution to this issue is to use a promise. `waitForFood`, in the preceding example, can return a promise object that is basically saying that when it's finished processing or when it gets a result from the API that it's calling, it promises to call a function. What function? You have to let the promise object know that.

In ECMAScript 6, promises are going to be a native part of the language. Until then, though, a number of different promise libraries allow you to solve this problem. Angular's promises are based on the Q library, which was written by Kris Kowal.

In Listing 2.4, waitForFood is now returning a promise object. You'll delve deeper into how you can make a function return a promise object, and what exactly that means, in Hour 8, "Discovering Services: Part II." For now, you just know that waitForFood is returning a promise, and you need to know what to do with it.

You can handle a promise object in two ways. One is to use success and error functions after the call.

LISTING 2.4 Synchronous Call with Promises Using success and error

```
1:  function haveLunch(){
2:    waitForFood().success(function(){
3:      eat();
4:    }).error(function(){
5:      //show an error.
6:      //maybe the kitchen messed up the order?
7:    });
8:  }
```

Here, we're chaining function calls together. Because waitForFood is returning a promise, the success function belongs to that promise object, so you're able to call it on the returned promise from waitForFood. The parameter that the success function takes in is a function that is called once the promise is resolved. And because each function on the promise object also returns a promise, we can also call the error function on the returned promise from success. The error function also takes in a function, but in this case, it's only called if the promise is rejected.

The other way to handle a promise object is to use a then function. The idea of chaining is the same as when you use the success and error functions, but instead of having both of those separate functions, the then function takes in two functions that are executed either when the promise is resolved or when it is rejected (see Listing 2.5).

LISTING 2.5 Synchronous Call with Promises Using then

```
1:  function haveLunch(){
2:    waitForFood().then(function(){
3:      eat();
4:    }, function(){
5:      //show an error.
6:    });
7:  }
```

Whether you use then or `success` and `error` is a matter of preference. However, then might make the code a little more readable. After all, you `waitForFood`, then you do something else.

Pub/Sub

In general, all your code should consist of small chunks or components that focus on doing one thing really well. These small chunks should operate as independently as possible, because it helps maintainability when you're able to change a component without affecting any others. This is known as *decoupling* or *loosely coupled code*.

When you have multiple, independently operating components making up a bigger application, one of the challenges you run into is that of communication between those components.

Inevitably, you'll need to let one component know when something happens so that it can do its job. In a lot of those instances, you could just include a reference to another component, but then the first component depends on the second, and they become tightly coupled. They no longer work independently of each other.

One mechanism or design pattern you can use to solve this problem is using events with the Pub/Sub pattern, or Publish/Subscribe. You're likely used to the concept of event-driven development any time a button is pressed or a text box's value changes. You can also use events to communicate between different parts of your code. .NET events and delegates use Pub/Sub, so if you're familiar with events and delegates, you're all set. If not, read on.

Pretend that you have two components, neither of which knows the other even exists. The first component needs to let the other know when it has finished a particular task. Once Component1 has finished its task, it will "publish" an event. Component2 previously "subscribed" to or listened for an event to let it know when it can start its job. In fact, multiple components can listen for events. You can think of the Pub/Sub pattern as a channel that broadcasts events that other components can tune in and listen for. When you listen to the radio, the station doesn't know you exist. It just broadcasts out a signal that you can tune in and listen to if you know the appropriate channel.

MV*

You might be familiar with the MVC design pattern from .NET MVC. If not, that's okay, because you've probably used the pattern without ever realizing it. You see the term *MV** or *MVW* sometimes when reading about JavaScript frameworks. This is an acronym for Model-View-Whatever, meaning that other than having a model and a view, the * or W can vary so that the exact implementation of the pattern doesn't matter all that much.

That might seem strange, but the idea of an MV* pattern or framework is to ensure separation of concerns. The mechanism you use to ensure the separation of concerns can vary from framework to framework and implementation to implementation. The exact pattern that most front-end frameworks use is kind of fuzzy. You might see some people talk about Angular as an MVVM framework, or an MVC framework. There are great bar debates over what constitutes certain patterns and what pattern a certain framework follows. It's not really worth debating, because, again, exactly what the pattern is doesn't really matter. Use what makes sense to you and what is the most extensible and maintainable. The way you use the framework might fit one pattern, and the way someone else architects his or her solution might follow a slightly different pattern. The important part is that you've separated your application into individual components that are focused on one thing. MV* is another tool in your utility belt to help make that happen.

Because of that, this discussion does not examine every variation of MV*. Instead, the focus here is on the individual pieces that could make up an MV* pattern.

Model

The *M* stands for model, which is the data your application uses. Across technologies, there are a lot of ways to separate your data from the rest of your code. In .NET's Entity Framework, you might have `Entity` classes that represent your data model. JavaScript doesn't have classes, but we can emulate that behavior with functions. Even in using functions, though, you can use a variety of methods to represent a data model object in JavaScript. No particular way is any better than another, as long as the method you use encapsulates data that should be private and is extensible in case you need to expand the model or have nested models.

The `RestaurantModel` in Listing 2.6 has three model properties and one method.

LISTING 2.6 Model Object in JavaScript

```
 1:   function RestaurantModel(name, address){
 2:     var reviews = [];
 3:
 4:     return {
 5:       name: name,
 6:       address: address,
 7:       reviews: reviews,
 8:       addReview: addReview
 9:     }
10:
11:     function addReview(review){
12:       reviews.push(review);
13:     }
14:
15:   }
16:
17:   function ReviewModel(author,
```

```
18:                     body,
19:                     restaurantName,
20:                     rating){
21:     return{
22:       author: author,
23:       body: body,
24:       restaurantName, restaurantName,
25:       rating: rating
26:     }
27:   }
```

If you want to create a new restaurant object, we can do that by calling the RestaurantModel function and assigning the return result to an object. The same function that creates the restaurant model object can also create a ReviewModel object for that restaurant. The result of that function call can then be sent to the RestaurantModel's addReview method, as shown in Listing 2.7.

LISTING 2.7 Using a Model Object in JavaScript

```
1:    function RestaurantManager(){
2:      var coolNewRestaurant =
3:          RestaurantModel('Blackwood', '123 Park Ave');
4:      var reviewText =
5:          document.getElementById('review_body').text;
6:      var newRestaurantReview =
7:          ReviewModel('Art Vandelay', reviewText,
8:                              'Blackwood', '5');
9:      coolNewRestaurant.addReview(newRestaurantReview);
10:   }
```

View

The *V* stands for view. This is simply how you'll display your model data. Typically, this is going to be the HTML part of a web application. You'll learn more about views in Hour 7, "Discovering Services: Part I."

Whatever's and *'s

The *Whatever* part of MV* is just a way to show that the exact implementation can be a variety of things. Candidates for this include the following:

▶ Controller

▶ ViewModel

▶ Presenter

Controllers

Controllers are one of the central parts of how Angular applications are structured, but that will eventually change in Angular2. You'll learn how Angular 1.x uses controllers in Hour 8, but for now the theory behind controllers is more important.

A controller is the object that dictates how the view is updated with model data. It also handles user input and updates the model accordingly. You can think of a controller as a traffic cop of the application. It tells the app what to do, helps create and manipulate the data, and helps the data get to where it needs to go.

ViewModels

You'll be using ViewModels a lot on your journey through Angular here. Many consider Angular more of an MVVM (where *VM* is ViewModel) framework because your controller is basically acting as a ViewModel. ViewModels are just more UI-friendly representations of your data model. It's likely that your data model contains a lot of raw data that you wouldn't display to the user. You might first need to manipulate that data or format it so that it displays in a pretty format. That manipulated data is represented in a ViewModel.

When you read about $scope in Hour 6, "Understanding Views, Data Binding, and Event Handling," you'll learn how that is, more or less, Angular's implementation of a ViewModel.

Presenters

A presenter is very similar to a ViewModel, and there is a lot of ambiguity around what exactly the differences are. Now is not the time to get into the subtle differences, but suffice it to say that a presenter falls somewhere between a controller and a ViewModel. The view can call methods that exist on a presenter object, much like a controller, but it also holds data the view displays, much like a ViewModel.

Summary

In this hour, you had a brief explanation of five important things to know about JavaScript. You then learned several JavaScript patterns that you'll use throughout the remainder of the book. The hour concluded with a discussion about MV*, where Angular fits in, and why MV* is really kind of a fuzzy, debate-filled concept that doesn't actually matter. Just do what works!

Q&A

Q. Why are design patterns important?

A. Design patterns are time-tested solutions to repeatable problems. They aren't a cure-all, and you shouldn't attempt to force a pattern into just any situation and hope it works. They're tools just like any other, and you should use the right tool for the job. Many of these tools are used to write better, more maintainable applications, and that's definitely the case with Angular.

Q. **Which is the correct MV* pattern for giant enterprise applications? What about for small applications?**

A. There is no "correct" pattern. Just like mentioned earlier, these patterns are just tools you can use for different problems. If you were fixing a car or building a treehouse, there wouldn't be a general "correct tool." You have a tool belt and need to recognize if you need a Phillips head screwdriver or a flathead. If you learn how the tools work, you can much more easily choose the right one for the job.

Workshop
Quiz

1. How does double equals (==) differ from triple equals (===)?

2. What is a common strategy for keeping your functions out of the global scope?

3. How do you implement C# style public and private methods and properties in JavaScript?

4. True or False: Variables in JavaScript are scoped only to the function in which they're created.

5. What design pattern could you use for component communication?

6. True or False: An outer function has access to variables declared in an inner function thanks to closure.

Answers

1. Triple equals performs type checking as well. Whereas `'1'` `==` `1` would evaluate to `true`, `'1'` `===` `1` would not.

2. Using an immediately invoked function expression, or IIFE.

3. Using the Revealing Module pattern. Public members are included in the `return` statement; private ones are not.

4. True. While C# uses block scoping, in JavaScript, any variable created inside of a function is only scoped to that function.

5. Pub/Sub.

6. False, oh so false. Closure is when an inner function has access to variables declared in an outer function, even after the outer function has returned. Outer functions definitely do not have access to inner function variables. Check out quiz item 4.

Exercise

Think about implementing a typical 52-card playing deck using the Revealing Module pattern. What methods would you make public and which private? How would you do it?

HOUR 3
Tinkering with Tools for Modern Front-End Development

What You'll Learn in This Hour:

▶ The current tool landscape

▶ Node

▶ NPM

▶ Bower

▶ Grunt

▶ JSHint

▶ Yeoman and Angular scaffolding

Why tools? Well, in short, tools are awesome! They simplify our lives and make the overall development experience easier, quicker, and less prone to errors. The tools discussed this hour represent a set of great tools that on their own provide a huge amount of value, but when combined create a robust development experience to rival any other.

If you're coming from the .NET world, many of these tools will seem familiar, and if you're not, don't worry. All of these tools are fairly simple to use, and once you get the hang of them, you won't imagine web development without them.

The Tool Landscape

Before we dive into the tools, let's briefly discuss the current tool landscape. The front-end community is thriving and growing, which has brought about tremendous evolution in the past few years; but this has created a bit of an issue. Because the community is innovating so quickly, keeping up with the latest tools is becoming difficult. Also, these tools and libraries seem to burst on to the scene with tremendous force, bringing with them new and exciting ideas that quickly catch on, only to have a new tool innovate on top of the innovation. You might hear talk of the package manager wars, or the task manager wars. These "wars" are a result of the rapid innovation that the community is currently undergoing. Don't let this scare you, though; the results of these innovations are well worth the constant change.

Node

Node is a huge topic that can, and has, filled books in its own right. So, it's not covered much here, but it's important to know about. From the Node team: "As an asynchronous event-driven framework, Node.js is designed to build scalable network applications." Well, that sounds all fine and dandy, but what are you going to use Node for? The answer to this is, you won't really.

To clarify, almost all the tools covered this hour are built on top of Node or require Node in some way or another. Node is a highly flexible module-based platform built on top of the Google Chrome V8 engine and ECMAscript, which means that almost all of JavaScript's native functions, objects, and methods are supported. This has enabled developers to quickly build amazing tools using the language they are already comfortable with.

It is important to note that Node.js is a "server-side" framework that you can use for all sorts of applications, and the use of it in this book is to enable front-end development tools. For the uses covered in this book, install Node on your development machine and not on your web server.

To install Node, visit the Node website at https://nodejs.org.

Package Management

For those who have a .NET background, package management should already be familiar. If you are comfortable with the concept of package management, feel free to skip the next paragraph, although you might learn a thing or two even if you are already comfortable.

There is a saying that if you don't manage your packages, your packages will manage you. (In my experience, this is certainly true.) In the extremely innovative front-end community, libraries are constantly being updated, and many of these libraries rely on other libraries, which in turn rely on other libraries. This can cause a mess of dependencies that either forces you to spend hours resolving these dependencies or ultimately forces you to give up. This is where package managers come in. They maintain a list of libraries and their dependencies, and will help you automatically resolve these dependencies.

The first package manager discussed here is NPM.

NPM

The first thing you should know about NPM (Node Package Manager) is that's automatically installed when you install Node. So, take the next 10 seconds to celebrate not having to install anything for this topic.

NPM is by far one of the most common tools for web developers. Where Node allows developers to build great development tools, NPM allows the developers to share their libraries, while simultaneously making it easy for people to install and update. NPM is by far the largest package manager for JavaScript libraries, boasting more than 125,000 packages at the time of this writing, with over a billion installs (that's right, a billion, with a *B*) per month.

NPM can be accessed via command line. So, if you are on a Windows PC, open the command prompt. If you're running OS X or Linux, open Terminal and type **npm**.

If you are experiencing errors, see the information about Node earlier (what it is and how to install it.).

Now that you have NPM up and running, let's install a package.

If you closed the command prompt or Terminal, open it again and run the following command:

```
npm install -g bower
```

Let's break this command down so that you better understand what it's doing. By typing npm install, you are invoking NPM and telling it to install a package called Bower. The -g flag is telling Node to install this package globally. The reason you install Bower globally is that it is not project dependent.

If you receive an error message when trying to install Bower, you may need to run the command with elevated privileges. On a Windows computer, try running the command prompt as an administrator. If you are on OS X or Linux, try running the command with the sudo modifier:

```
sudo npm install -g bower
```

That should prompt you for your password, and even though it doesn't look like you are typing anything, you are.

Follow these tips if you run into any problems installing packages throughout the remainder of this hour.

Bower

Bower is a package manager. Wait, didn't you just learn that was what NPM is? That's right! At this point, you might be thinking that the web development community just likes to complicate things (or that somebody is pulling your leg), and you would be partially right.

Bower is indeed another package manager, but one that focuses on installing front-end frameworks, libraries, and assets. While NPM can indeed install all of these things, it does so in a much different way. The following sidebar covers the differences between NPM and Bower.

BY THE WAY

Bower Versus NPM

As mentioned earlier, NPM and Bower are both package managers, so what's the point in having two? Doesn't that just get confusing? It certainly has caused and will continue to cause confusion and arguments. This discussion does not take sides, and instead explains why there are two and what each one brings to the table.

The biggest difference between the two is the way they manage dependencies. NPM uses a nested dependency tree structure, which allows the developer of the package you are installing to request specific versions of libraries. This ensures that the package you are installing will work no matter what other versions of its dependencies you already have installed. This is really great for those writing server-side applications because size and download speed are not really issues. However, if you are developing front-end applications, making your end user download three separate versions of jQuery is simply unacceptable.

This is where Bower comes in. Bower uses a flat dependency structure, ensuring that your end user is downloading only one version of each library. This greatly reduces the number of files your users have to download, which in turn decreases the load time of your application. However, Bower can't ensure that when you install a new package that relies on one you already have it will work. This puts the burden of resolving dependencies on you, the developer.

Don't feel that you need to pick only one of these. In fact, you should use both. NPM for development dependencies like Bower, Grunt, Gulp, and so on, and use Bower for application dependencies such as jQuery and Underscore.

To get started with Bower, create a new folder somewhere easily accessible, and navigate to it using your operating system's terminal. Bower works just like NPM, where all you have to do is type **bower install**, but it can also grab files from other places. Here are some examples of ways to install libraries, assets, or even git repositories.

```
#### registered package
$ bower install jquery
#### GitHub shorthand
$ bower install desandro/masonry
#### Git endpoint
$ bower install git://github.com/user/package.git
#### URL
$ bower install http://example.com/script.js
```

Bower packages are installed in a subfolder called bower_components inside whatever folder you are currently in when you run the command.

Grunt

Grunt, at its core, is a task runner. Add a few of the hundreds of community-made plug-ins and you can automate your entire build process with just a few lines of code. Grunt uses Node's require() system, along with adding some things to the package.json file. So, make sure to install Grunt as follows:

```
sudo npm install -g grunt-cli
```

This installs the Grunt command-line interface (CLI) globally so that it's available to use in any of your projects. After you have it installed, you can start using it in your projects. To set it up, first make sure that you have a package.json file in your project directory. If you don't, you can easily create one by answering a few questions after running the following command:

```
npm init
```

After answering questions from Node, you need to generate a Gruntfile, which is where you can set up tasks. To do that, run the following command:

```
npm install grunt --save-dev
```

The `--save-dev` flag tells the Grunt CLI that you want to make Grunt a development dependency.

WATCH OUT!

Installation Trouble!

If for some reason this command fails to generate a Gruntfile, visit http://gruntjs.com/getting-started to view the latest example Gruntfile.

This allows your fellow teammates, with just a single command, to make sure that they have all the necessary Node packages installed:

```
npm install
```

To add other premade Grunt tasks to your project, simply install them the same way you did Grunt. Here is the command to install JSHint, which is a code-validation task that ensures you write both valid and good JavaScript code:

```
npm install grunt-contrib-jshint --save-dev
```

Now that you have JSHint installed, let's take a look at your Gruntfile. It should look something like this:

```
module.exports = function(grunt) {

  grunt.initConfig({
  });

};
```

To configure JSHint and set up a task to run it, modify your Gruntfile like so:

```
module.exports = function(grunt) {

  grunt.initConfig({
    jshint: {
      files: ['Gruntfile.js', 'src/**/*.js', 'test/**/*.js'],
```

```
    options: {
      globals: {
        jQuery: true
      }
    }
  }
});

grunt.loadNpmTasks('grunt-contrib-jshint');

grunt.registerTask('default', ['jshint']);

};
```

This sets some options for JSHint, like what files it should examine and what globals you will have defined. Grunt then needs to make sure it loads the tasks, and finally, you register a task called default that will run JSHint. To actually run JSHint, just run the following:

```
grunt
```

This executes the default task that you just set up to run JSHint! While your IDE of choice may come with some built-in tools for front-end development, thousands of plug-ins can be used in any combination, providing you with the flexibility to automate your entire build. Grunt is an amazingly powerful task runner that can save you loads of time with your build and deployment process.

Yeoman

After reading through this hour, you might be thinking that it takes a lot of work to get all these tools set up for every new project you work on, and you wouldn't be wrong. This is where Yeoman comes in. Yeoman is a scaffolding tool that allows anyone to write plug-ins for it. It's simple to use and infinitely extensible. If you find yourself creating the same config files, installing the same packages, and scaffolding out the same folder structure every time you start a new project, you're going to love Yeoman. If this is your first foray into JavaScript programming, you could probably use a little jumpstart. Let's use Yeoman to scaffold out a brand new Angular application. To do so, let's first install Yeoman, as follows:

```
npm install -g yo
```

Just like when you use -g in the Grunt install command, this ensures that Yeoman is installed globally so that you can use it wherever you are.

Let's also run the following command to install the Yeoman Angular generator globally:

```
npm install -g generator-angular
```

At this point, make a new project folder and `cd` into it from your command prompt. Then run the following command:

```
yo angular MySweetNewAppName
```

Yeoman is going to ask you a few questions to make sure that it installs all the features you want. Once you complete all the prompts, Yeoman installs all the dependencies it needs and scaffolds a simple Angular application for you. To view what's created, run the following Grunt command:

```
grunt serve
```

This command starts the Angular application within a locally running Node server where you can play with the app and debug it.

Summary

In this hour, you learned about the ever-shifting landscape of JavaScript and the open source community, dug into Node and its super-useful NPM (which was then compared to its rising alternative, Bower). You also set up Grunt to help you run a code-hinting tool called JSHint, and installed Yeoman to help scaffold out an entire Angular application.

Q&A

Q. **NPM and Bower do similar things; is there a competing tool to Grunt?**

A. Yes! It's called Gulp, and is very similar to Grunt, but has different syntax and some extra features. It's really up to you which you choose to use, as the installation processes and setup are almost identical.

Workshop

Quiz

1. What command creates a new package.json file?

2. How do you save a dependency when using Bower?

3. What's the command for running the default Grunt task?

Answers

1. `npm init`

2. `bower install --save-dev`

3. `grunt`

Exercise

For the book management system mentioned in the Introduction, set up your project by running `npm init`, `bower init`, `bower install angular`, and `bower install bootstrap`.

Mastering Modules

What You'll Learn in This Hour:

▶ What a module is

▶ Why modules are important

▶ Defining and referencing a module

In this hour, you learn what defines a module and why they are important when creating an easy-to-maintain and scalable application. You also learn about namespacing, to show that it provides context around what your module does. This hour also explains how to define modules, along with how to use them.

Angular Modules

You can think of Angular modules as containers. Modules separate the different logical parts of your application. This allows you to separate concerns within your application, and provides you with easy-to-test pieces. It also allows you to easily use different self-contained pieces of code throughout your application. This might not seem important when creating small applications, but as your code base starts to grow, it is vital that you decouple your application logic from other sections of your application.

You'll learn more about how best to architect and organize your code in Hour 15, "Approaching Angular Patterns" but you should know now that when building an Angular project, you should group your folder structure by application logic, not by type. In .NET, it's very common to have a folder structure that looks like this:

-Application

    -Controllers

        -LoginController.cs

        -SongController.cs

        -ArtistController.cs

```
-Views
        -Login.html
        -Home.html
        -Song.html
        -Artist.html
-Models
        -Login.cs
        -Song.cs
        -Artist.cs
```

The preceding folder structure represents grouping by type. There is a folder just for controllers, view, and models. In Angular, the recommended way to organize your application is by functionality, as follows:

```
-Application
     -Login
            -LoginController.js
            -Login.js
            -Login.html
     -Song
            -SongController.js
            -Song.js
            -Song.html
     -Artist
            -ArtistController.js
            -Artist.js
            -Artist.html
```

As you can see from this diagram, you have a folder for logical parts of our application. This logical grouping lends itself to Angular's modules. As a general rule, you should create modules for the following: any logical grouping (feature), for each reusable component, such as directives and filters, and then one "application" module that depends on your other modules and contains the application initialization logic.

Creating Modules

The first part of creating your Application module is by using ng-app, like so:

```
<div ng-app="music">
     <div>
```

```
        {{ defaultGreeting }}
      </div>
</div>
```

Here you are using the `ng-app` directive to bootstrap your application; the directive signifies the root of your application. You can also specify a module as your root module as follows:

```
angular.module("music", []);
```

Notice that the first parameter matches the parameter to `ng-app`. This tells Angular that you will use this module as your root module for your application. You might have noticed the second parameter is an empty array. This is your application's dependency array, where you will add both external modules, along with your own application modules.

Now that you have an application module, let's reexamine the Artist folder from the Application folder structure shown earlier:

-Application

    -Artist

        -ArtistController.js

        -Artist.js

        -Artist.html

You'll learn about controllers in the next hour, but first let's look at how to define a controller within a module called Artist:

```
angular.module('music.artist', [])
  .controller("artist.controller");
```

This defines a new module called music.artist and creates a controller on that module called artist.controller. Let's also add a service to the module. (Hour 7, "Discovering Services: Part I," and Hour 8, "Discovering Services: Part II," cover services in depth.)

```
angular.module('music.artist', [])
  .service("artist.model");
```

Here you've added a service to your music.artist module. To then use these modules throughout your application, you can add it as a dependency to your application module as follows:

```
angular.module('music', ['music.artist']);
```

This tells Angular that your music application depends on our music.artist module.

BY THE WAY

Dot Notation

You name your application modules using dot notation to represent namespaces. This allows developers to understand what modules are used for and what they belong to.

Some modules require or allow you to configure specific behavior of that module using the `config` function. You generally do this configuration only once when your application is bootstrapped. Each module configuration will differ, so you'll have to read the documentation, but here is an example of how to configure the `$http` service to accept JSON by default:

```
var musicApp = angular.module('music', ['music.artist']);]

muiscApp.config(['$httpProvider', function ($httpProvider) {
    $httpProvider.defaults.headers.post['Accept'] = 'application/json,
text/javascript';
}]);
```

Summary

In this hour, you learned what a module actually is and how it plays an integral part in large-scale applications. This hour also covered the best way to organize your Angular application to separate it into modules. This hour concluded by walking you through creating and configuring a module.

Q&A

Q. What happens in a naming collision?

A. Naming collisions in Angular fail silently, and because Angular has only one injector for your entire application, whichever module was loaded last will come out victorious.

Workshop

Quiz

1. Why are modules important?
2. How should you organize your application files?
3. What directive bootstraps your angular application?

Answers

1. Modules force both separation of concerns and provide you with self-contained reusable components that can be used across your entire app, or even across projects.
2. You should organize your application by feature, which will lend itself to modules and allow for easier maintenance in large projects.
3. `ng-app`

Exercise

For the book management system mentioned in the Introduction, create your index.html file, add `ng-app` to an element, and set up your book application module.

Covering Controllers

What You'll Learn in This Hour:

► What an Angular controller is

► What $scope is

► How controller inheritance works

► What should and shouldn't go in a controller

► Controller best practices

Coming from a .NET background, you might already be familiar with the concept of an MVC (Model-View-Controller) controller. On the surface, Angular appears to share a similar role to .NET MVC controllers, but as you delve deeper, you will probably find that Angular is more MVVM (Model-View-ViewModel) than MVC.

Angular Controllers

You define Angular controllers using the module pattern discussed in the preceding hour by using the controller construction function. Let's take a look at what that looks like:

```
angular.module('musicApp')
  .controller('ArtistController', ['$scope', function($scope) {

  }]);
```

Here we are defining an ArtistController on the module musicApp, which in our case is our root module. Notice that the second parameter in the controller constructor is an array. This is called the *dependency array*, which is covered in depth in Hour 11, "Depending on Dependency Injection." The first index of that array is requesting the $scope object, and the second index is a function defining our controller logic. The preceding code will work, but it is a best practice to use a named function inside an immediately invoked function expression (IIFE) as follows:

```
(function() {

angular.module('musicApp')
    .controller('ArtistController', ['$scope', ArtistController]);

    function ArtistController($scope) {

    };

}();
```

Note that instead of using an anonymous function inside your dependency array to define your controller instead, you define a named function below and inject the $scope object as a parameter. Now you will look at how to tie a controller to a view.

You can attached your controller to the DOM (view) by using the ng-controller directive. You will learn about directives in detail in Hour 9, "Using Built-In Directives." Here is code that links your controller and your view:

```
<div ng-controller="ArtistController">

</div>
```

This tells your Angular app that the ArtistController will define the scope of this view, and provides certain functionality. Scope has been mentioned multiple times already during this hour, but you have not really learned about it yet, so let's get to that now.

$scope

As mentioned at the beginning of this hour, Angular feels a lot more like MVVM than MVC, and it's $scope that's really responsible for that. You can think of $scope kind of like the viewbag in .NET MVC. Don't get too attached to that comparison, though, because $scope also exposes functions.

Suppose, for instance, that you want to display an artist to your user. You can write something like this

```
<div ng-controller="ArtistController">
  {{artist}}
</div>

angular.module('musicApp')
    .controller('ArtistController', ['$scope', artistController]);
```

```
function artistController($scope) {
  $scope.artist = 'Foo Fighters'
};
```

This will result in Foo Fighters being shown in the DOM where {{artist}} is. It's great that you can show a static artist name, but let's take a look at how you could let the user, using a button, pick the artist:

```
<div ng-controller="ArtistController">
        {{artist}}
        <button ng-click="pumpkins()">Pumpkins</button>
        <button ng-click="rise()">Rise</button>
</div>
```

Notice the two new lines of code added to show buttons. These buttons use the built-in ng-click directive, which will call a function in your controller. Now you have to add those functions in your controller for anything to happen, so let's do that:

```
app.controller('ArtistController', ['$scope', artistController]);

function artistController($scope) {
  $scope.artist = 'Foo Fighters'

  $scope.pumpkins = function(){
    $scope.artist = 'Smashing Pumpkins';
  }

  $scope.rise = function(){
    $scope.artist = 'Rise Against';
  }
};
```

Notice that we've added two new functions and attached them to $scope like so:

```
$scope.function = function(){};
```

Now when your user clicks a button, {{artist}}, which is set to Foo Fighters by default, will change to Smashing Pumpkins or Rise Against, based on the button they click. Now let's take a look at how to incorporate user input by creating a text box and search button:

```
<div ng-controller="ArtistController">
 <div>{{artist}}</div>
 <input ng-model="artistBox">
<button ng-click="search(artistBox)">Search</button>
</div>
```

We're now using the built-in Angular directive ng-model, which will set a value on the $scope object called artistBox to be the value of the input box. Below that, we're using the same `ng-click` directive, and calling a function like before, but now we are passing a parameter called `artistBox`. This will actually send the value of the text box to the search function in your controller, which looks like this:

```
function artistController($scope) {
  $scope.artist = 'Foo Fighters'

  $scope.search = function(artist){
    $scope.artist = artist;
  }
}
```

Now, users can type anything they want in the text box, and when they click Search, their text will appear above the box. Now that you've learned the basics of controllers, let's talk about the more complex topic of controller inheritance.

Controller Inheritance

When you use the `ng-controller` directive to link your view to your controller, Angular creates a new child scope that has access to all of its parent's scope properties. Consider the following code:

```
<div ng-controller="RootController">
  <p>Time: {{showTime}}, {{bandName}}!</p>

  <div ng-controller="ChildController">
    <p>Time: {{showTime}}, {{bandName}}!</p>

    <div ng-controller="GrandChildController">
      <p>Time: {{showTime}}, {{bandName}}!</p>
    </div>
  </div>
</div>
```

We've defined three controllers, nested within each other: `Root`, `Child`, and `GrandChild`, and they all bind to `showTime` and `bandName`. Now, we will implement their controllers and see how they share values:

```
app.controller('RootController', ['$scope', function($scope) {
  $scope.showTime = '11 AM';
  $scope.bandName = 'Foo Fighters';
}]);
app.controller('ChildController', ['$scope', function($scope) {
  $scope.showTime = '1PM'
  $scope.bandName = 'Smashing Pumpkins';
}]);
```

```
app.controller('GrandChildController', ['$scope', function($scope) {
  $scope.bandName = 'Rise Against';
}]);
```

This will result in the following HTML:

```
<div ng-controller="RootController">
  <p>Time: 11 AM, Foo Fighters!</p>

  <div ng-controller="ChildController">
    <p>Time: 1PM, Smashing Pumpkins!</p>

    <div ng-controller="GrandChildController">
      <p>Time: 1PM, Rise Against!</p>
    </div>
  </div>
</div>
```

Notice that the `GrandChildController` never defines `showTime`; instead, it gets bound to its parent's property called `showTime`.

Now that you understand scope inheritance, let's shift gears and talk about what does and doesn't belong in a controller.

What Should and Shouldn't Go into a Controller

Controllers really only have two things they should be responsible for: setting up the initial state of the view and providing functionality to the view via functions. The second one of those responsibilities can cause a lot of trouble. What most novice Angular developers tend to do is give their controllers far too much responsibility. They start adding service calls into controllers, DOM manipulation, and try to use them to share code across their applications.

In the preceding hour, we talked about the single responsibility principle and how the different pieces of your application should be responsible for only one thing. This allows us to write simple, maintainable, and easily testable code, which should result in a scalable application. You haven't yet learned about many of the built-in Angular tools that enable you to remove logic from your controllers, but you will; this book covers (eventually) the proper way to do everything mentioned earlier. That said, you can do a few things to your controller to make it less likely that you do things incorrectly.

Best Practices

You have already learned about using `$scope` as a view model within your controller, but `$scope` actually has a lot of extra functionality. For the most part, though, that extra functionality shouldn't exist inside a controller. Luckily, Angular has provided a way to avoid using $scope as your view model. This functionality is called *ControllerAs* and is used as follows:

```
<div ng-controller="ArtistController as artist">
    {{ artist.name }}
</div>
```

Notice that when you use ControllerAs syntax, you now use dot notation for your properties. This can prove useful for readability, especially when you get into nested controllers.

Now that you have made the switch to use ControllerAs syntax in your view, you can avoid using $scope in your controller. Instead, you can use the this keyword, as follows:

```
app.controller('ArtistController', [artistController]);

function artistController() {
  this.name = 'Foo Fighters'

  this.search = function(artist){
    this.name = artist;
  }
};
```

Using the preceding code, you no longer have to inject $scope into your controller, which allows you to limit the number of dependencies the controller has. Another common practice is to always us vm when using ControllerAs, like so:

```
<div ng-controller="ArtistController as vm">
    {{ vm.name }}
</div>
```

By using vm, which stands for "view model," for all your ControllerAs definitions, you can provide a consistent and easy-to-understand way of accessing bindable properties. The final tip for using the ControllerAs syntax is to assign your as to this at the top of your controller, as follows:

```
app.controller('ArtistController', [artistController]);

function artistController() {
  var vm = this;

  vm.name = 'Foo Fighters'

  vm.search = function(artist){
    vm.name = artist;
  }
};
```

Assigning the value of `this` to a variable captures the current representation of your context, which could change when you are inside of a JavaScript callback or nested function. (Remember, the `this` keyword represents the object calling the function, so it changes depending on the function caller.) This can prove especially useful when using promises, which are covered in Hour 8, "Discovering Services: Part II."

Summary

This hour covered using and creating Angular controllers, `$scope`, controller inheritance, and best practices. It's important to keep in mind that Angular controllers share some similarities to their .NET counterpart, but behave more like view models do in the MVVM pattern.

Q&A

Q. **If I shouldn't perform DOM manipulation in my controller, where should I do it?**

A. You should perform DOM manipulation inside directives, which can bind to properties on your controller (view model). For more information on directives, see Hour 9, "Using Built-In Directives," and 10, "Conquering Custom Directives."

Workshop

Quiz

1. What syntax is used to bind a property to a view?

2. How do you call a controller function when a user clicks a button?

3. How do you define a controller so that you don't have to inject `$scope`?

Answers

1. `{{ propertyName }}`

2. `<button ng-click="vm.search()">Search</button>`

3. `<div ng-controller="ArtistController as artist">`

Exercise

For the book management system mentioned in the Introduction, create your first controller using the ControllerAs syntax, add a list of example books to your controller, and create CRUD (create, read, update, delete) methods like `vm.addBook()` and `vm.deleteBook()` on your controller.

Understanding Views, Data Binding, and Event Handling

What You'll Learn in This Hour

- ▶ How Angular views compare to .NET MVC's Razor views and ASP.NET Web Forms
- ▶ How Angular data binding works
- ▶ Using ViewModels in Angular
- ▶ How and why to use ControllerAs syntax
- ▶ What two-way data binding is and why it's awesome
- ▶ Tips for excellent data binding performance
- ▶ Using multiple controllers in a view
- ▶ How to set up your view to use multiple templates
- ▶ Event handling in Angular
- ▶ Best practices for writing amazing and maintainable views

Most applications consist of displaying and transforming data. Whether that data is a list of news articles, a screen full of gadgets for you to purchase, or a grid of pictures of places you could go to lunch, it all boils down to showing users the data they want to see and allowing them to interact with it to get the information they need. In Angular, this user interface is done through views mostly made up of HTML data binding, which is just a way to get the data to the HTML, and event handling, which consists of a way to deal with user interactions.

Angular Views

At a high level, views in Angular are directly analogous to a .NET Model-View-Controller (MVC) view or a .NET .aspx page. Views are your application's user interface. In a view, your application displays data, buttons, links, lists, and anything else the user needs to interact with the app.

Both .NET MVC views and Angular views contain Hypertext Markup Language (HTML) and Cascading Style Sheets (CSS) class references, but they differ in two important ways:

▶ First, one of the main pillars and goals of Angular is to extend the capabilities of HTML so that it becomes a markup language designed for building web applications. Angular views are the same HTML files you know and love, but with new superpowers. Those superpowers are mainly in the form of *directives*, which you can think of as components or widgets that either encapsulate functionality (much like a Web Form user control) or bring additional functionality to existing elements. You'll learn more about Angular directives during Hour 9, "Using Built-in Directives," and Hour 10, "Conquering Custom Directives."

▶ The second way in which Angular views differ from .NET views is how data is bound to a page.

Data Binding

In a .NET Web Forms page, you might set the text of an element in an .aspx page's code behind:

```
<!-- .NET view (page.aspx)-->
<asp:Literal id="ordertotal" runat="server" />
// Code behind (page.cs)
orderTotal.text = "$17.50";
```

In a .NET MVC view, you can display text from your model in numerous ways. One method you might use is the @ symbol with the `model` keyword:

```
<span>@model.orderTotal</span>
```

Here your model has a property on it describing what the order total is. This is probably closest to Angular's syntax, except instead of the @ symbol, Angular uses double curly braces, which is a common front-end templating syntax:

```
<span>{{ vm.orderTotal }}</span>
```

Aside from the curly braces, the main difference between .NET MVC binding and Angular's is that *vm* is the name you've assigned your ViewModel. You could call this *ViewModel*, *myModel*, *fluffyPuppy*, or anything you like. .NET MVC uses a standard *model* as a keyword.

But where does *vm* come from in the Angular example? In a .NET view, you simply declare your model near the top of the page:

```
@model Ecommerce.Models.Order

<span>@model.orderTotal</span>
```

In Angular, though, you can declare your controller in your view, and your ViewModel (vm) is an alias for that controller.

```
<!-- View to show declaring a controller in a view.-->
<div ng-controller="Order as vm">
    <p>{{ vm.orderTotal }}</p>
</div>
```

The ng-controller attribute on the div is a built-in Angular directive that links your view to its corresponding controller. (For bonus points, think about how a view is linked to a controller in .NET MVC.) Order is the name of the controller, and vm is the alias. This type of Angular syntax is called *ControllerAs* syntax because we're referring to the controller by its alias and treating that alias as the controller's view model. The ViewModel's orderTotal property is populated inside the controller:

```
// Controller that assigns a value to the orderTotal property
function Order() {
    var vm = this;
    vm.orderTotal = '$17.00';
}
```

In this example, we've created a vm variable in the controller that is assigned to this, a reference to the controller. That vm, however, is not the same variable as the one created in the view. They can actually have two different names, or you could even just use this in your controller. You should use vm in the controller, though, for a couple of reasons:

▶ First, vm is more representative of what the variable holds. Anything assigned to vm is part of your ViewModel.

▶ Second, just using this in your controller has the potential to be confusing, especially when you start using nested functions. Aliasing *this* with *vm* allows you to later avoid syntax such as the following:

```
var that = this;
```

which becomes necessary when the scope object changes in a nested function but you still need access to the original or outer scope.

Also notice that you no longer need to inject $scope into the controller, because you're not binding anything directly to it. You might use $scope for other things down the road (as discussed later), but for the purposes of your data model, you no longer need it.

You're not required to use ControllerAs syntax in your views, but it is considered a best practice. Most important, it removes the necessity of binding your model directly to $scope, which really cleans up your syntax. You would much rather see

```
vm.orderTotal = getTotal(order);
```

than

```
$scope.vm.orderTotal = getTotal(order);
```

However, if you're reading other examples or someone else's code and it looks like this, don't freak out:

```
<!-- View that does not use controllerAs.-->
<div ng-controller="Order">
    <p>{{ orderTotal }}</p>
</div>
```

This might seem like an easier, more direct approach. And in the simplest of your applications, it is. However, just like use of .NET MVC's `Viewbag` in large applications is typically not a good idea, binding directly to `$scope` also tends to be a bad idea.

As you can see in the view, there is a single variable between the curly braces. In the ControllerAs examples, though, we're binding to the `vm` object. What's the difference?

In JavaScript, values assigned to primitive types (strings, numbers, Booleans) are *immutable*. If you try to change one of these values, JavaScript actually creates a copy of the variable with the new value. However, properties on JavaScript objects are *mutable* values. Those values can be changed without creating a copy.

This is important because when your application needs to change the value of a property, you typically don't want to create a copy of that property; you just need to update the value.

Another important reason to use ControllerAs to alias your controller is due to the way JavaScript's prototypal inheritance works. In Angular, this shows up when you have nested scopes. A nested scope happens any time you have a directive inside a controller, or a nested controller (as discussed in the last chapter). Not binding your values to a controller's alias can lead to some confusing results when you have nested scopes. Consider the following example:

```
<!-- View without ControllerAs syntax that has nested scopes.-->
<div ng-controller="Order">
    <input type="text" ng-model="orderTotal" />
    <div ng-if="showDetails">
        <input type="text" ng-model="orderTotal" />
    </div>
</div>
```

BY THE WAY

A Note on `ng-model`

We'll discuss `ng-model` more in a bit. For this example, just know that it's a property tied to `$scope`.

Assuming we set `showDetails` to true somewhere else in the application, you would expect both inputs to mirror each other, because they share an `ng-model`. And as long as you type in the first text box before the second, you'd be correct. However, if you type in the second text box before the first, the models are distinct. "That's crazy!" I hear you saying. Take a moment and try to think about why this happens.

Give up?

This craziness happens because `ng-if` has its own scope that's a child of the `Order` controller's scope. If you type in the first text box before the second, the child scope inherits the value from the parent scope (the `Order` controller's scope). However, typing in the second text box before the first gives the child scope a distinct value from the first text box, and it won't inherit the first scope's value.

This isn't due to any special properties of `ng-if`, in particular. This scope inheritance happens with anything that would have its own scope, including directives or nested controllers. You'll learn about directive scope later.

DID YOU KNOW?

Prototypal Inheritance

Prototypal inheritance is a concept that gives a lot of JavaScript developers problems, especially coming from a classical inheritance background. It's a vitally important concept, though. To read more about prototypal inheritance, check out the *Mozilla Developer Network's JavaScript Guide*. It's full of great information on JavaScript.

You can avoid all of that mess by using ControllerAs syntax:

```
<!-- View with nested scopes, but with ControllerAs.-->
<div ng-controller="Order as vm">
    <input type="text" ng-model="vm.orderTotal" />
    <div ng-if="showDetails">
        <input type="text" ng-model="vm.orderTotal" />
    </div>
</div>
```

Now the two models explicitly share the same scope of the controller's alias, `vm`, and we've tamed the scope craziness.

Two-Way Data Binding with ng-model

Surrounding a view model property with curly braces is one way to display data from your model in your view. With static data that can't be updated by the user, that method usually suffices. Curly braces provide your view with *one-way data binding,* so called because once data is sent to the view, there is no mechanism with which to send back any updated property values to the controller.

However, in the case of input fields or any other data that might be manipulated by the user, you should use the built-in Angular directive ng-model:

```
<!-- View showing ng-model.-->
<div ng-controller="Order as vm">
    <input type="text" ng-model="vm.orderTotal" />
</div>
```

This directive directly ties that text box's value to the orderTotal property on your ViewModel if one exists. The ng-model directive doesn't require a corresponding property on the ViewModel, though. If one doesn't exist, it will create one. However, in larger real-world applications, this is probably not the best idea because it could lead to confusing code and maintenance issues.

The important takeaway with ng-model is that when the text box is updated, the ViewModel's orderTotal property value is also immediately updated. Conversely, when the ViewModel's orderTotal property value is updated, so is the text in the text box. This is what's known as *two-way data binding*, a really cool feature found in a lot of front-end frameworks.

BY THE WAY

If you're new to the concept of two-way data binding, read the preceding paragraph again. Let that sink in. Why do you think this is such a powerful feature of a framework?

The big deal about two-way binding is that it allows your UI to be updated immediately when a model property changes, without having to write additional code to bring that refreshed data to the front of the application. You can think of it as your data syncing across your model and UI automatically.

Figure 6.1 is directly from the Angular documentation, illustrating precisely how two-way binding works at a high level.

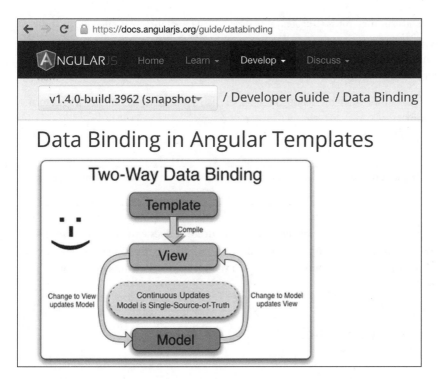

FIGURE 6.1
AngularJS two-way binding.

DID YOU KNOW?

Three-Way Data Binding

It's actually possible to implement three-way data binding in which your database is also updated immediately as soon as the model and UI are updated. One excellent implementation of this is done by Firebase (www.firebase.com), which recently became part of Google. We don't get into Firebase in this book, but it's definitely worth checking out as you further your Angular expertise.

Data Binding Performance

Unfortunately, data binding in Angular does come at a cost. It's likely not usually a concern except in the largest applications, but data binding takes a toll on performance. It's generally accepted that around 2,000 elements on a page can use Angular's data binding before you notice performance issues. You might think that 2,000 elements seems like a lot, but if you think about an application with rows of data in a list and the pieces of data that might also live in these rows, 2,000 isn't out of the realm of possibility.

The reason for this performance hit is that Angular uses "dirty checking." Angular keeps track of a property's value and compares it to its previous value. If the value is different, Angular fires a change event. This is a part of what is known as Angular's `$digest` cycle. Each value that is data bound is added to a `$watch` list.

When Angular has thousands of elements on the `$watch` list, your application isn't going to be as speedy as you want.

BY THE WAY

Take a moment and think about what you could do to make sure that you limit the elements on the `$watch` list.

In Angular 1.3, a feature called *one-time binding* was introduced. It does exactly what it sounds like. When you add a double colon in front of your binding expression, the property is removed from the `$watch` list as soon as the value is rendered in the view. First look at syntax you're already familiar with:

```
<!-- View showing two-way binding.-->
<div ng-controller="Order as vm">
    <input type="text" ng-model="vm.orderTotal" />
    <p>{{ vm.orderTotal }}</p>
</div>
```

In this example, text will be rendered directly below the text box, mirroring what's in the text box. If you edit what's in the text box, the text below it will change instantly. This is because `vm.orderTotal` is two-way bound.

However, in the next example, the bottom text will only match what's in the text box on the first render. Any changes made to the text box after the page is rendered won't be reflected in the text below it. This is because we've added the double colon syntax to the binding expression, telling Angular to bind that expression only once and then remove it from the `$watch` list.

```
<!-- View showing one-time binding.-->
<div ng-controller="Order as vm">
    <input type="text" ng-model="vm.orderTotal" />
    <p>{{ ::vm.orderTotal }}</p>
</div>
```

Using this could potentially increase the performance of your Angular applications when you're using a lot of two-way data binding.

You might be wondering, "If double curly braces is already one-way binding, why do we need the double colon syntax?"

Let's experiment with both and see what we find out.

1. Using plnkr.co or jsfiddle.net, create a view using ControllerAs syntax and give it two `div` elements and a button. In the `div`s, add in curly braces for both, and a double colon for only one. Give the button an `ng-click` attribute with a method name:

```
<body ng-app="myApp">
  <div ng-controller="Order as vm">
    <input type="button" ng-click="vm.addItemToCart()" />
    <div>Order Total: {{ ::vm.orderTotal }}</div>
    <div>Items in cart: {{ vm.itemsInCart }}</div>
  </div>
</body>
```

2. Create a controller with the same name you used in the view. In the controller, create a function with the same name you put into the `ng-click`:

```
angular.module('myApp', [])
  .controller('Order', function(){
    var vm = this;
    vm.orderTotal = "$70.23";
    vm.itemsInCart = 5;

    vm.addItemToCart = function(){
      vm.itemsInCart++;
      // normally we would get the new order total
      // from the server, but for this example, we'll
      // just set it ourselves.
      vm.orderTotal = "$83.92";
    };

  });
```

3. Click the Add Item button several times and notice that the number of items in the cart increases, but the order total never changes. As long as you have the double colons next to `vm.orderTotal`, it will never change. It was bound to the view just once (hence *one-time binding*) and removed from the list of items Angular needed to watch. So even if the `orderTotal` property updates, Angular will never notice.

Multiple Controllers in a View

In smaller applications, each view typically only has one controller. In larger apps, though, a view could have multiple controllers (perhaps one that controls a sidebar and another that controls the main content).

Your view can also have nested controllers, resulting in a parent-child relationship between your controllers. In those cases, simply reuse the `ng-controller` syntax:

```
<!-- View with multiple controllers.-->
<div ng-controller="Shell as shellVM">
    <nav-bar></nav-bar>
    <div ng-controller="Main as mainVM">
       Main Content
    </div>
    <div ng-controller="Sidebar as sidebarVM">
       Sidebar Content
    </div>
</div>
```

Here, the `Shell` controller acts as the parent controller to the two sibling controllers of `Main` and `Sidebar`.

These controllers should each have a specific responsibility. Often, you'll need these controllers to communicate or share data. You'll learn how to do that in Hour 16, "Making Components Communicate."

BY THE WAY

What are some other reasons or scenarios where you might need multiple controllers or nested controllers in a single view?

Multiple Templates

As discussed in the first hour, single-page apps don't need to refresh in the browser. The UI is displayed on a single page, and the content inside of that page lives in your various templates that get shuffled in and out depending on the state of your application.

Out of the box, Angular allows you to include the following syntax that injects your templates' content into the HTML:

```
<!-- View with ng-view.-->
<div ng-app="exampleApp">
```

```
    <div ng-controller="Shell as shellVM">
        <div ng-view></div>
    </div>
</div>
```

Here `ng-view` acts as the window into the rest of your application. All your content gets injected inside of that `div` and is dynamically updated. If you've used partial views in .NET MVC, the concept is similar, but here instead of specifying a particular partial view to include, `ng-view` acts as a dynamic partial view. You'll use routing to tell Angular which template or page should be injected into that `div` at any given point in your app based on the current URL. You'll learn more about routing in Hour 12, "Rationalizing Routing." You could also include multiple templates in your view by using the `ng-include` directive, as covered in Hour 9.

Angular Event Binding

Event binding in Angular follows one of the core tenets of the framework that we've touched on a few times: adding functionality to HTML. Instead of using a jQuery selector to find an element and bind an event to it

```
$('#submitOrderBtn').on('click', function(){
    // post data to server
});
```

Angular's syntax is much more declarative:

```
<input type="button" id="submitOrderBtn" value="Submit"
        ng-click="vm.submitOrder" />
```

In fact, it's pretty similar to ASP.NET Web Forms syntax:

```
<asp:Button id="submitOrderBtn" Text="Submit"
        OnClick="SubmitOrderBtn_Click" runat="server"/>
```

and .NET MVC syntax (without a form):

```
<input type="button" value="Submit"
    onclick="location.href='@Url.Action("Submit", "Order")'" />
```

Angular's syntax is also similar to .NET MVC when using a `<form>` tag to submit data.

.NET MVC:

```
@using (Html.BeginForm())
{
    @Html.TextboxFor(model => model.orderTotal)
    <input type="submit" value="Submit">
}
```

AngularJS:

```
<!-- View using a form.-->
<form ng-submit="vm.submitOrder()">
    <input type="text box" ng-model="vm.OrderTotal" />
    <input type="submit" id="submit" value="Submit" />
</form>
```

Notice the `ng-click` and `ng-submit` directives in the Angular example. That tells Angular that you want to link the event of clicking this button or submitting this form to the method on the vm object.

There are other event handling directives in Angular such as `ng-focus`, `ng-blur`, and mouse-driven events like `ng-mouseover`. These all work just like `ng-click`, where you can either evaluate an expression after the equals sign or call a method on your ViewModel.

You can reference any of the data you see on the view in the controller's event handler function, because all of that data is part of the vm object.

View Best Practices

View code often doesn't get the same love and care as JavaScript code because it's HTML markup. Developers can often get sloppy with markup code and treat it as an afterthought. To avoid sloppy views, check out some of these best practices.

Template File Organization

Each page of your application typically should have its own template, so you should break your views into different files. Because Angular inserts each template into `ng-view`, there's no need for your templates to have their own html, head, or body tags. Those will remain in your index.html file while your templates have their own files.

How you separate the CSS for styling your views is a matter of preference. A common solution is to have a shared CSS file for common styling across templates and then a CSS file either for each view or each application feature area.

Element Attributes

Because Angular adds a significant amount of syntax to your markup, it's important that your view is consistent with the order of each of the element's attributes. For instance, you could keep the id attribute of an element as far to the left as possible, while keeping any built-in Angular directives as far to the right as possible:

```
<input id="orderTotalTextbox" class="form-input"
    placeholder="Order Total" ng-model="vm.orderTotal" />
```

There's no right or wrong way, as long as you're consistent and make it easy to find attributes you're looking for.

Hiding a Template's Raw Content

Most of the time, the double-curly brace data binding syntax will work exactly how you want it to. Sometimes, though, the user of your application could see a flash of the braces at the very beginning of a page load before Angular has had a chance to traverse the page and render your elements.

There are two solutions to this problem:

▶ The first is using the ng-bind directive instead of the curly brace syntax. The usage of ng-bind is identical to ng-model. The difference in these two is simply that ng-bind, like the double curly-braces, uses one-way data binding.

▶ The second solution to the flashing of your prerendered content is to use the ng-cloak directive in an enclosing parent element. This directive simply hides any of the children elements' raw content until Angular has finished processing.

Summary

Think of views in Angular just like Razor views in .NET: They consist of the UI and UI logic of your application. Views have one or more templates and one or more controllers that typically consist of a way to show users data they care about. The way that's done in Angular is through data binding. Data can be bound to a view in either two-way binding, in which data in the view is kept in sync with other parts of the application, or via one-time binding that keeps the variable off of Angular's $watch list. One-time binding was introduced in version 1.3 and can help improve the performance of your applications. The manner in which users interact with the data they care about is handled through events. If you've bound an event to a particular element or action on a page, Angular fires the event when the user performs that action. You can then handle or respond to the event.

Q&A

Q. Can I declare my model at the top of my view like I do in .NET MVC Razor views?

A. No, you don't specifically tell the view your model at the top of the file, but if you use the ControllerAs syntax, that's kind of what you're doing. The alias you assign to your controller is essentially the ViewModel that you're referencing. If you don't use ControllerAs syntax (you really should), your model is going to consist of any properties tied to $scope. So in neither case do you call out your model at the top of the view like in .NET MVC, but it should still be clear what model you're tying to your view.

Q. Can I still bind events in code like I do in jQuery, or is that all handled inside the view in Angular?

A. You are able to bind events in code. For example, you might need to bind events programmatically depending on some condition. If that's the case, that conditional logic and event binding will typically happen in a custom directive, which you learn about in Hour 10.

Q. What's an example of a time it would be better to use one-time binding instead of two-way binding?

A. You should use one-time binding whenever possible to avoid adding items that Angular needs to watch. So any time you don't need data to be updated in the view based on user interaction, use one-time binding. The number of items in a shopping cart, for instance, will change and update based on user behavior. That's definitely a valid use of two-way binding. The description or price of a product, the user's name, or the current date are all examples of data that can probably use one-time binding in your view.

Workshop

Quiz

1. What symbols does Angular use to bind data onto a view?

2. What is the name of the syntax in Angular when you use an alias to refer to your controller?

3. How do you specify a property should use one-time binding in the view?

4. What directive can you use to keep unprocessed content from appearing before Angular has a chance to process your view?

Answers

1. Double curly braces: {{ }}

2. ControllerAs syntax

3. Double colons: ::

4. `ng-cloak`

Exercise

For the book management system mentioned in the Introduction, first create the book list view. Then, inside a `<div>` tag in your view, use the data binding expression syntax to bind the data from the first book in your controller's list of books.

HOUR 7
Discovering Services: Part I

What You'll Learn in This Hour:

▶ What Angular services are
▶ The five types of Angular services
▶ How services are used in controllers
▶ Using services as models

This first Angular services hour shows how services are used to separate concerns, much like different projects or "layers" in a .NET application. In this hour, you learn how services are used to contain an application's logic and how services communicate with other parts of the application. You then learn the different ways to create an Angular service, and when to use each. This hour concludes by showing how you can use Angular services to hold and store an application's data, much in the same way a .NET entity would.

Angular Services

Angular services are the backbone of your application, and will do the majority of the heavy lifting. They are responsible for all of your business logic, and should follow the single-responsibility principle to ensure that your code is easy to understand and maintain. The concept of services should be very familiar if you are already comfortable using .NET class libraries to encapsulate your business logic. Listing 7.1 shows an Angular service that returns the name of a beer:

LISTING 7.1 Angular Service

```
 1: angular
 2:    .module('app')
 3:       .service('beerService', beer);
 4:
 5: function beer() {
 6:    var _brewery = 'Three Floyds'
 7:    var _beer = 'Dark Lord';
 8:    this.getBeer = function() {
 9:       return _brewery + ' ' + _beer;
10:       };
11: }
```

As you can see from these examples, services are really no different from a .NET class that is responsible for some business logic.

BY THE WAY

All Angular Services Are Singletons

Each component of your Angular application that is dependent on a particular service is provided a reference to the sole instance of that service via the service's factory.

Angular has some confusing terminology for services that should be clarified. There are actually five types of services in Angular, one of which is unfortunately called `Service`:

- ▶ `Service`

- ▶ `Factory`

- ▶ `Value`

- ▶ `Constant`

- ▶ `Provider`

It's important to understand the differences between these to make sure that you use the one that fits your needs best. One thing to keep in mind is that each of these service types is actually a provider, which informs the Injector how they should be instantiated. The two most common Angular services are `Service` and `Factory`, so let's take a look at those first.

Service Versus Factory

`Service` and `Factory` are almost identical to each other, so much so that it technically doesn't matter which one you use. That said, you'll learn here a few reasons one might be better than the other. Before that, though, let's take a look at the same service written as a `Service` and then a `Factory` (see Listing 7.2):

LISTING 7.2 Service Versus Factory

```
// Service
 1:    angular
 2:     .module('app')
 3:        .service('beerService', beer);
 4:
 5:  function beer() {
 6:     var _brewery = 'Three Floyds'
 7:     var _beer = 'Alpha King';
 8:     this.getBeer = function() {
 9:        return _brewery + ' ' + _beer;
10:        };
11:  }
12:
13:  // Factory
```

```
14:   angular
15:   .module('app')
16:     .factory('beerFactory', beer);
17:
18:   function beer() {
19:     var _ brewer = 'Three Floyds'
20:     var _beer = 'Alpha King';
21:     var getBeer = function () {
22:       return _brewer + ' ' + _beer;
23:     }
24:
25:   return {
26:     getBeer: getBeer
27:   };
28: }
```

As you can see, the code for both types is almost identical, with the big difference being that
Service uses the this keyword and that Factory returns an object with the publicly available methods. That's because services are instantiated behind the scenes using the new keyword,
whereas factories are not. You should typically use Factory over Service because it allows you
to use the revealing module pattern, which provides an easy-to-read interface for what methods
are publicly available to use (and are easy to read.).

Value Versus Constant

Now that you know a bit about the two most common types of Angular services, let's take
a look at the Value and Constant services. Just like Service and Factory, these two services are also almost identical. Both are used to provide your application with a reusable way to
share static values across your application. Listing 7.3 defines a Value and a Constant:

LISTING 7.3   Value Versus Constant

```
//Value
1:   angular
2:     .module('app')
3:       .value('breweryValue', 'Three Floyds');

//Constant
1:   angular
2:     .module('app')
3:       .constant('breweryConstant', 'Three Floyds');
```

At this point, you're probably wondering what the difference is between the two. You might have
even reread the two pieces of code and come to the conclusion that the folks behind Angular
have a screw loose. Although that may or may not be true, the difference between the two types
is when they are available to use. The Constant service is available during Angular's configuration phase of the application lifecycle, whereas Value services are available only during the run
phase. You'll learn about the differences in phases next when we discuss Angular providers.

Providers

Angular providers are by far the most complex type of service in Angular, and as mentioned earlier are the basis for all the services just covered. They are very similar to the `Service` and `Factory` types, with the key difference being that providers are the only type that can be passed into the app.config. This allows you to set values on the service application-wide before they are injected into any part of your application.

Providers will look like a hybrid of both the `Service` and `Factory` type utilizing the `this` keyword along with returning an object with the publicly available methods. Listing 7.4 is an example of a `Provider`:

LISTING 7.4   Angular Provider

```
 1:  angular
 2:    .module('app')
 3:      .provider('beerProvider', beer);
 4:
 5:  function beer() {
 6:    var brewery = 'Three Floyds'
 7:    this.beer = '';
 8:
 9:    var getBeer = function () {
10:      return _brewery + ' ' + _beer;
11:    }
12:    var beer = {
13:      getBeer: getBeer
14:    };
15:    this.$get = function(){
16:      return beer;
17:    };
18:  }
```

A couple of things to note are the mix of `var` and `this` on variables, and the addition of `this.$get`. Variables that are attached to `this` are able to be set in the app.config, whereas variables declared using `var` are not. The `this.$get` is required on all providers and must return an object containing all publicly available methods.

An example of how to set the value of `this.beer` in your app.config is shown here:

```
1:  app.config(function(beerProvider){
2:    beerProvider.beer = 'Alpha King';
3:  });
```

In review, there are five types of Angular services: `Service`, `Factory`, `Value`, `Constant`, and `Provider`. The first four types are actually just simplified versions of `Provider`, and all five types are singletons. `Factory` and `Service` are almost identical, and `Factory` should be used over `Service` because it is more readable and allows you to use the revealing module pattern.

Value and Constant are also very similar; the difference is that Constant is available during the configuration portion of the application lifecycle and Value is not available until the run portion of the lifecycle. Providers are the most complex version of service and allow you to set properties within your app.config that will be used across your entire application.

Now that you understand the five types of Angular services, let's take a look at how they are used within other portions of your application.

Using Services

One of the most powerful things about services is that they are reusable throughout your application to perform common tasks. Listing 7.5 shows a primitive logger service that you can use throughout your application:

LISTING 7.5   Creating a logger Factory

```
 1:  angular
 2:  .module('app')
 3:  .factory('logger', logger);
 4:
 5:  function logger() {
 6:    var info = function (msg) {
 7:      console.log('INFO: ' + msg);
 8:    }
 9:
10:    return {
11:      info: info
12:    };
13:  }
```

Let's take a look at how to use this logger service in a controller (see Listing 7.6):

LISTING 7.6   Using the logger Factory

```
 1:  angular
 2:  .module('app')
 3:  .controller('BeerController', ['beerService', 'logger']);
 4:
 5:  function BeerController(beerService, logger) {
 6:    var vm = this;
 7:    vm.beer = '';
 8:    vm.title = 'Controller Using a Service';
 9:    activate();
10:    function activate() {
11:      return getBeer().then(function() {
12:        logger.info('Activated Beer Controller');
13:      });
14:    }
15:
```

```
16:     function getBeer() {
17:       return beerService.getBeer().then(function(data) {
18:         vm.beer = data;
19:         logger.info(vm.beer + ' returned from service';
20:           return vm.beer;
21:       });
22:     }
23:   }
```

In this example, we inject two services into our controller via its dependency array: the
`beerService` from earlier in the chapter and the `logger` service we just wrote. (For more
on dependencies, see Hour 11, "Depending on Dependency Injection") We use the `getBeer`
function to retrieve our current beer, and then we use the `logger` service to log the result of the
service and that our controller has been activated.

BY THE WAY

Services Everywhere!

You've learned how to use services in a controller, but they can also be used in directives, filters,
and even other services.

▼ TRY IT YOURSELF

Using a Service in a Service (Serviceception)

Because Services can be used for many different things, you will definitely run into using a service within another service, so let's take a look at how we would use the `logger` service we
wrote and use it in the `beerFactory` from earlier in this hour. Using plnkr.co, jsfiddle.net, or
even on your own in Visual Studio, set up a shell of an Angular app:

1. In a JavaScript file, or in a `<script>` tag, create an app module with the `beer` service:

```
1:   angular
2:     .module('app')
3:       .factory('beerFactory', beer);
4:
5:   function beer() {
6:     var _ brewer = 'Three Floyds'
7:     var _beer = 'Alpha King';
8:     var getBeer = function () {
9:       return _brewer + ' ' + _beer;
10:    }
11:    return {
12:      getBeer: getBeer
13:    };
14:  }
```

2. Inject the `logger` service into the `beerFactory`:

```
1:   angular
2:     .module('app')
3:       .factory('beerFactory', beer);
4:   beer.$inject = ['logger'];
5:   function beer(logger) {
6:     var _ brewer = 'Three Floyds'
7:     var _beer = 'Alpha King';
8:     var getBeer = function () {
9:       return _brewer + ' ' + _beer;
10:    }
11:    return {
12:      getBeer: getBeer
13:    };
14:  }
```

3. Now that you have injected the `logger` service into the `beerService`, let's modify the `beerService` to log information:

```
1:   function beer(logger) {
2:     var brewer = 'Three Floyds';
3:     var beer = 'Alpha King';
4:     var getBeer = function () {
5:       logger.info("We're in the getBeer function");
6:       return brewer + ' ' + beer;
7:     }
8:     return {
9:       getBeer: getBeer
10:    };
11:  }
```

Summary

In this first hour exploring services, you learned the various types of Angular services and learned the difference between them, along with when to use them. You wrote a `beerService` that returns the current beer and a `logger` service that you can use throughout your application. As the hour concluded, you learned about using services in a controller and then within another service.

Q&A

Q. Does Angular provide any built-in services?

A. Yes! Angular has provided a few very useful services that you can use throughout your application, and you'll learn about some of them in the next hour.

Workshop

Quiz

1. How many types of Angular services are there, and what are they?

2. How do you inject a service into another service?

3. Why should you use a `Factory` instead of a `Service`?

Answers

1. Five: `Service`, `Factory`, `Value`, `Constant`, and `Provider`.

2. `firstFactory.$inject = ['secondFactory'];` and pass in 'secondFactory' as an argument to 'firstFactory'.

3. `Factory` allows you to use the revealing module pattern, which provides an easy-to-understand interface declaration.

Exercise

For the book management system mentioned in the Introduction, move your book object and your book CRUD methods into a factory. This keeps your controller light and moves reusable logic into another component.

HOUR 8
Discovering Services: Part II

What You'll Learn in This Hour:

▶ Using services as a DAL

▶ Fetch data from a RESTful service with $http and $resource

▶ Using $q and promises for async programming

The first Angular services hour showed how services are used to separate concerns, much like different projects or "layers" in a .NET application. This hour shows how services can be used as a data access layer (DAL) using the built-in Angular services $http and $resource. This hour also covers asynchronous programming in JavaScript using $q and promises.

Using Services for a DAL

In the preceding hour, we built an Angular service to return static information about beer. In this hour, we write a service that fetches beers from an application programming interface (API), along with creating, updating, and deleting beers. Here is a refresher on the service from the preceding hour:

```
 1:  angular
 2:  .module('app')
 3:    .service('beerService', beer);
 4:
 5:  function beer() {
 6:    var _brewery = 'Three Floyds'
 7:    var _beer = 'Alpha King';
 8:    this.getBeer = function() {
 9:      return _brewery + ' ' + _beer;
10:    };
11:  }
```

Angular provides a simple but powerful built-in service called $http that takes a request object, which will carry out the requested action against the URL you provide and return a promise. You'll learn about promises a little later this hour, but for now, take a look at an example for retrieving a beer from a RESTful service with the ID of 53:

```
 1:  var request = {
 2:    method: 'GET',
 3:    url: 'http://beerapi.com/beer/53'
 4:  }
 5:
 6:  $http(request).success(function(){
 7:      alert("Beer Retrieved Successfully");
 8:    })
 9:    .error(function(){
10:      alert("Beer Retrieval Was Unsuccessful");
11:    }
12:  );
```

In this code, we create a simple `request` object with two values: `method`, which relates to the HTTP verb you want to use, and a `url` that you want to make the request against. We then execute the request by calling $http and passing our `request` object in as a parameter. Angular provides extensive configuration options for $http. The following table from the official Angular documentation shows all the configuration options available to use:

TABLE 8.1 Angular Configuration Options

`method`	`{string}`	HTTP method (for example, `'GET'`, `'POST'`).
`url`	`{string}`	Absolute or relative URL of the resource that is being requested.
`Params`	`{Object.<string|Object>}`	Map of strings or objects that will be turned to `?key1=value1&key2=value2` after the `url`. If the value is not a string, it will be JSONified.
`data`	`{string|Object}`	Data to be sent as the request message data.

headers	{Object}	Map of strings or functions that return strings representing HTTP headers to send to the server. If the return value of a function is `null`, the header will not be sent. Functions accept a `config` object as an argument.
xsrfHeaderName	{string}	Name of HTTP header to populate with the XSRF token.
xsrfCookieName	{string}	Name of cookie containing the XSRF token.
transformRequest	{function(data, headersGetter) | Array.<function(data, headersGetter)>}	`transform` function or an array of such functions. The `transform` function takes the `http` request body and headers and returns its transformed (typically serialized) version.
transformResponse	{function(data, headersGetter, status) |Array. <function(data, headersGetter, status)>}	`transform` function or an array of such functions. The transform function takes the `http` response body, headers, and status and returns its transformed (typically deserialized) version.
paramSerializer	{string|function (Object): string}	A function used to prepare string representation of request parameters (specified as an object). If specified as `string`, it is interpreted as a function registered in with the {$injector}.
cache	{boolean|Cache}	If true, a default $http cache will be used to cache the GET request; otherwise, if a cache instance is built with $cacheFactory, this cache will be used for caching.
timeout	{number|Promise}	Timeout in milliseconds, or promise that should abort the request when resolved.
withCredentials	{boolean}	Whether to set the `withCredentials` flag on the XHR object.

As you can see in the table, `$http(config)` gives you complete control over how you make HTTP requests. However, it may prove to be overkill, so Angular provides shortcut methods for GET, PUT, POST, DELETE, HEAD, PATCH, and JSONP. For example, you can write the same GET request from earlier like this:

```
 1:  $http.get('http://beerapi.com/beer/53')
 2:    .success(function(data, status, headers, config) {
 3:      alert("Beer Retrieved Successfully");
 4:    })
 5:    .error(function(data, status, headers, config) {
 6:      alert("Beer Retrieval Was Unsuccessful");
 7:  });
```

The PUT and POST verbs take an additional parameter for the object you want to update or create. Here is an example of calling `$http.post` to POST a new beer to the beer API:

```
 1:  var newBeer = {
 2:    name: 'Awesome New Beer',
 3:    brewery: 'Angular Brews'
 4:  }
 5:
 6:  $http.post('http://beerapi.com/beer/', newBeer)
 7:    .success(function(data, status, headers, config) {
 8:      alert("Beer Created Successfully");
 9:    })
10:    .error(function(data, status, headers, config) {
11:      alert("An Error Occurred When Creating A Beer");
12:  });
```

These shorthand methods can end up saving you a lot of time, but the Angular team has actually taken it one step further with the inclusion of `$resource`. Note, however, that `$resource` is not included in the standard Angular core, but can be installed in the following ways:

- `npm install angular-resource`

- `bower install angular-resource`

- Include it in your index file: `<script src="/bower_components/angular-resource/angular-resource.js"></script>`

After you have it included in your application, don't forget to add it as a dependency to your app module, as follows:

```
angular.module('app', ['ngResource']);
```

Now that you have angular-Angular resource all set up, you are ready to inject it into your services, and reduce the code you need to write even more. Let's consider the following API signature for our beer service:

```
GET All /beer

GET ID /beer/{beerId}

POST/PUT /beer/{beerId}

DELETE /beer/{beerId}
```

Using `$resource`, we can write the following code that allows Angular to generate CRUD (create, read, update, and delete) methods for us based on our convention, like so:

```
var Beer = $resource('http://beerapi.com/beer/:beerId', {beerId:'@id'});
```

The preceding code sets `Beer` equal to the following object:

```
{
  'get':    {method:'GET'},
  'save':   {method:'POST'},
  'query':  {method:'GET', isArray:true},
  'remove': {method:'DELETE'},
  'delete': {method:'DELETE'}
}
```

Let's take a look at each one of these key-value pairs in turn. The first: `'get'` will execute a GET request using `$http` behind the scenes. By specifying: `beerId:'@id'` in our setup of the resource, when we call `Beer.get` and pass in an object with a property called `id`, Angular will replace `:/beerId` in our route with the value of `id` on your object. You can make this GET request as follows:

```
1:  var beer = Beer.get({idbeerId:53}, function() {
2:    alert(beer.name);
3:  });
```

The preceding code would result in a GET request made to http://beerapi.com/beer/53.

Suppose that you make that same request, and want to update the `brewery` property for that particular beer. You can do the following:

```
1:  var beer = Beer.get({idbeerId:53}, function() {
2:    beer.brewery = "Some Different Brewery";
3:    beer.$save();
4:  });
5:
6:  You can create a new beer like so:
7:
8:  var newBeer = new Beer({name: 'New Beer'});
9:  newBeer.brewery = "Super Awesome Beer Company";
10: beer.$save();
```

Create a Custom Method Using $resource

Angular's $resource returns you a simple object with a handful of standard HTTP requests to use, but you may find that the API you are using doesn't follow Angular's expected convention. $resouce allows you to pass in an options object to specify the creation of additional methods that correspond to other HTTP verbs:

1. In a JavaScript file, or in a `<script>` tag, create a new $resource with a PUT parameter with a default bool set to true in the query string:

```
1:  var Beer = $resource('http://beerapi.com/beer/:beerId', {beerId:'@id'}{
2:      markOutOfStock: {method:'PUT', params:{outOfStock:true}
3:  });
```

2. Call the new method:

```
1:   var beer = Beer.get({idbeerId:53}, function() {
2:       beer.$markOutOfStock(expectedDate: '6/5/2015');
3:   });
```

3. This makes a request to our beer service that looks like this:

```
PUT http://beerapi.com/beer/53/?expectedDate='6/5/2015'&markOutOfStock=true
{id:53, name:'A Beer Name', Brewery:'Cool Brewery Name'}
```

GO TO ▶ If you would like to set up a back end to test this on, see Chapter 22, "Using Angular with ASP.NET Web API," and change your $resource to follow the examples there.

Promises and $q

You may have noticed earlier that whenever we make an $http request, we then write `.success(function).error(function)`. This is because $http requests are asynchronous and return a promise to a specific method for $http called, you guessed it, success and error.

When you make an $http request, it kicks off the request and continues code execution, just like async does in C#. When the request has returned, $http interprets the status code that was returned and either resolves for success (for 2xx codes) or rejects (for 4xx codes). If resolve is called, your success function executes, and if reject is called, the error function is called. Let's take a closer look at Angular's $q service.

$q is a built-in Angular service that enables you to do asynchronous operations using promises. We looked at how $http uses a special version that calls .success or .error, but let's now take a look at using it ourselves with the standard methods. Consider the following code:

```
1:   function asyncCheers(group) {
2:      var deferred = $q.defer();
3:
4:      setTimeout(function() {
5:        deferred.notify('Contemplating a Cheers!');
6:
7:        if (vibeIsRight(group)) {
8:          deferred.resolve('Give a funny toast!');
9:        } else {
10:          deferred.reject("The group doesn't seem ready for a toast
             yet!");
11:        }
12:      }, 1000);
13:
14:      return deferred.promise;
15:   }
16:
17:   var promise = asyncCheers({spirit: 'high', drunk: true});
18:   promise.then(function(response) {
19:      alert('Success'Succes ' + responserespone);
20:   }, function(reason) {
21:      alert('Failed: ' + reason);
22:   }, function(notification) {
23:      alert('Notification receivedrecieved: ' + notification);
24:   });
```

First we create a deferred using $q.defer(), and create a timeout function (because it's an async process), and add logic to notify that we are contemplating making a toast. Then we create logic to either resolve or reject the deferred. Finally, we return the deferred promise.

The next line of code sets a variable called promise equal to the result of asyncCheers, which is a promise object. Because it's a promise, we can create functions for each of the three scenarios. The first, called .then, executes when the deferred is resolved (success), the second is called when the deferred is rejected, and the last is when the deferred is notified of some action.

BY THE WAY

You Can Chain Deferred Calls

Because you have complete control over what functions get called when a promise is resolved, you can actually set it to be a promise, which would be immediately resolved when the first promise is resolved. This allows you to chain as many asynchronous requests as you want!

Summary

This second hour about services covered using the built-in $http Angular service to make HTTP requests. You also learned about using ngResource's $resource, which added a layer of abstraction over $http to save us a lot of code. The hour concluded with a discussion about $q and promises for creating your own asynchronous methods.

Q&A

Q. Does Angular support SOAP services?

A. Angular doesn't support consuming SOAP services out of the box, but the Angular community has a few open source modules that you can use.

Q. Does the object $resource returns include a PUT?

A. No! $resource by default does not return a method for PUT. Follow the section on adding a custom method for an example of how you can add a PUT method to $resource.

Workshop

Quiz

1. How do you install Angular's Resource module?

2. What two methods are returned in the $http promise?

3. How would you trigger an error callback when using a deferred?

Answers

1. `bower install angular-resource`

2. `success` and `error`

3. `deferred.reject()`

Exercise

For the book management system mentioned in the Introduction, use $resource or $http to interact with the open Google Books API. Specifically, wire up an ISBN search when the user is adding a book and has populated the Author and Title fields. Save the ISBN with the book. For example, https://www.googleapis.com/books/v1/volumes?q=flowers+inauthor:keyes will search for any title containing the string "flowers" by an author that matches the name "keyes", such as *Flowers for Algernon*.

Using Built-In Directives

What You'll Learn in This Hour:

▶ What Angular directives are

▶ How to use directives

▶ What the most commonly used directives are

One of the major distinguishing features of Angular is directives. Directives are what give regular old Hypertext Markup Language (HTML) the superpowers it needs to allow you to quickly build dynamic web applications. This hour covers exactly how directives give HTML new and exciting powers. Of course, with great power comes great responsibility, so this hour also covers how to use directives responsibly. The hour concludes with the most common built-in Angular directives and what you can use them to do.

Angular Directives

Angular directives are attributes you can add to HTML elements to give them additional functionality. This can be anything from event binding to giving an element a dynamic Cascading Style Sheets (CSS) class. Instead of explicitly tying your JavaScript code to your HTML like you might with jQuery, Angular uses declarative markup to extend HTML. This is similar to how you'd accomplish a similar task with ASP.NET's MVC (Model-Viewer-Controller) or Web Forms. The following example shows how to bind a button click event using MVC, Web Forms, jQuery, and finally Angular directives:

```
@*.NET MVC*@
@Html.ActionLink("Add Friend", "addFriend")

<%-- .NET Web Forms --%>
<asp:Button ID="addFriendBtn" runat="server" Text="Add Friend" OnClick="addFriend"
/>

// jQuery event binding
  $('#addFriendBtn').on('click', addFriend);
```

```
<!-- Angular event binding -->
<input type="button" id="addFriendBtn" value="Add Friend" ng-click="addFriend()">
```

As you can see from these examples, if you're familiar and comfortable with how .NET handles event binding, you should feel right at home with using Angular directives.

In general, there are two types of directives in Angular:

- Attribute directives

- Element directives

You've already seen an example of an attribute directive. These are any directives that add functionality to an HTML element via an attribute. In fact, you've been using these types of directives all throughout this book already. The first thing you have to do to create an Angular application is add the ng-app directive to an element. Then, everything inside of that element is considered part of your Angular application. You've also seen how to give a template a controller using the ng-controller directive. You'll see more examples of these types of directives a little later, but for now, think about what other kinds of functionality you'd like to give a button if it had additional powers.

Element directives are just like user controls in .NET Web Forms or partial views in MVC. They're an encapsulated and reusable piece of functionality that you can put in your view. You simply use the name of the directive as you would any other HTML element. The following example shows how a .NET Web Forms user control and a .NET MVC partial view compare to an element directive in Angular:

```
<%-- .NET Web Forms User Control --%>
<uc:FriendProfile id="profile" runat="server" />

@*.NET MVC Partial View*@
@Html.RenderPartial("_FriendProfile")

<!-- Angular Element Directive -->
<FriendProfile id="profile"></FriendProfile>
```

Once again, if you're familiar and comfortable with .NET partial views or user controls, you should have no problem with the concept of an Angular component-style directive.

GO TO ▶ You'll learn how to create your own element directives in Hour 10, "Conquering Custom Directives."

BY THE WAY

Other Directive Types

There are actually two other types of Angular directives: class directives and comment directives. Both of these directive types, however, are widely considered to be bad practices. It's very difficult to tell these types of directives apart from a regular class or regular comment, and they provide no benefits over attribute or element directives.

Built-In Angular Directives

Angular comes with a number of directives you've already seen, such as `ng-app`, `ng-controller`, and `ng-model`. You use these directives to bootstrap your application or assign data to your model. This section covers some of the most commonly used directives. These range from DOM manipulation to event handling to repeaters.

BY THE WAY

Full List of Directives

This hour covers some of the directives you're most likely to see and use as you're getting started on your Angular journey. You'll likely see and need more eventually. So for a full list, including examples, check out the Angular docs at https://docs.angularjs.org/api/ng/directive.

---

ng-hide and ng-show

These two attribute directives do just what you think they would do: They hide or show the elements they're placed on. To use these, you supply an expression to the directive that evaluates to a truthy or falsy value:

```
<!-- ng-hide Directive -->
<input type="button" value="Add Friend" ng-hide="vm.isFriend" />
```

In this example, we'd like to hide the Add Friend button if `vm.isFriend` evaluates to `true`. We don't want the button to show if they're already our friend! You could accomplish this same thing if you were to use `ng-show` and the expression evaluates to `false`.

When the element is hidden using `ng-hide` or `ng-show`, it's still in the DOM, but with an `ng-hide` CSS class added to the element:

```
<!-- rendered HTML -->
<input type="button" value="Add Friend" ng-hide="vm.isFriend" class="ng-hide" />
```

ng-if

This directive allows you to accomplish the same thing as `ng-hide` or `ng-show`, but instead of Angular adding a class to the element to hide it, the element isn't added to the DOM at all.

The usage for `ng-if` is identical to that of `ng-hide` and `ng-show`:

```
<!-- ng-if Directive -->
<input type="button" value="Add Friend" ng-if="!vm.isFriend" />
```

Here we're telling Angular that we only want this button added to the DOM if `vm.isFriend` evaluates as `false`.

▼ TRY IT YOURSELF

Using DOM Manipulation Directives

Wanting to hide or show an element in your view is very common. Using plnkr.co, jsfiddle.net, or even on your own in Visual Studio, set up a shell of an Angular app:

1. In a JavaScript file, or in a `<script>` tag, create an `app` module with a controller:

```
angular.module('app', [])
.controller('ctrl', function(){
  var vm = this;
  vm.isFriend = true;
});
```

2. In an HTML file, add a `<body>` tag with an `ng-app` directive along with a controller that has two buttons: one that has an `ng-hide` attribute and one with an `ng-show` attribute:

```
<body ng-app='app'>
  <div ng-controller='ctrl as vm'>
    <h2>Albert Einstein</h2>
    <input type="button" value="Add Friend" ng-hide="vm.isFriend" />
    <input type="button" value="Send Message" ng-if="!vm.isFriend" />
  </div>
</body>
```

Now we have a button that will hide if Albert is already our friend, and another button for sending messages that is only added to the DOM if Albert is not yet our friend.

3. When you run this in the browser, right-click Mr. Einstein's name to inspect the DOM. You should notice that the Add Friend button is there with an `ng-hide` class, while the Send Message button is nowhere to be found. In its place is a comment letting you know that's where the button would be if the expression in the `ng-if` directive had evaluated to `true` (see Figure 9.1).

```
| Elements | Network  Sources  Timeline  Profiles  Resources »        >Ξ  ⚙

        ▼<body ng-app="app" class="ng-scope">
          ▼<div ng-controller="ctrl as vm" class="ng-scope">
              <h2>Albert Einstein</h2>
              <input type="button" value="Add Friend" ng-hide=
              "vm.isFriend" class="ng-hide">
              <!-- ngIf: !vm.isFriend -->
          </div>
        </body>
```

FIGURE 9.1
Add Friend button with the `ng-hide` class.

ng-class

ng-class enables you to dynamically add or remove CSS classes on an element, dependent on the Boolean evaluation of an expression. The syntax for ng-class is a little different, in that you use single curly braces to surround the expression. Then you start with the class name followed by a colon and the expression. If the expression evaluates as true, the class is added to the element:

```
<h2>Albert Einstein<i ng-class="{'fa fa-user': vm.isFriend}"></i></h2>
```

We'd like to add a little user icon next to dear Albert if we've determined he's our friend. The output of this if vm.isFriend evaluates as true is the same as above but with the class attribute added along with fa and fa-user (see Figure 9.2).

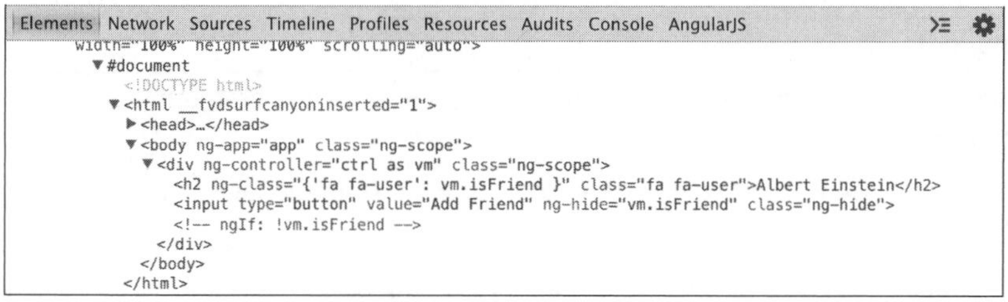

FIGURE 9.2
Classes fa and fa-user added thanks to ng-class.

BY THE WAY

Font Awesome

The class we added to the Albert Einstein heading above (fa and fa-user) is part of the font library called *Font Awesome*. It is, indeed, an awesome library and worth checking out for all of your icon needs: http://fortawesome.github.io/Font-Awesome/.

ng-repeat

One of the directives that you'll use in almost every application you build is ng-repeat. This one also does what its name implies: It repeats the element you attach it to. Use this directive to generate lists and menu items and lots of other stuff. It's directly analogous to the .NET Web Forms Repeater control or .NET Razor view's foreach:

```
<%-- .NET Web Forms Repeater Control --%>
<asp:Repeater id="FriendList" runat="server" DataSource="MyFriends">
  <ItemTemplate>
     <asp:Label runat="server" ID="FriendLabel" text='<%# Eval("FriendName") %>' />
  </ItemTemplate>
</asp:Repeater>
```

```
@*.NET MVC foreach *@
@foreach (var friend in Model.MyFriends)
{
    <div>@friend.Name</div>
}
```

```
<!-- Angular ng-repeat Directive -->
<div ng-repeat="friend in vm.MyFriends">
  {{friend}}
</div>
```

You can use several options with ng-repeat to decorate your repeater, as described in Table 9.1.

TABLE 9.1 `ng-repeat` Properties

Variable	Description
$first	Evaluates as true if the current item in the ng-repeat is the first item in the collection.
$last	Evaluates as true if the current item in the ng-repeat is the last item in the collection.
$index	The 0th-based index of the current item in the ng-repeat.
$odd	Evaluates as true if the index of the current item in the ng-repeat is odd.
$even	Evaluates as true if the index of the current item in the ng-repeat is even.

▼ TRY IT YOURSELF

Using ng-repeat

Depending on your stylistic preferences, you may want to give alternate rows in a list a different background color. Or maybe alternate rows would use a totally different layout. This is a common use case, and is achievable in the Web Forms Repeater user control using <AlternatingItemTemplate>. Here, you learn how to accomplish the same thing with Angular:

1. You can use the same module, controller, and view from the previous Try It Yourself, or feel free to start a new one.

2. In your HTML file, add a <div> tag with an ng-repeat directive that will repeat over a list of friends. (If you're starting a new HTML file, add in an ng-app and an ng-controller directive as in the previous Try It Yourself.)

```
<div ng-repeat='friend in vm.friends'>
  {{friend}}
</div>
```

Now we have a list of our friends ready to display as soon as we create the list in the controller. Onward and upward!

3. In your controller, you'll add an array with your list of friends and assign it to a `vm` property we'll just happen to call `friends`. If you're starting this .js file from scratch, go ahead and create an Angular module and controller just like we did before:

```
angular.module('app', [])
.controller('ctrl', function(){
  var vm = this;
  vm.friends = ['Drew', 'Emily', 'Kailin', 'Letteer',
'Mary', 'Tyler', 'Verite'];
});
```

4. At this point, if you run this, you'll see the list of friends, and you have yourself an `ng-repeat`. We're going to really stretch our legs here, though, and see how we can make each alternating friend in our list have a background color. There are many ways you can do this, but we'll use a combination of `ng-class` and the `$odd` and `$even` variable to assign a different class to every other friend.

We'll start by wrapping our `friend` expression in a `<div>` tag with an `ng-class` directive on it, and assign a class to friends with an `odd` index in the array we created in the previous step:

```
<div ng-repeat='friend in vm.friends'>
  <div ng-class='{"odd-friend": $odd}'>{{friend}}</div>
</div>
```

5. Let's say for the odd-numbered friends that we want them to be highlighted with a light blue (but feel free to get a little crazy with it and add your own color). So, create a small CSS file (or go ahead and do it right in your HTML file; we won't tell anyone) and assign a light blue color to the `odd-friend` class:

```
.odd-friend { color: #CCFFFF; }
```

6. Fire this up in your browser of choice, and you should have something resembling Figure 9.3.

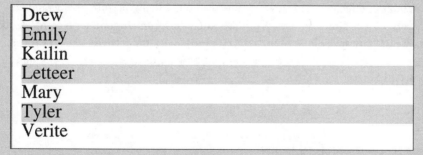

FIGURE 9.3
List of friends with the 'odd-friend' class applied.

ng-click

You read a little bit about this at the beginning of the hour. One important piece to note, though, is that this directive (and other event-based directives like ng-blur, ng-mouseover, ng-keypress, and so on) requires that you pass in a function that you want Angular to call when that event happens.

In the case of ng-click, it's a function we want to call when a user clicks the element containing this directive. This trend holds for all event-based directives:

```
<!-- Angular event binding -->
<input type="button" id="addFriendBtn" value="Add Friend"
      ng-click="vm.addFriend()">
<input type="search" id="searchFriend" ng-model="vm.searchKey"
      ng-keypress="vm.searchForFriend()">
```

In both of the cases above, we're calling a function on the view model when the user either clicks the button or types in the search box. And if you're paying especially close attention, you'll notice that we slipped in a new directive on that second input, which leads us to ng-model.

ng-model

This directive ties the value of an element to its corresponding property on $scope or on your view model. In the preceding example, the value in the search box is assigned to vm.search-Key. We can then reference that ng-model property in our controller.

Summary

This was your first exposure to directives! Hopefully, it's not as scary as it seemed at first. After discussing how directives add special abilities to HTML elements, this hour covered the various types of directives and how you can use them. You then took a tour of some of Angular's most common built-in directives. This hour didn't cover all of them, because that would be silly; Angular has a lot of directives! Check out the Angular documentation for a complete list. Here, though, we did pay special attention to DOM manipulation directives, like ng-class, ng-if, and ng-repeat, along with a couple of event-based directives like ng-click and ng-keypress.

Q&A

Q. Are there special directives for forms?

A. Yep. There are a lot of directives for forms, ranging from ng-submit to submit a form, all the way to directives for input elements like ng-blur or ng-disabled and even validation directives like ng-required. Again, check the Angular documentation for a comprehensive list.

Q. Event-based directives take in a function that Angular calls, but can directives that depend on a Boolean value like `ng-if` call a function to get the value for the expression?

A. Definitely. Just remember to create the function in your controller, and reference it as the directive's value in the view:

```
<!-- ng-if Directive calling a function to get value -->
<input type="button" value="Add Friend" ng-if="vm.checkFriend()" />
```

Q. I did a little research of my own and sometimes see directives mentioned in this chapter, but they have 'data-' before them. What's up with that?

A. First off, good for you for doing additional research! You'll be an Angular expert in no time! By prefixing a directive with 'data-' the developer is making sure the HTML validates. Technically, having attributes that browsers don't inherently know about, such as *ng-app, ng-controller*, or any other Angular directive, is invalid markup. However, the vast majority of modern browsers don't have a problem with leaving off the 'data-' prefix. If you're concerned with validating your HTML, though, by all means add 'data-'!

Workshop

Quiz

1. What are the two main types of Angular directives?

2. What are the two types of Angular directives you should avoid using?

3. What directive is the equivalent of .NET MVC's `@foreach` structure in Razor views?

Answers

1. Attribute and element

2. Class and comment

3. `ng-repeat`

Exercise

For the book management system mentioned in the Introduction, first create the book list view. Then, inside a `<div>` tag in your view, use the data binding expression syntax to bind the data from the first book in your controller's list of books.

HOUR 10
Conquering Custom Directives

What You'll Learn in This Hour:

▸ Why you would ever need to write custom directives

▸ What the link function is

▸ Where to perform DOM manipulation in your Angular app

▸ All about directive scope

▸ Deciding which directive type to use

▸ How to make your directives super reusable

In the preceding hour, you learned about the incredible power of directives. Hopefully, that chapter was enough to sell you on how cool directives are. But if not, that's okay because this hour will definitely close the deal.

This hour covers why you need to write custom directives. The word *custom* can be scary. But don't let it intimidate you; it's awesome, and we'll do it together.

You'll likely need to take control of the DOM at some point in your app. Directives are the place to do it, and you'll learn about where and how.

One of the most confusing parts of directives is scope. We'll clear that up, and by the end of this hour, you'll have a doctorate in directive scopes.[1]

In the preceding hour, we talked about the two main types of Angular directives: element and attribute directives. Now you'll learn when to use each type.

This hour concludes with a discussion on making sure that the directives we write are reusable components.

Sound good? Let's get to it!

---

1. *This is completely untrue.*

Why Custom Directives?

We already talked about the superpowers directives give HTML. But can you imagine if Superman could create his own custom superpowers? He'd be writing an insane amount of code.

Using `ng-click` and `ng-repeat` is obviously essential to writing Angular applications, but there are directives you'll need that Angular doesn't include. In fact, there are entire directive libraries you can drop right into your apps.

BY THE WAY

Directive Libraries

You can search for Angular directives and be hard-pressed not to find dozens of directives other devs have written that you can use (everything from directives on top of Twitter Bootstrap to graphing and charting libraries). Most are free, some are not. For a lot of really useful UI components, check out Angular UI (https://angular-ui.github.io/) and AngularStrap (http://mgcrea.github.io/angular-strap/).

The list of reasons why custom directives are important is long, and we won't beat the point into submission. However, encapsulation of logic and code reuse are the two big reasons.

Imagine you have a text box. You would love for that text box to do something cool when the user presses the Enter key. Sure, you could write some jQuery:

```
// jQuery enter binding
 $('#myAwesomeTextbox').keypress(function(e) {
   if(e.which == 13) {
     //something cool!
   }
});
```

That's some solid code. Where should it go, though, and do you need to copy and paste that code block every time you want to do the same thing in a different place? What if you want to use that in an entirely different app? More copying and pasting? Blasphemy!

We can encapsulate that code block in a directive and reuse it whenever we need. So, let's go ahead and create our first directive.

▼ TRY IT YOURSELF

Your First Custom Directive

Angular's specialty is giving superpowers to HTML. Let's give HTML our own custom superpower by creating a directive that calls a function when a user presses the Enter key in an input. Using plnkr.co, jsfiddle.net, or even on your own in Visual Studio, set up a shell of an Angular app.

1. Create an `app` module with a controller and a function that does something, maybe an alert:

```
angular.module('app', [])
.controller('ctrl', function(){
 var vm = this;
 vm.enterSuperpower = function(){
  alert('You pressed enter!');
 };
});
```

2. In an HTML file, add a `<body>` tag with an `ng-app` directive along with a controller that has an input text box. Add an attribute to the input box that we'll call `on-enter` and assign it to the function you created in step 1:

```
<body ng-app='app'>
 <div ng-controller='ctrl as vm'>
  <input type="textbox" on-enter="vm.enterSuperpower()" />
 </div>
</body>
```

Now we have a text box with our own custom directive on it. Next, we'll create the `on-enter` directive.

3. In a new file (or after your controller), create a directive the same way you created a controller in step 1. We'll call it `'onEnter'`.

WATCH OUT!

Directive Naming

Notice that we camelCase (first letter of the first word is lowercase) the directive name in JavaScript, but snake-case (first letter of all words are lower, and the words are joined with a hyphen) it in the HTML. Angular requires that. In the future when you're debugging your directive because it doesn't seem to be working, the first thing to check should be the naming.

WATCH OUT!

More About Directive Naming

It might seem like a good idea to name your directive with a prefix of *ng* just like Angular does. It's not. *ng* is reserved for Angular directives. If the Angular authors ever get as smart as you are and implement a directive with the same name as yours, you'll run into naming conflicts. Come up with some other, better, cooler prefix and stick with that one.

```
angular.module('app')
.directive('onEnter', function(){
 return{
  link: function(scope, element, attrs){
```

```
element.bind('keypress', function(e){
  if(e.which === 13){
    scope.$apply(function(){
      scope.$eval(attrs.onEnter);
    });
    e.preventDefault();
  }
  });
  }
}
});
```

There's a lot of code in there that we haven't talked about yet. Go ahead and type it in like that and get it working; then we'll talk about it.

Link Function

In the Try it Yourself in the previous section, you wrote a directive that returned what we call the *directive definition object*. That's an object that contains all the properties and configuration of a directive. In the case of our `on-enter` directive, all the logic is in the `link` function. The `link` function is the default place to put your logic. The `link` function executes while the directive is attached to the DOM. This makes it the perfect place to perform any DOM manipulation you need or to bind any events to elements.

You also see that the `link` function is passed three parameters: `scope`, `element`, and `attrs`.

`scope` is the scope you know and love. But the scope of what? Ah, don't get ahead of yourself, young dev. All in time. You'll learn more about directive scope later in this hour. Skip ahead if you can't handle the suspense.

`element` is the element the directive belongs to. In `on-enter`, that means the input box. So, we're able to bind an event right to the element.

`attrs` is short for *attributes*. That is a collection of the attributes on the element. In our `on-enter` directive, we passed in a function as the value of an attribute, so we fetch it using `attrs.onEnter`, and execute the function using `$eval`.

That's probably a lot to take in, but step through the code in a debugger and inspect values. If you take nothing else away, just know that the link function is typically where you would perform DOM manipulation or bind events to elements. The link function is the last piece of a directive that Angular executes. Additionally, Angular doesn't call a directive's link function until it's finished executing all of the link functions of a directive's children. Because it's the last function Angular will call, it's the safest place to put your DOM manipulation logic, since you know the DOM will be ready.

scope.$apply

You probably also noticed the `scope.$apply` line in the `on-enter` directive. Because you bind events with plain JavaScript or jQuery, Angular doesn't know about them. When the event fires, you need a way to let Angular know it has to run a digest cycle, and `scope.$apply` does just the trick.

DOM Manipulation

The most common type of DOM manipulation in most applications is hiding and showing things. When a user clicks a button, show this text. Or if a user selects this option, show a new field. That kind of stuff is all taken care of with the built-in directives `ng-hide` and `ng-show`.

What if there was some other kind of DOM manipulation you needed to do in your application? Can you just put it in the controller? Controllers are just JavaScript, so you could. But it's a bad idea. It's a controller's responsibility to manage the `viewmodel` as well as respond to user input and delegate tasks to services. It's important to keep logic out of controllers so that they're easy to test and maintain.

DOM manipulation code (what you might be used to using jQuery for) should go in the `link` function.

Do you remember the old HTML `<blink>` tag? It made any text inside of it blink. It was an awful abomination, and it was amazing. It's sadly/thankfully no longer supported by most modern browsers. What if you want to bring it back? You'd need to do some DOM manipulation, and we know just the place to do that.

TRY IT YOURSELF ▼

The Blink Tag Makes Its Triumphant Return

The `<blink>` tag is a relic from web development long ago. It simply made the text inside of it blink for no real reason at all. Let's create a `<blink>` tag with an Angular directive.

1. Create an `app` module with a directive and directive definition object that has a `link` function:

```
angular.module('app')
.directive('blink', function(){
return{
  link: function(scope, element, attrs){

  }
 };
 };
});
```

2. Create a view that has an `ng-app` directive in the body tag. Inside the body, create a `<blink>` tag and put some text in it:

```
<body ng-app="app">
 <blink>Hi guys!</blink>
</body>
```

3. We're going to add three new properties to the directive definition object: `restrict`, `template`, and `transclude`. `restrict` just tells the directive whether it should be an element or an attribute. Here, our `<blink>` tag is an element, and we need to give it a template so that Angular knows what we want to display. `transclude` sounds super fancy, but it's just telling the directive to use whatever is between the two element tags. While we're at it in this step, we'll go ahead and put in the DOM manipulation logic that makes our element blink. We'll want our text to blink every 500ms, so we want to use an `interval`. Angular provides a wrapper around `interval` that will do the trick. Finally, the `link` function has access to the directive element, and that's all we need to make this `<blink>` tag rise from the grave:

```
angular.module('app')
.directive('blink', function($interval){
 return{
  restrict: 'E',
  transclude: true,
  link: function(scope, element, attrs){
   $interval(function(){
    var visibilityState =
    element.css('visibility') === 'hidden' ?
    'visible' :
    'hidden';
    element.css('visibility', visibilityState);
   }, 500);
  },
  template: '<span ng-transclude></span>'
  };
 };
});
```

Run this and watch the beautiful blinking magic happen.

Directive Scope

As mentioned before, the `link` function used scope. But what controller's scope is it? By default, directives have a *shared scope* with the parent the directive belongs to. In the case of our `on-enter` directive, that means that the directive will share the scope with whatever controller the directive is inside.

In the case of a directive like on-enter, that's okay because we're not using any of the properties on the parent scope, so you can freely reuse on-enter wherever you need to.

Suppose, however, that you want to create a component-style directive, like you would in an ASP.NET Web Forms user control or an ASP.NET MVC partial.

We have this nifty new on-enter directive that you can put on text boxes. So, let's create a directive that's a text box with on-enter already on it. We'll call it a super-textbox, and we want to use it to allow superheroes to enter their name on the official superhero meetup form so that we know who is attending our meetup. We'll change the function that's called when the user presses Enter to nameEntered, and it will do something super cool like alert the page when the superhero presses the Enter button. So if you're following along, make sure you change your controller to have that function instead.

LISTING 10.1   superTextbox: **An Element Directive with Shared Scope**

```
1: app.module('app')
2: .directive('superTextbox', function(){
3:  return{
4:   restrict: 'E',
5:   template: '<input ng-model="name" on-enter=vm.nameEntered()">{{name}}
6:  }
7:
```

If you skipped the last Try It Yourself (don't do that!), you might notice a couple of new properties on the directive definition object: restrict and template. restrict are telling the directive whether it should be an attribute or an element (or a class or a comment, but we don't like to talk about those). template is telling the directive what to display in the DOM in place of the directive. Our super-textbox is restricted to an element (so we can't use it as an attribute like we did with on-enter), and it's going to be an input.

GO TO ▶ Check out Hour 9, "Using Built-In Directives," for the reason we don't like to talk about class and comment directive types.

If you add this new directive to our app module that we already have from the on-enter example, and then throw a few of those new super-textbox directives in the view (just put a super-textbox element in your HTML like this: <super-textbox>), we should be all set, right?

Check out in Figure 10.1 what we get as we start to type.

What's going on here? Our super-textbox directives are all sharing a scope. When the user updates the name property in the model by typing in the text box, it updates the same property, because the scope is shared by all of the directives. That clearly isn't what we wanted. Surely, we can do something to fix this mess, right? Isolate scope to the rescue!

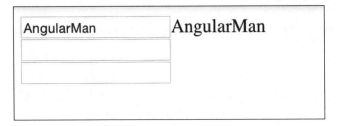

FIGURE 10.1
Multiple copies of a directive sharing scope.

Isolate scope allows you to give each directive its own scope so that the superheroes can all sign in to the meetup. Let's modify the earlier example to use isolate scope.

LISTING 10.2   `superTextbox`: **An Element Directive with Isolate Scope**

```
1: app.module('app')
2: .directive('superTextbox', function(){
3:   return{
4:     restrict: 'E',
5:     scope: {},
6:     template: '<input ng-model="name" on-enter=vm.nameEntered()">{{name}}
7:   }
```

That's a pretty subtle change. We've just added a `scope` property to the directive definition object and assigned it to an empty object. That's basically telling the directive that it's got its own scope at its disposal. So now if we run this and try to use it, we get what we would expect, as shown in Figure 10.2.

AngularMan   **AngularMan**

FIGURE 10.2
Multiple directives using isolate scope.

That's great! But wait, when the user presses Enter, there's no alert. What's up with that?

It makes sense if you think about it. The `nameEntered` function was on the controller's scope, and we gave all the directives their own scope. So, the directive has no idea what you're talking about when you put in `nameEntered`. We think that's perfectly reasonable. In fact, the directive shouldn't know, because then it's not tied to that one controller so tightly. If there were some way for us to just tell the directive what function to call instead of having the scope shared, we could reuse this directive in other parts of our application.

Lucky for us, there is. The view that is using our `super-textbox` directive could just tell us what function to call when the user presses Enter. Then the directive just looks for that function and calls it.

LISTING 10.3   `superTextbox`: **An Element Directive with Isolate Scope and Passed Function**

```
1: app.module('app')
2: .directive('superTextbox', function(){
3:  return{
4:   restrict: 'E',
5:   scope: {
6:    enterFunction: '&'
7:   },
8:   template: '<input ng-model="name" on-enter="enterFunction()">{{name}}
9:  }
```

Then make your view pass in the function you want the directive to call, like this:

```
<super-textbox enter-function='vm.nameEntered()'><super-textbox>
```

Sweet. This is looking good. What's that & symbol all about, though? That tells the directive that you want to assign that scope property to a function. It knows which function because the name on the scope property is the same as the name we used in the view. You can make them different names by telling the directive which property from the view you want to assign to that particular scope.

LISTING 10.4   `superTextbox`: **An Element Directive with Isolate Scope and Passed Function with Different Names**

```
1: app.module('app')
2: .directive('superTextbox', function(){
3:  return{
4:   restrict: 'E',
5:   scope: {
6:    myFunc: '&enterFunction'
7:   },
8:   template: '<input ng-model="name" on-enter="myFunc()">{{name}}
9:  }
```

If you want to customize your `super-textbox`, though, with some fancy placeholder text, can you just pass a string into the directive like we did with a function? Sure can. You would just use an @ symbol instead of the &.

LISTING 10.5   superTextbox: **An Element Directive with Isolate Scope, Passed Function with Different Name, and a Passed String**

```
 1: app.module('app')
 2: .directive('superTextbox', function(){
 3:  return{
 4:    restrict: 'E',
 5:    scope: {
 6:     myFunc: '&enterFunction',
 7:     placeholder: '@'
 8:    },
 9:    template: '<input ng-model="name" on-enter="myFunc()" placeholder=
"{{placeholder}}">{{name}}
10:  }
```

Don't forget to update your view to pass in the placeholder:

```
<super-textbox enter-function='vm.nameEntered()' placeholder='Enter Name'>
<super-textbox>
```

Okay, we're on a roll. There is one last thing we might want to do. A generic alert when the superhero enters his or her name is great, but it'd be a much more welcoming meetup if we could give them a nice message with their name in it. To do that, we need to bind a controller viewmodel property with a property in the isolate scope in the directive. We can do that with the = symbol.

We'll also use this example as an opportunity to introduce a few last properties on the directive definition. That template is getting kind of long. Let's pull that into its own HTML file and reference it. Also, we're going to have a little bit of data logic with our property that we're two-way binding. Let's put that in the directive's controller instead of the link function. Directive controllers are just like the controllers you already know; you just use them to control the directive instead of a view.

LISTING 10.6   superTextbox: **An Element Directive with Isolate Scope, Passed Function with Different Name, a Passed String, and a Two-Way Bound Object**

```
 1: ///controller.js
 2: angular.module('app', [])
 3: .controller('ctrl', function(){
 4:  var vm = this;
 5:  vm.hero = {};
 6:  vm.nameEntered = function(){
 7:   alert('Welcome, ' + vm.hero.name + '!');
 8:  };
 9: });
10:
11:
```

```
12: ///super-textbox.js
13: angular.module('app')
14: .directive('superTextbox', function(){
15:  return{
16:   restrict: 'E',
17:   scope: {
18:    sayHi: '&enterFunction',
19:    placeholder: '@',
20:    hero: '='
21:   },
22:   templateUrl: 'super-textbox.html',
23:   controller: function($scope){
24:    $scope.updateName = function(){
25:     $scope.hero.name = $scope.name;
26:     $scope.sayHi($scope.name);
27:    }
28:   }
29:  };
30: });
31:
32:
33: ///onEnter.js
34: angular.module('app')
35: .directive('onEnter',function(){
36:  return {
37:   link: function(scope,element,attrs) {
38:       element.bind("keypress", function(event) {
39:     if(event.which === 13) {
40:      scope.$apply(function() {
41:         scope.$eval(attrs.onEnter);
42:      });
43:      event.preventDefault();
44:     }
45:    });
46:      }
47:  };
48: });
49:
50:
51: <--super-textbox.html-->
52: <input ng-model="name" on-enter="updateName()" placeholder="{{placeholder}}">
53:
54:
55: <--index.html-->
56:  <body ng-app='app'>
57:  <div ng-controller='ctrl as vm'>
58:
59:   <div>
```

```
60:     <super-textbox
61:     enter-function='vm.nameEntered()'
62:     placeholder='Enter Name'
63:     hero='vm.hero'></super-textbox>
64:   </div>
65:   <div>
66:    <super-textbox
67:    enter-function='vm.nameEntered()'
68:    placeholder='Enter Name'
69:    hero='vm.hero'></super-textbox>
70:   </div>
71:   <div>
72:    <super-textbox
73:    enter-function='vm.nameEntered()'
74:    placeholder='Enter Name'
75:    hero='vm.hero'></super-textbox>
76:   </div>
77:  </div>
78: </body>
```

In `index.html` we're passing `vm.hero` into the `super-textbox` directive using the `hero` attribute. In the directive, we use the = symbol to bind the `vm.hero` to the directive scope's `hero` property. So, when `hero.name` is updated in the directive controller, it's also updated in the parent controller.

We're getting into the directive's controller because we changed the `on-enter` function of the `super-textbox` to call a function that's created in the directive controller. Then the controller takes the `name` property from the directive's `ng-model` and assigns it to the directive scope's `hero.name` property.

Finally, we've renamed the directive scope's function that `index.html` passes in to `sayHi`. The controller calls `sayHi`, which is the function called `vm.nameEntered` in the original controller. That function shows an alert welcoming `vm.hero.name` to the meetup. That's the same `vm.hero.name` we updated in the directive's controller with two-way binding.

That was a long example! Feel free to read it over a couple of times and put all of it in a plnkr or fiddle.

It might help if we summarize your scope options (see Table 10.1).

TABLE 10.1 Directive Isolate Scope Options

Symbol	Description	Common Use Case
&	Allows you to pass a function to the directive and bind it to the directive's isolate scope	A function to call on an attribute directive (like `on-enter`)

Symbol	Description	Common Use Case
@	Allows you to pass a string value to the directive and bind it on the directive's isolate scope	Passing in a customization option for your directive
=	Allows you to pass an object to the directive that is two-way bound to the controller the object belongs to	For use on any property that a directive is in charge of updating and the changes need to be reflected in the original controller

Element Versus Attribute

We've now built a pretty sweet attribute style directive and a pretty sweet element style directive. But how do you know which one your directive should be?

Generally, if you have a component with its own template, that should be an element. That is analogous to using a partial view in ASP.NET MVC or a user control in ASP.NET Web Forms. Attributes add existing functionality to existing elements.

For times when you just can't decide, or you want extra flexibility, you can allow your directive to use either. You can do this by specifying both A and E:

```
restrict: 'AE'
```

Summary

This hour covered why you need custom directives. Sometimes you need custom functionality that Angular directives don't provide. This hour also covered the `link` function and talked about how any DOM manipulation in your application should go in there. That led into a long section on directive scope, which covered isolate scope and passing properties into a directive to add to the directive's isolate scope. The hour concluded by covering when to make your directive an element or an attribute.

Q&A

Q. Is there a difference in the scopes used in the `link` function and the `controller` function of a directive? Why does one have the $ symbol and the other doesn't?

A. It's the same scope. The difference in naming is to indicate that scope is actually injected into the controller, whereas Angular passes it into the `link` function. You can test this out by changing the name of the `scope` parameter in the `link` function. It will still work. If you change `$scope` in the `controller` function, you'll get an error.

Workshop

Quiz

1. What symbol do you use to pass a function into a directive?

2. What is the difference between using the = symbol and the @ symbol?

3. True or False: DOM manipulation should go in the controller.

4. Where should DOM logic go in a directive?

Answers

1. The & symbol

2. The = symbol two-way binds a property between the directive and the controller the directive is a child of. The @ symbol simply passes a string value into the directive.

3. False. Any time you need to manipulate the DOM, put it in a directive! This allows your controllers to be free of DOM logic, allowing them to be more easily tested.

4. The `link` function

GO TO ▶ Check out Hour 18, "Unraveling Unit Tests," to learn more about unit testing in AngularJS.

Exercise

For the book management system mentioned in the Introduction, move the book view properties from within the `ng-repeat` into a book info directive and repeat the directive.

Depending on Dependency Injection

What You'll Learn in This Hour:

▶ A basic overview of dependencies, inversion of control, and dependency injection
▶ Dependency injection strategies in .NET
▶ Why you should use dependency injection in Angular
▶ How you should use dependency injection in Angular

At a high level, modern application development is essentially the art of "connecting" many different components to do something of value. You write some of these components specifically for your project (for example, your Angular services or your .NET business logic manager classes), and you include other components that are written by others (for example, UnderscoreJS or ASP. NET Identity). As a .NET developer, you have tools like NuGet Package Manager so that you can easily install, use, and update openly distributed components. On the front end, tools like NPM and Bower enable developers to do the same. Regardless of where these components originate, your application code connects different components with the goal of achieving loose coupling and high cohesiveness between these components. Your application code has *dependencies* on these different components.

Inversion of Control and Dependency Injection

In any enterprise application, it can become a nightmare to manage all these dependencies because your application code is responsible for creating implementations for these dependencies. *Inversion of control* (IoC) is a design pattern by which a software component leans on an external service to provide implementations of the other required components (dependencies) at runtime. Eek! What does that mean?! Essentially, if you subscribe to the IoC way of thinking, your software component isn't responsible for handling the creation of any other components that it needs to do its work. It delegates that responsibility to something else: an *IoC container*. Your software component can still achieve great power without that great responsibility.

Dependency injection (DI) is a form of IoC by which a DI framework injects component implementations into the constructors of application components. Rather than these components constructing dependent objects themselves, the DI framework assembles the dependencies necessary for your software component to work and provides them. (Martin Fowler calls this object an *assembler*.) Typically, developers refer to IoC and DI (and the terms *IoC container* and *DI container*) interchangeably, but IoC more generically refers to the concept that dependencies are managed outside of the software component, and DI refers specifically to injection of implementations into the software component's constructor.

Dependency Injection in .NET

.NET developers have been using DI for years. Some developers prefer to roll their own DI container, but many third-party DI containers are well supported and are in use in many production applications. These include Castle Windsor, Ninject, and Autofac, among many others. Unity, or the Unity Application Block as it is also known, is Microsoft's DI container developed by the Microsoft Patterns and Practices (MS PnP) group. In the following code sample (Listing 11.1), we're instantiating a `UnityContainer`, the DI container class from Microsoft Unity, during the OWIN Startup process for our ASP.NET Web API project. (OWIN applications have a startup class where you configure components for the application pipeline.) After we instantiate our container, we use it to tie interfaces to implementations. After this configuration, any time either the `IApplicationManager` or `IFileManager` interfaces are used as constructor parameters in any component, Unity will inject the concrete implementations of `ApplicationManager` and `FileManager`, respectively.

LISTING 11.1   OWIN Startup Class with Unity Container Registration

```
1: public partial class Startup
2: {
3:    public void Configuration(IAppBuilder app)
4:    {
5:      var container = new UnityContainer();
6:      container.RegisterType<IApplicationManager, ApplicationManager>()
7:            .RegisterType<IFileManager, FileManager>();
8:    }
9: }
```

After configuring your Unity container, you can simply add dependencies to your component's constructor and Unity will automatically inject the mapped implementations from the configuration. In the following ASP.NET Web API controller, these two dependencies are made available by Unity at runtime, and we save them off as private `readonly` fields for usage by controller methods shown in Listing 11.2.

LISTING 11.2   Sample Controller with Dependencies

```
 1: public class ApplicationController : ApiController
 2: {
 3:    private readonly IApplicationManager _applicationManager;
 4:    private readonly IFileManager _fileManager;
 5:
 6:    public ApplicationController(IApplicationManager applicationManager,
       IFileManager fileManager)
 7:    {
 8:      _applicationManager = applicationManager;
 9:      _fileManager = fileManager;
10:    }
11:
12:    //TODO: Write controller actions that use _applicationManager and _
       fileManager
13: }
```

Currently, the only way to implement Unity (or any other DI container, other than one you build yourself) is to pull third-party code into your project yourself, ideally using NuGet Package Manager. Moving forward, ASP.NET 5 will actually include a (small and limited) DI container out of the box. Although it won't be able to handle more complex features offered by other frameworks such as lifetime management and multiple constructor resolution, it will be useful for teaching newer developers the tenets of DI as they create .NET projects.

The Case for DI on the Front End

Given the rising amount of logic being performed on the front end, testability of your Angular code should be a concern for any project. Proponents of DI often tout increased testability as the pattern's main benefit. Because a component's dependencies are injected at runtime, the developer can easily create mock implementations of these dependencies. This way, tests can be written that actually test the component itself, not the dependencies (which could then have their own tests).

GO TO ▶ See Hour 18, "Unravelling Unit Tests," for more on testing.

In addition, JavaScript function closure around your components forces you to make no assumptions about the components you use. Any JavaScript not wrapped in functions will execute in the global scope. This means that any created variables will remain in the global scope. Rather than calling other components from the global scope, and assuming the implementation that you get back will be the same each time, you can lean on Angular's injector to ensure the same implementation of a component is available for your code to use.

GO TO ▶ Immediately invoked function expressions (IIFEs) are the standard for handling JavaScript function closure. For more on IIFEs, check out Hour 2, "Presenting JavaScript Patterns."

Using Angular's DI

Every Angular component, including controllers, services, and directives, is created and made available to your custom components using Angular's built-in DI container: the Angular injector. Similar to the .NET example shown earlier, if you want to use dependencies in your component, you must configure the DI container so that it can provide the correct implementation. To use Angular's DI, you must annotate your components with their dependencies. This is how the injector knows what dependencies need to be injected. There are three ways to annotate your application component with information about dependent components:

1. Implicitly from the function parameter names (has caveats related to minification)

2. Using the inline array annotation (preferred by the AngularJS team)

3. Using the $inject property annotation (preferred by some developers)

Implicit Annotation

Implicit annotation is the easiest option for annotating dependencies, but has caveats. With this style of annotation, the developer simply inserts the names of the dependencies directly into the component's constructor. In the example in Listing 11.3, notice how we haven't defined the $scope or $window variables; the Angular injector will automatically inject implementations for these dependencies when this component is used.

LISTING 11.3 Sample Controller with Implicit Annotation of Dependencies

```
1: (function () {
2:
3:   angular.module('app').controller('SampleController', function($scope, $window)
     {
4:     $scope.online = $window.navigator.onLine;
5:   });
6:
7: })();
```

DID YOU KNOW?

How Implicit Annotation Works Under the Hood

What's happening behind the scenes here is that the Angular injector is actually calling .toString() on your function, parsing the resulting string representation of your function for the signature (the part after function that is in parentheses), and extracting the parameter names into an array to be used in a similar fashion to the other two annotation methods.

Because these parameter names end up in an array, the order of the parameters does not matter. The example in Listing 11.4 switches the two $scope and $window parameters and is functionally the same as the previous example.

LISTING 11.4 Sample Controller with Implicit Annotation of Dependencies Showing Switched Parameters

```
1: (function () {
2:
3:   angular.module('app').controller('SampleController', function($window,
     $scope) {
4:     $scope.online = $window.navigator.onLine;
5:   });
6:
7: })();
```

Sounds great, right? Unfortunately, the implicit annotation method has a fatal flaw. Because these parameters are JavaScript variables and are not strings, running your code through a minification tool will result in Angular being unable to inject the dependencies you intend. In the minified example in Listing 11.5 (whitespace added for readability), JavaScript variable names are shortened to single letters. Angular now has no reference to know that you want the $scope and $window dependencies to be loaded.

GO TO ▶ For more on minification, see Hour 17, "Demonstrating Deployment."

LISTING 11.5 Sample Controller with Implicit Annotation of Dependencies After Minification

```
1: (function () {
2:
3:   angular.module('app').controller('SampleController', function(a, b) {
4:     a.online = b.navigator.onLine;
5:   });
6:
7: })();
```

Inline Array Annotation

This is the method preferred by the Angular team itself; all official AngularJS documentation uses this method. In the example in Listing 11.6, we are passing an array as the second parameter to .controller(). The first parameter is the controller name of SampleController, and the second parameter is an array that lists each dependent component's name as a string and ultimately includes the actual controller constructor function with its parameters. Because the dependencies are defined as strings, any minification efforts will retain the intended dependency name in the array but will correctly replace the function parameters with single letters. Unlike the implicit annotation method, the developer must keep both the list of dependency names as strings and the actual parameters of the component's constructor in order when using the inline array method.

LISTING 11.6 Sample Controller with Inline Array Annotation of Dependencies

```
 1: (function () {
 2:
 3:   angular.module('app').controller('SampleController', ['$scope', '$window',
       function($scope, $window) {
 4:     $scope.online = $window.navigator.onLine;
 5:   }]);
 6:
 7: })();
```

$inject Property Annotation

The final method is preferred by some Angular developers, including John Papa, the author of the *AngularJS Style Guide*. Functionally, this is similar to the inline array annotation method but has the advantage of readability. If your component has many dependencies, the inline array annotation method may get unwieldy. This method allows the developer to separate the controller constructor function from the dependency list. Similar to the inline array annotation method, the developer must keep the controller constructor function parameters and the $inject array in the same order.

LISTING 11.7 Sample Controller with $inject Property Annotation of Dependencies

```
 1: (function () {
 2:
 3:   angular.module('app').controller('SampleController', SampleController);
 4:
 5:   SampleController.$inject = ['$scope', '$window'];
 6:
 7:   function SampleController($scope, $window) {
 8:     $scope.online = $window.navigator.onLine;
 9:   }
10:
11: })();
```

Summary

This hour discussed software component dependencies and the ideas of inversion of control and dependency injection. Next, we briefly drew comparisons to DI implementations in .NET before uncovering the true benefits to injecting dependencies in front-end code. The hour concluded by discussing three methods for dependency annotation in Angular: implicit annotation, inline array annotation, and $inject property annotation.

Q&A

Q. How can injecting my dependencies help the testability of my components?

A. Consider a custom component that creates a bunch of objects before performing valuable work using those objects. A useful test of this component would test this valuable work without relying on the implementations of these objects or any kind of global state. When creating a test, you can easily mock the dependencies because you aren't testing the dependencies; you're testing the code that performs the valuable work.

Q. In .NET, I have many choices for a DI container, including Unity, Autofac, and Ninject. What are my choices for Angular?

A. Although Angular's injector is similar to these .NET tools in that all are used to provide components with concrete implementations of dependencies at runtime, there are no extension points in Angular for you to swap out the injector for a different DI tool.

Workshop

Quiz

1. What are the three methods of dependency annotation in Angular?

2. Why is the implicit annotation method considered poor practice for production applications?

3. On what object can I set the `$inject` property to an array of my dependency names?

Answers

1. Implicit, inline array, and `$inject` property annotation

2. Typically, in production applications, you will minify your JavaScript for performance benefits. When this occurs, implicit annotation will fail due to variable renaming.

3. An Angular controller

Exercise

For the book management system mentioned in the Introduction, change your dependency injection to use `$inject` so that your code is minification safe. Specifically, this applies to your controller and service you created in Hours 5, "Covering Controllers," and 7, "Discovering Services: Part I," respectively.

Rationalizing Routing

What You'll Learn in This Hour:

▶ Why single-page apps need routing

▶ How to set up routing

▶ How to make your URLs look great with `$locationProvider` and HTML5 mode

▶ How to make a route change wait for something else to execute by using a resolve

Any complex application is going to have more than one area or page to look at. How your application navigates from page to page is something you should think about and plan for. Angular provides an optional router that lets you do just that.

This hour explains why single-page applications need a router, and then shows you how to set up the Angular router. It's really not too different from the routing you might be used to with ASP.NET.

You'll also learn how to clean up your URLs with `$locationProvider` and HTML5 mode, and the hour concludes by showing you how and when to use resolves.

By the end of this hour, you should be routing your way around Angular like a pro.

Routing in a Single-Page App

Just based on the name *single-page app*, it might seem counterintuitive that you need a router to take you to different pages. However, the idea behind a single-page app isn't that there's only one view in your entire application. Instead, you have only one page that gets updated with different views. As far as the browser is concerned, only one base page is loaded, and then all of your HTML is inserted and removed to give the appearance of multiple pages.

There are a couple of different ways to accomplish that.

▶ One is to delete the parent DOM node of a view as soon as you show a new one. This keeps from cluttering up the DOM with unnecessary HTML, but when navigating back to a page, the DOM has to construct it from scratch.

▶ Another way to update the page with new view content is to hide a view as soon as a user navigates away, and show the new view. Leaving the old view in the DOM can make everything a little more complex, but it's sometimes easier to just toggle the display state of a view instead of completely removing it and adding it back.

A router also manages where an application should go if a user types a URL into the address bar of the browser. That's definitely more complex to handle on your own. You would need to parse the URL yourself and determine what view should be visible.

You could manage and coordinate all of those HTML insertions and removals yourself, plus handle and parse URLs to load up views in your application. But that's what a router does for you.

Setting Up Routing with Angular

ngRoute isn't included with Angular out of the box. It requires a separate install. You can install ngRoute a few different ways:

1. From bower with the following command:

   ```
   bower install angular-route@1.3.15
   ```

   Instead of 1.3.15, use whatever version of Angular you'd like and include it in a script tag like this:

   ```
   <script src="bower_components/angular-route/angular-route.js"></script>
   ```

2. Download a local copy from https://code.angularjs.org/ and reference it in a script tag like the following:

   ```
   <script src="angular_components/angular-route.js"></script>
   ```

   Instead of angular_components, use whatever folder you downloaded angular-route.js to.

3. Reference a CDN copy of ngRoute inside of a script tag like this:

   ```
   <script src=" ajax.googleapis.com/ajax/libs/angularjs/X.Y.Z/angular-route.js
   "></script>
   ```

After you have it installed, you need to add ngRoute as a dependency to your module, as shown in Listing 12.1.

LISTING 12.1   Including the `ngRoute` Dependency

```
1: //app.js
2: angular.module('app', [
3:   'ngRoute'
4: ]);
```

GO TO ▶ Check out Hour 11, "Depending on Dependency Injection," for more on dependency injection.

Now we can begin setting up routes. We'll be using $routeProvider to do that, and because Angular only allows you to inject providers in a config function, that's exactly what we'll do, as shown in Listing 12.2

LISTING 12.2   Injecting $routeProvider into the App's config Function

```
1: //app.js
2: angular.module('app', [
3:   'ngRoute'
4: ])
5: .config(function ($routeProvider) {
6:   // implement routes
7: });
```

Now that we've got the $routeProvider all set up, let's take a look at adding a few routes. Suppose, for instance, that we have an application with a login view and a home page. We need to decide what URL would map to the login view and its controller, and what URL would map to the home page and its controller. You can implement those mappings by using the when() function on the $routeProvider. Think about what URLs you would use to map to our login and home views, and then take a look at our solution in Listing 12.3.

LISTING 12.3   Mapping URLs to Views Using the when Function

```
1:  //app.js
2:  angular.module('app', [
3:    'ngRoute'
4:  ])
5:  .config(function ($routeProvider) {
6:    $routeProvider
7:     .when('/login',{
8:       templateUrl: 'login/login.html',
9:       controller: 'Login',
10:      controllerAs: 'vm'
11:    })
12:     .when('/home',{
13:       templateUrl: 'home/home.html',
14:       controller: 'Home',
15:      controllerAs: 'vm'
16:    });
17:  });
```

GO TO ▶ Check out Hour 11, "Depending on Dependency Injection," for more on dependency injection.

Well, that was actually pretty straightforward, wasn't it? We map the login controller and view to a URL that is just '/login', and the home controller and view to a URL that is 'home'. So, when you run this app locally, the URL would look something like "http://localhost:63342/login", where the port number is whatever port you're using locally. In a production environment or on a remote server, the URL might look like "http://www.myangularapp.com/login". What the when function is concerned with is the path after the domain/port.

BY THE WAY

.NET Routing's URLs Versus Angular Routing's URLs

Whereas .NET's routing system is essentially a pattern-matching system, where you can define the pattern of the URL to map to your controller and action, Angular's routing is a bit more manual and direct. You define the actual name of the route for the URL and what controller it should use.

Before any of our views show up, though, we have to include the ngView directive in our view. That directive tells the router where we want to insert the template that we specify in the routing config:

```
<div ng-view></div>
```

The router will now insert your template between those two div tags.

BY THE WAY

ngView Directive Takes Many Forms

You can use the ngView directive as an attribute directive like we did here, but you can also make it a standalone element.

BY THE WAY

You're Only Allowed One ngView per App

One of the major drawbacks of ngRoute is it's difficult to have nested views in your application. There might be times when only part of your application changes, like if you're using a tab bar. If you want URLs to correspond to those pages, you have to use some hacks like using URL parameters.

An alternative to ngRoute is ui-router. This is an open source replacement for ngRoute, and it allows you to have nested views. In addition, it's a bit of a different mindset as far as routing goes. Instead of thinking about routing in matching URLs to controllers, ui-router uses the concept of application *states*. ui-router uses whatever *state* your application is in to route the user. ui-router is a very robust and viable alternative to ngRoute. It is, however, still in beta and under active development, so we do not go into detail about it in this book. If you want more information about it, check out the GitHub for ui-router: https://github.com/angular-ui/ui-router.

Now if you have any content in your templates and you navigate to one of the URLs we've mapped to the template, you should see your content.

But what happens if someone tries to type in a path that we haven't accounted for? There's no view to render, so you'll just get a blank page. We can account for this using the otherwise function on the $routeProvider. Any time there's a URL that doesn't meet one of our rules, we can have the router redirect us to the home page. Let's add that into our example and give it a shot, as shown in Listing 12.4.

LISTING 12.4   **Mapping a Redirect for All Other URLs Using the otherwise Function**

```
 1:  //app.js
 2:  angular.module('app', [
 3:   'ngRoute'
 4:  ])
 5:  .config(function ($routeProvider) {
 6:   $routeProvider
 7:    .when('/login',{
 8:     templateUrl: 'login/login.html',
 9:     controller: 'Login',
10:     controllerAs: 'vm'
11:    })
12:    .when('/home',{
13:     templateUrl: 'home/home.html',
14:     controller: 'Home',
15:     controllerAs: 'vm'
16:    })
17:    .otherwise({
18:     redirectTo: '/home'
19:    });
20: });
```

Now, any time the user enters a path in our app that doesn't match 'home' or 'login', the user will be redirected to 'home'.

To this point, Angular routing shouldn't look very different from ASP.NET routing.

With ASP.NET MVC routing, you have a RouteCollection in a RegisterRoutes method inside of a RouteConfig class. With Angular, you also have a config (even though it's a function) that acts like the RegisterRoutes method. And instead of the RouteCollection, we have the $routeProvider.

Let's take a look in Listing 12.5 at how you might accomplish the same kind of routing we've done so far in Angular with ASP.NET's router.

LISTING 12.5   ASP.NET Routing

```
1: public static void RegisterRoutes(RouteCollection routes)
2: {
3:   routes.MapRoute(
4:     "Default", // Route name
5:     "{controller}/{action}", // Route Pattern
6:     new { controller = "Home", action = "Index" } // Default values
7:   );
8: }
```

ASP.NET routing is actually able to accomplish everything we have in Angular so far in significantly less code, thanks to the pattern-matching system it uses. With this routing, the first parameter in the path automatically maps to the controller. Home is the default controller if it isn't specified. This is exactly what we're doing with Angular's routing.

The when function is accomplishing the same thing that the MapRoute method in ASP.NET routing is. They both specify a URL and some configuration values. In .NET, you can name your routes to reference them in your code later on, but you don't really need to do that with Angular; the URL path you specify will suffice.

If you're familiar with ASP.NET routing, one other difference you might have noticed so far is that in .NET routing; you can use routing to set up parameters. We can actually do this with Angular, as well.

In the URL in the when function, you can specify the name of a parameter prefaced with a colon. That will enable you to fetch those parameters in the controller using the $routeParams service. In this example, let's say that on our home page we want to be able to set a selected product with a parameter in the URL. We can add that parameter to our URL, and then access it in the home controller after we inject the $routeParams service (see Listing 12.6). The name of the parameter in the controller will be whatever name we give it in the when function.

LISTING 12.6   Using Parameters in ngRoute

```
1:  //app.js
2:  angular.module('app', [
3:    'ngRoute'
4:  ])
5:  .config(function ($routeProvider) {
6:    $routeProvider
7:    .when('/login',{
8:      templateUrl: 'login/login.html',
9:      controller: 'Login',
10:     controllerAs: 'vm'
11:   })
12:   .when('/home/:productId',{
```

```
13:    templateUrl: 'home/home.html',
14:    controller: 'Home',
15:    controllerAs: 'vm'
16:  })
17:  .otherwise({
18:    redirectTo: '/home'
19:  });
20: });
21: // home.js
22: angular.module('app')
23:  .controller('Home', Home);
24:
25: Home.$inject = ['$routeParams'];
26:
27: function Home($routeParams){
28:  var vm = this;
29:  var selectedProduct = $routeParams.productId;
30: }
```

Cleaning Up Your URLs with HTML5 Mode

You might have noticed another big difference between .NET routing URLs and Angular URLs: To this point, all of our URLs have a hash mark (#) in them. It's usually not ideal to have symbols in your URL. We can make URLs look like .NET routing URLs with HTML5 mode and the $locationProvider.

We start by injecting $locationProvider into the config function right alongside $routeProvider. Inside the config function, we just call the html5Mode function on the $locationProvider and pass in true (see Listing 12.7).

LISTING 12.7 Setting html5Mode to Remove Hashes from URLs

```
1: //app.js
2: angular.module('app', [
3:  'ngRoute'
4: ])
5: .config(function ($routeProvider, $locationProvider) {
6:  $routeProvider
7:  .when('/login',{
8:    templateUrl: 'login/login.html',
9:    controller: 'Login',
10:   controllerAs: 'vm'
11:  })
12:  .when('/home/:productId',{
13:   templateUrl: 'home/home.html',
14:   controller: 'Home',
```

```
15:    controllerAs: 'vm'
16:  })
17:  .otherwise({
18:    redirectTo: '/home'
19:  });
20:
21:  $locationProvider.html5Mode(true);
22:
23: });
```

BY THE WAY

HTML5 History API

HTML5 mode enables you to use the HTML5 history API, which is a way to manipulate the browser's history using JavaScript. For older browsers that don't support the HTML5 history API, Angular falls back to using the hashtags in your URLs automatically.

Executing Code Before a Route Change with a Resolve

You might sometimes need something else to happen before you navigate to a new page. Perhaps, as in our example, you have a login page and a home page. Maybe before the user can navigate to the home page, the app needs to check with the server to ensure that the user is logged in and then wait for the response. You can do this with a resolve. A resolve contains a promise that must complete successfully before the route will change.

To use a resolve, we just add a `resolve` property to our when function. That property is an object whose property is the name of the value you need to resolve. You assign that property to a function that returns the value. If we need to inject a service into that function, we can do so in the function. Let's do it (see Listing 12.8).

LISTING 12.8   Using a Resolve with `ngRoute`

```
 1: //app.js
 2: angular.module('app', [
 3:   'ngRoute'
 4: ])
 5: .config(function ($routeProvider, $locationProvider) {
 6:   $routeProvider
 7:   .when('/login',{
 8:     templateUrl: 'login/login.html',
 9:     controller: 'Login',
10:     controllerAs: 'vm',
```

```
11:    resolve: {
12:      isLoggedIn: function(userService){
13:        return userService.isUserLoggedIn();
14:      }
15:    }
16:  })
17:  .when('/home/:productId',{
18:    templateUrl: 'home/home.html',
19:    controller: 'Home',
20:    controllerAs: 'vm'
21:  })
22:  .otherwise({
23:    redirectTo: '/home'
24:  });
25:
26:  $locationProvider.html5Mode(true);
27:
28: });
29:
30: // home.js
31: angular.module('app')
32:   .controller('Home', Home);
33:
34: Home.$inject = ['$routeParams', '$location', 'isLoggedIn'];
35:
36: function Home($routeParams, $location, isLoggedIn){
37:   var vm = this;
38:   if(!isLoggedIn){
39:     $location.path('login');
40:     return;
41:   }
42:   var selectedProduct = $routeParams.productId;
43: }
```

Here we've set up the resolve with a property called isLoggedIn. That will call our UserService to check whether a user is logged in. We didn't implement the UserService here, but let's pretend it returns a promise. When that promise completes successfully, the value is assigned to isLoggedIn. That value is then visible to our controller via dependency injection using the same name we gave it in the resolve.

Also notice that we injected $location into the home controller. We can check the value of isLoggedIn, and if the user isn't logged in, we use $location to route the user back to login. Pretty clean, huh?

Summary

This hour covered the ins and outs of Angular routing. You also learned why single-page apps need routing. The hour provided a few different examples of how to implement routing using ngRoute, including using the when function, otherwise function, parameters, and HTML5 mode. The hour concluded with a discussion about resolves and how to use them.

Q&A

Q. If `ui-router` is more powerful than `ngRoute`, and Angular made `ngRoute` a separate module, are there plans to improve it?

A. The Angular team is well aware of the feedback around the current shortcomings of ngRoute. That's part of the reason why it's a separate module. In addition, the team developed an entirely new router for the next major release of Angular. The plan is to back port the new router to the next release of Angular 1. That release is still pending, though, so we aren't ready to talk about it just yet. It's likely that by the time you read this, that new router is released and ready to go. So, look up Angular's Component router for more information.

Q. ASP.NET MVC also has attribute-based routing. Is there any equivalent in Angular?

A. Attribute routing in ASP.NET is a really cool feature that allows you to decorate your action methods with attributes to map routes to those controller actions. Unfortunately, Angular doesn't have anything like this.

Workshop

Quiz

1. What function takes in the path for a route for ngRoute?

2. What directive tells the view where to insert templates for ngRoute?

3. True or False: ngRoute is the only routing solution Angular supports.

4. In a controller, how do you access the property defined with an ngRoute resolve?

Answers

1. when

2. ngView

3. False. `ui-router` is a common and robust routing solution. In addition, the Angular team is working on releasing their new component router.

4. You inject the property into the controller function.

Exercise

For the book management system mentioned in the Introduction, cut and paste your view from Hour 6, "Understanding Views, Data Binding, and Event Handling," into a separate HTML file, reference it using `ng-view`, and create a route for your new view.

Actualizing Application Organization

What You'll Learn in This Hour:

▶ Angular in a single file
▶ Breaking your application into separate files
▶ Organizing your application by file type
▶ Organizing your application by feature
▶ Application pro tips

This hour is all about how to organize your application for scalability, modularity, readability, and maintainability. If you haven't experienced a project that has no organization, poor naming conventions, and little modularity, you're very lucky. Most of us have not been so lucky. This hour covers common pitfalls for angular novices, ways to avoid those pitfalls, and great pro tips to really set your project apart.

Angular in a Single File

Probably the worst thing you could possibly do in an Angular application, or pretty much any other application, is to put everything in one file. That said, your angular application will still work, and unfortunately this happens more often than it should. For simple applications, it might be very tempting to do the following:

```
<html ng-app="taskApp">

  <head>
    <script data-require="angular.js@1.4.0-rc.2" data-server="1.4.0-rc.2"
src="https://code.angularjs.org/1.4.0-rc.2/angular.js"></script>
    <link rel="stylesheet" href="style.css" />

    <script type='text/javascript'>
      var app = angular.module('taskApp', []);
```

```
    app.controller('TaskController', ['$scope','TaskService', function($scope,
taskService){

      var vm = this;
      vm.tasks = taskService.getTasks();
      vm.title = 'Tasks';
    }]);

    app.factory('TaskService', function(){
      function getTasks(){
        return [ {name:'Read a Book'},{name:'Write Email'},{name:'Volunteer'}];
      }

      return {
        getTasks: getTasks
      }
    });
  </script>
</head>

<body>
    <div ng-controller="TaskController as vm">
      <div>{{vm.title}}</div>
      <div ng-repeat="task in vm.tasks">
        <div>{{ task.name }}</div>
      </div>
    </div>
</body>

</html>
```

To be clear, the preceding code absolutely works. However, this is pretty much the worst thing you could ever do. End of story. Please do not under any circumstances try to write an entire application inside your index.html file.

Breaking Your Application into Separate Files

A much better way to write this application is to split it up into multiple files. You can do this logically based on file type. Let's break out this application into separate files, as follows:

```
/*index.html*/
<html>
  <head>
    <script data-require="angular.js@1.4.0-rc.2" data-semver="1.4.0-rc.2"
src="https://code.angularjs.org/1.4.0-rc.2/angular.js"></script>
    <link rel="stylesheet" href="style.css" />
    <script src="task.module.js"></script>
```

```
    <script src="task.controller.js"></script>
    <script src="task.factory.js"></script>
  </head>

  <body  ng-app="taskApp">
      <div ng-controller="TaskController as vm">
        <div>{{vm.title}}</div>
        <div ng-repeat="task in vm.tasks">
          <div>{{ task.name }}</div>
        </div>
      </div>
  </body>
</html>

/*task.module*/
(function(){
  var app = angular.module('taskApp', []);
})();

/*task.controller.js*/
(function(){
  var app = angular.module('taskApp')
    .controller('TaskController', ['$scope','TaskService', function($scope,
taskService){
      var vm = this;
      vm.tasks = taskService.getTasks();
      vm.title = 'Tasks';
    }]);
})();

/*task.factory.js*/
(function(){
  angular.module('taskApp')
    .factory('TaskService', function(){
      function getTasks(){
        return [ {name:'Read a Book'},{name:'Write Email'},{name:'Volunteer'}];
      }

      return {
        getTasks: getTasks
      }
    });
})();
```

This application turns out exactly the same as the first one, but it's now broken into smaller parts that are much easier to understand and maintain. Notice that the scripts all point to the root folder when loading the individual script files, which will really become a nightmare when this application starts to grow.

Organizing Your Application by File Type

There are a couple different strategies for organizing files within your Angular application. The first one will be very familiar to those who have written .NET Model-View-Controller (MVC) applications, which is to organize your files by type. For example, the earlier application would look like this:

-TaskApplication

|-Controllers

|-task.controller.js

|- Services

|- task.service.js

|- Modules

|-task.module.js

This isn't a bad way to organize your files when building really small applications, but can become really unwieldy as your application starts to grow. The preferred way to organize your application is by feature.

Organizing Your Application by Feature

Organizing your application by feature plays right into Angular's modular design, and also allows developers to quickly guess where your logic may be when maintaining your application down the road. Let's add some login files to the application, and reorganize the files based on feature:

-TaskApplication

|-Login

|-login.controller.js

|-login.module.js

|-login.service.js

|-login.html

|-Task

|-task.controller.js

|-task.module.js

|-task.service.js

|-task.html

If you are diligent in organizing your files this way, your application should stay modular and maintainable as your code base grows.

Application Pro Tips

You've already learned some best practices for organizing your application, and those are a great start, but you can do some other simple things to ensure that as your application grows it doesn't become impossible to maintain.

John Papa in his Angular style guide introduces the LIFT principle, which you should keep in mind at all times, not just when building Angular applications, but whenever you are developing. LIFT is an acronym for

▸ Locate your code easily.

▸ Identify code at a glance.

▸ Flat structure as long as we can.

▸ Try to stay DRY (Don't Repeat Yourself).

You've already learned about the first one. As a reminder, however, it's important to be able to easily locate the code you are looking for. You can best achieve this by organizing your application by feature, not by file type.

Identifying code at a glance can be thought of in two parts. The first part is to name your f iles appropriately. You're going to end up with a lot of JavaScript files, even within one feature, so it's important to name them appropriately, such as feature.controller.js and feature. service.js. Make sure to be consistent in your naming conventions. It's also important to have one and only one Angular component within a file. You should never have multiple services, controllers, or other Angular components within the same file.

"Flat structure as long as we can" is similar to the first bullet point, but even if you are organizing your application by feature, you might get carried away and start adding folders when you don't necessarily need to. This could lead to creating files 5+ directories deep, which makes finding a file very tedious. John Papa recommends creating a new nested folder once you hit the 7 to 10 file range, but do what you are comfortable with; after all, this isn't a hard-and-fast rule.

The last bullet, "Try to stay DRY," might be a bit confusing because he isn't talking about code reuse here (although you should absolutely try for code reuse). Instead, he's referring to not making things more complex than they need to be when it comes to naming conventions. He suggests that you don't need to name your view feature.view.html because it's obvious that your .html file is a view. However, he also explains that if you find yourself in a situation when you are torn between *T* and *L*, *I*, or *F*, *T* is the least important.

Summary

This hour talked about what a module actually is, and how it plays an integral part in large-scale applications. The hour also covered the best way to organize your Angular application to separate it into modules.

Q&A

Q. Do I have to follow these principles?

A. No, however, these are industry best practices and help to reduce complexity, increase code reuse, and provide an easy-to-understand application structure.

Q. Where would I put a component that doesn't belong to any one feature?

A. This depends largely on what the component does, but a common practice is to create a Utility module that is shared across other modules.

Workshop

Quiz

1. What's the worst thing you could do in an Angular application?

2. How should your application files be organized?

3. What does LIFT stand for?

Answers

1. Write the whole thing in a single file.

2. You should organize your application by feature, which will lend itself to modules and allow for easier maintenance in large projects.

3. Locate your code easily.

   Identify code at a glance.

   Flat structure as long as we can.

   Try to stay DRY (Don't Repeat Yourself).

Exercise

For the book management system mentioned in the Introduction, move all your files into a module-organized file structure.

HOUR 14
Figuring Out Filters

What You'll Learn in This Hour:

▶ What Angular filters are

▶ Why Angular filters are useful as a data transformation tool

▶ What built-in filters are available

▶ How to create a custom filter

▶ How to use Angular filters for both formatting and searching

During the software requirements gathering phases, stakeholders always have inputs about how certain data should be displayed to the end user. Whether it's string formatting for consistency (for example, always showing things in lowercase), changing dates to the same format, applying the correct currency format to monetary amounts, or any level of custom formatting, developers often find themselves applying various transformations to the raw data before presentation to the user. In unmanaged front-end code, the implementation of this quickly becomes a spaghetti of many single-purpose functions and lots of presentation logic directly in the view.

Fortunately, Angular provides *filters* as a way to quickly and concisely format data for presentation. In addition, filters provide much more functionality than simple formatting; they can be used to, well, filter your data. Angular filters make implementing a simple list search a breeze. By the time you are finished with this hour, you will be able to use both built-in and custom Angular filters for both data formatting and searching through data in your applications.

Examples of Formatting with Built-In Angular Filters

Let's take a look at how we can start using Angular filters to format our data. The examples below can be used directly in your view binding logic (your HTML).

String Casing

Consider a situation in which you are rendering previously entered user data and want to ensure presentation consistency for data that could have been entered differently by different people (for example, "John Doe", "jOHN dOE", and "john doe" all render as "john doe").

In the .NET world, strings can easily be made lowercase by using the `System.string.toLower()` method (and can likewise be made uppercase with the `System.string.toUpper()` method).

Angular has a few built-in filters as well, one of which is `lowercase`. In the following example, we assign a string to a variable on the `$scope` and run it through the `lowercase` filter in our view to yield john doe. Notice the Angular filter syntax, which uses a pipe character and the filter name:

```
<!-- View to show a name in lower case-->
<div ng-app>
    <div ng-controller="ExampleCtrl">
        <p>{{ name | lowercase }}</p>
    </div>
</div>
// Controller that assigns a string.
function ExampleCtrl($scope) {
    $scope.name = "JoHn DoE";
}
```

With the pipe syntax, we can actually run the data through multiple filters. Below, we apply `lowercase` and then apply `uppercase` to yield JOHN DOE. In .NET, this is akin to writing `name.toLower().toUpper()`.

In this specific example, the `uppercase` filter basically undoes the work performed by the `lowercase` filter; however, if the first filter were to append `"- name"` to the string instead of making it lowercase, the result would be JOHN DOE - NAME:

```
<!-- View to show a name in lowercase-->
<div ng-app>
    <div ng-controller="ExampleCtrl">
        <p>{{ name | lowercase | uppercase }}</p>
    </div>
</div>
// Controller that assigns a string.
function ExampleCtrl($scope) {
    $scope.name = "JoHn DoE";
}
```

Dates

Date presentation can be a huge headache for a developer. Fortunately, Angular developers can lean on the framework to do the heavy lifting when it comes to date formatting in Angular apps.

For the following example, consider a situation in which the same date and time data from the server must be shown as just a date on one view, but as a date with the time as well on another view. We take a full date with time information and format it in two different instances: once with just the date, and once with the date and time. Here, we're using the built-in date filter. Notice the filter syntax here for the parameter to the date filter: After the filter name, you include a colon and then the variable you'd like to pass in. In these two instances, we're passing in the shortDate and medium formats.

In .NET, the System.DateTime structure provides two helper methods for accomplishing similar tasks. The System.DateTime.toShortDateString() applied to the same sample date in the following example would yield 3/3/2015. Likewise, the System.DateTime.toLongDateString() method would yield Tuesday, March 3, 2015. When combined with the System.DateTime.toLongTimeString() method, we could get to the full date and time:

```
<!-- View to show two date formats.-->
<div ng-app>
    <div ng-controller="ExampleCtrl">
        <p>Just date: {{ transactionDateTime | date:"shortDate"}}</p>
        <p>Date and time: {{ transactionDateTime | date:"medium" }}</p>
    </div>
</div>
// Controller that assigns a string representation of a date.
function ExampleCtrl($scope) {
    $scope.transactionDateTime = "2015-03-03T23:15:12.8258574";
}
```

The preceding example yields the following:

> Just date: 3/3/15
>
> Date and time: Mar 3, 2015 11:15:12 PM

Currencies

Imagine that you're building a system that shows financial transactions in various currencies. Part of what can make currency formatting a challenge is all of the inconsistencies across currencies. For example, whereas U.S. dollars are printed like $X,XXX.XX with a comma separating thousands and a decimal point separating dollars and cents, euros are printed like €Y.YYY,YY, with the punctuation reversed. In addition, whereas U.S. dollars and euros print the symbol first, other currencies like Swedish krona print the symbol last (for example, 2 495 kr).

We'll dive into a deeper example later, but in the following example, we use Angular's built-in `currency` filter to handle the addition of the symbol and rounding. Notice that we're optionally setting the currency symbol as the first parameter to the `currency` filter because it automatically assumes $ if no symbol is sent.

In .NET, you can get basic currency formatting by passing the `"C"` format specifier to the `.toString()` method. Later, we'll look at a more advanced example:

```
<!-- View to show two monetary amounts.-->
<div ng-app>
    <div ng-controller="ExampleCtrl">
        <p>EUR amount: {{ transactionFromAmount | currency:"€"}}</p>
        <p>USD amount: {{ transactionToAmount | currency }}</p>
    </div>
</div>
// Controller that assigns two monetary amounts.
function ExampleCtrl($scope) {
    $scope.transactionFromAmount = "1234.56"; //EUR
    $scope.transactionToAmount = "1295.6099870987"; //USD
}
```

The preceding example yields the following:

> EUR amount: €1,234.56
>
> USD amount: $1,295.61

Create Your Own Angular Filter

Now that you've seen a few examples of using Angular's built-in filters, let's take a look at how you can build your own custom filters to satisfy more detailed requirements. The following three examples build on the previous three examples.

A Better Capitalization Filter

In the capitalization example earlier, we looked at Angular's built-in `lowercase` and `uppercase` filters. However, users prefer that we should actually show names as "John Doe," not "john doe." Because first-letter capitalization (known as *title casing*) isn't a built-in Angular filter, we'll have to build one ourselves.

In the following example, we first grab a reference to our app module with `angular.module('app', [])`. Then, we use the `.filter()` method to declare a new filter that will be accessible by any component within our module. We pass `'titlecase'` as the name of the filter along with the function that will execute when the view renders. Inside the filter's function, we're matching each contiguous word with a regular expression and passing in a function to run on each match:

```
<!-- View to capitalize a name.-->
<div ng-app="app">
    <div ng-controller="ExampleCtrl">
        <p>{{ name | titlecase }}</p>
    </div>
</div>
// Filter for titlecasing a string
// Adopted from http://stackoverflow.com/a/196991
angular.module('app', []).filter('titlecase', function () {
    return function (str) {
        return str.replace(/\w\S*/g, function(txt) {
            return txt.charAt(0).toUpperCase() + txt.substr(1).toLowerCase();
        });
    };
});

// Controller that assigns a string.
function ExampleCtrl($scope) {
    $scope.name = "JoHn DoE";
}
```

BY THE WAY

How Execution Works

Technically, this will be executed whenever Angular's `$digest()` runs, so changes to the backing `ng-model` will cause the view to be rerendered and your custom filter will be applied.

When this filter runs, the result is John Doe (a name in the format we wanted).

A Better Date Filter

The built-in Angular `date` filter is very versatile and will work in many date presentation situations; however, it will only work for formatting a date as a singular moment in time. If we want to calculate a time interval (.NET folks, this is a `TimeSpan`), we will need to build our own custom filter. Let's build upon our date example from earlier. Now, we will be storing three separate dates about our transactions: the created date, the submitted date, and the due date. After a user submits a transaction, we want to show how long ago this transaction was created and how long until it is due.

In the following example, we again grab a reference to our `app` module with `angular.module('app', [])` and use `.filter()` to declare a new filter with the name `'timespanfrom'`. This filter also depends on the excellent MomentJS library for date manipulation, so we inject it. The inner function takes the target date as the first parameter and the "anchor" date, the date from which to calculate the timespan, as the second parameter. Moment's `.from()` method takes an optional second parameter of `true` to return the value without a suffix like "ago":

```
<!-- View to show two date formats as timespans.-->
<div ng-app="app">
    <div ng-controller="ExampleCtrl">
        <p>
        Transaction was created
        {{ transactionCreationDate | timespanfrom:transactionSubmitDate }}
        before
        {{ transactionSubmitDate | date:"mediumDate" }}
        </p>
        <p>
        Transaction is due
        {{ transactionDueDate | timespanfrom:transactionSubmitDate }}
        after
        {{ transactionSubmitDate | date:"mediumDate" }}
        </p>
    </div>
</div>
// Filter for properly formatting dates as timespans.
angular.module('app', []).filter('timespanfrom', function (moment) {
    return function (date, anchor) {
        return moment(date).from(anchor, true);
    };
});

// Controller that assigns string representations of three dates.
function ExampleCtrl($scope) {
    $scope.transactionCreationDate = "2015-03-01";
    $scope.transactionSubmitDate = "2015-03-23";
    $scope.transactionDueDate = "2015-04-01";
}
```

This example yields the following:

> Transaction was created 22 days before Mar 23, 2015
>
> Transaction is due 9 days after Mar 23, 2015

A Better Currency Filter

Our currency filter example above is great for simple symbol concatenation and rounding, but the reality is that the international currency formatting landscape is much more complex. As mentioned earlier, there are many inconsistencies between U.S. dollar, euro, and Swedish krona including different punctuation for the thousands separator, different punctuation for the cents separator, and a different location of the symbol (prefix versus postfix). Let's build a better currency formatter that solves these issues.

In the following example, we have three transaction objects assigned to $scope that represent the same transaction in three different currencies. Each of these three objects has two parameters: amount representing the monetary value for the transaction and currency combination, and currency representing the three-letter ISO currency code for the transaction amount (either EUR, USD, or SEK):

```
// Controller that assigns monetary amounts in three currencies.
function ExampleCtrl($scope) {

    $scope.transactionFrom = {
        amount: 1234.56,
        currency: "EUR"
    };
    $scope.transactionTo = {
        amount: 1295.6099870987,
        currency: "USD"
    };
    $scope.transactionTransmit = {
        amount: 11296.7187340234,
        currency: "SEK"
    };
}
```

BY THE WAY

Overwriting Built-In Filters

We could have simply called our custom filter currency, but doing so would just overwrite the Angular built-in currency filter.

In our view, we print out all three of these objects' amount properties and run them through our custom customcurrency filter, passing in the currency ISO three-letter code as a parameter to the filter:

```
<!-- View to show monetary amounts for a transaction-->
<div ng-app="app">
    <div ng-controller="ExampleCtrl">
        <p>EUR amount: {{ transactionFrom.amount | customcurrency:transactionFrom.
currency}}</p>
        <p>USD amount: {{ transactionTo.amount | customcurrency:transactionTo.
currency }}</p>
        <p>SEK amount: {{ transactionTransmit.amount | customcurrency:transaction
Transmit.currency }}</p>
    </div>
</div>
```

Finally, let's examine the code for the filter itself. First, we use `.module()` to grab a reference to our module and use `.filter()` to create a custom filter. We give it the name of `customcurrency` and pass in `numberFilter` as a parameter. If you want to use other filters inside your custom filter, including Angular built-in ones, simply take the filter's identifier and append "Filter" to the end of it. Angular's injector will provide the right function for you.

Inside the filter's function, we first define a mapping of the three-letter currency code to an object with properties detailing the currency's inconsistencies, including the character to use for the thousands separator, the character to use for the decimal separator, the currency's symbol, and the placement of the symbol in the resulting formatted string (either prefix or postfix). Then we use the built-in number filter, which defaults the thousand and decimal separators to the default U.S. dollar standard, to round and format the amount. Next, we do some string replacements to change the default separators to letters and then to the correct separators defined in our mapping. Finally, we apply the symbol in the right position and return it:

```
// Filter for properly formatting currency.
angular.module('app', []).filter('customcurrency', function (numberFilter) {
    return function (amount, currencyISO) {

        // Define all currencies and their differences.
        var currencies = {
            "EUR": {
                thousandSeparator: '.',
                decimalSeparator: ',',
                symbol: '€',
                symbolIsPrefix: true
            },
            "USD": {
                thousandSeparator: ',',
                decimalSeparator: '.',
                symbol: '$',
                symbolIsPrefix: true
            },
            "SEK": {
                thousandSeparator: ' ',
                decimalSeparator: '.',
                symbol: 'kr',
                symbolIsPrefix: false
            }
        }

        // Round the number using Angular's built-in number filter.
        var strAmount = numberFilter(amount, 2);

        // Replace the default separators with letters to identify them.
        strAmount = strAmount.replace(/\,/g, "T");
        strAmount = strAmount.replace(/\./g, "D");
```

```
    // Replace the letters with the correct separator.
    strAmount = strAmount
            .replace(/T/g, currencies[currencyISO].thousandSeparator);
    strAmount = strAmount
            .replace(/D/g, currencies[currencyISO].decimalSeparator);

    // Apply the symbol.
    if (currencies[currencyISO].symbolIsPrefix) {
        strAmount = currencies[currencyISO].symbol + strAmount;
    } else {
        strAmount = strAmount + ' ' + currencies[currencyISO].symbol;
    }

    return strAmount;

    };
});
```

The preceding example yields the following:

    EUR amount: €1.234,56

    USD amount: $1,295.61

    SEK amount: 11 296.72 kr

In .NET, you can use the `"C"` format specifier as a parameter to the `.toString()` method and provide a `CultureInfo` as the optional second parameter. This culture info uses .NET's Culture Info Codes to automatically determine the currency symbol, symbol placement, thousands separator, and decimal separator for you. Consider this .NET example:

```
double money = 1234.56;

var us = CultureInfo.CreateSpecificCulture("en-US");
var italy = CultureInfo.CreateSpecificCulture("it-IT");
var sweden = CultureInfo.CreateSpecificCulture("sv-SE");

var usd = money.ToString("C", us);
var eur = money.ToString("C", italy);
var sek = money.ToString("C", sweden);

Console.WriteLine(usd);
Console.WriteLine(eur);
Console.WriteLine(sek);
```

This .NET example yields the following:

    $1,234.56

    € 1.234,56

    1.234,56 kr

▼ TRY IT YOURSELF

Building the UI for a Transaction Ledger Application

Here we'll combine our `titlecase` filter for enforcing capitalization consistency for user input (first and last names), the built-in Angular `date` filter for date formatting, and our `customcurrency` filter for localized currency formatting depending on the currency code. Specifically, we'll be building a user interface that shows data about investment transactions, including the investor's name, the transaction creation date, the transaction submission date, the transaction due date, the transaction's amount in the investor's currency (the person receiving the money), the transaction's amount in the investment's currency (the party receiving the money), and the transaction's amount in the currency in which the money was sent.

1. Create a view that shows the necessary data defined above. Because this is tabular data, you'll likely want to use a table to present the data. Don't forget to include an `ng-app` attribute on the root element and the `ng-controller` attribute to define the view scope for your controller:

```
<!-- View to show data for three transactions -->
<div ng-app="app">
    <table ng-controller="ExampleCtrl">
        <tr>
            <th>Investor Name</th>
            <th>Creation Date</th>
            <th>Submit Date</th>
            <th>Due Date</th>
            <th>From Amount</th>
            <th>To Amount</th>
            <th>Transmit Amount</th>
        </tr>
    </table>
</div>
```

2. Now that we've got the basics for our view, let's add a row that will repeat for each transaction. For this, we'll use the `ng-repeat` directive. We'll add a `<td>` for each data point we want to display. For now, just give each data point any name that makes sense; we'll tie them in the JavaScript later:

```
<!-- View to show data for three transactions -->
<div ng-app="app">
    <table ng-controller="ExampleCtrl">
        <tr>
            <th>Investor Name</th>
            <th>Creation Date</th>
            <th>Submit Date</th>
            <th>Due Date</th>
            <th>From Amount</th>
            <th>To Amount</th>
            <th>Transmit Amount</th>
        </tr>
```

```
        <tr ng-repeat="t in transactions">
            <td>{{ t.investorName }}</td>
            <td>{{ t.creationDate }}</td>
            <td>{{ t.submitDate }}</td>
            <td>{{ t.dueDate }}</td>
            <td>{{ t.from.amount }}</td>
            <td>{{ t.to.amount }}</td>
            <td>{{ t.transmit.amount }}</td>
        </tr>
    </table>
</div>
```

3. Let's wrap up our work on the view by implementing all of the filters that we've learned about in this chapter. Let's use our `titlecase` filter to present the investor's name correctly. The built-in Angular `shortDate` filter will work for the three dates: transaction creation, transaction submission, and transaction due date. For the three amounts, we'll use our `customcurrency` directive from earlier:

```
<!-- View to show data for three transactions -->
<div ng-app="app">
    <table ng-controller="ExampleCtrl">
        <tr>
            <th>Investor Name</th>
            <th>Creation Date</th>
            <th>Submit Date</th>
            <th>Due Date</th>
            <th>From Amount</th>
            <th>To Amount</th>
            <th>Transmit Amount</th>
        </tr>
        <tr ng-repeat="t in transactions">
            <td>{{ t.investorName | titlecase }}</td>
            <td>{{ t.creationDate | date:"shortDate" }}</td>
            <td>{{ t.submitDate | date:"shortDate" }}</td>
            <td>{{ t.dueDate | date:"shortDate" }}</td>
            <td>{{ t.from.amount | customcurrency:t.from.currency}}</td>
            <td>{{ t.to.amount | customcurrency:t.to.currency}}</td>
            <td>{{ t.transmit.amount | customcurrency:t.transmit.currency}}</td>
        </tr>
    </table>
</div>
```

4. Before we bind the data in a controller, let's set up our filters. We'll grab a reference to our Angular app with `angular.module('app', [])` and chain the filter definitions:

```
// Filter for titlecasing a string
// Adopted from http://stackoverflow.com/a/196991
angular.module('app', [])
    .filter('titlecase', function () {
        return function (str) {
            return str.replace(/\w\S*/g, function(txt) {
                return txt.charAt(0).toUpperCase() + txt.substr(1).toLowerCase();
            });
        };
    }) // Filter for properly formatting currency.
    .filter('customcurrency', function (numberFilter) {
        return function (amount, currencyISO) {

            // Define all currencies and their differences.
            var currencies = {
                "EUR": {
                    thousandSeparator: '.',
                    decimalSeparator: ',',
                    symbol: '€',
                    symbolIsPrefix: true
                },
                "USD": {
                    thousandSeparator: ',',
                    decimalSeparator: '.',
                    symbol: '$',
                    symbolIsPrefix: true
                },
                "SEK": {
                    thousandSeparator: ' ',
                    decimalSeparator: '.',
                    symbol: 'kr',
                    symbolIsPrefix: false
                }
            }

            // Round the number using Angular's built-in number filter.
            var strAmount = numberFilter(amount, 2);

            // Replace the default separators with letters to identify them.
            strAmount = strAmount.replace(/\,/g, "T");
            strAmount = strAmount.replace(/\./g, "D");
```

```
            // Replace the letters with the correct separator.
            strAmount = strAmount
                    .replace(/T/g, currencies[currencyISO].
                    thousandSeparator);
            strAmount = strAmount
                    .replace(/D/g, currencies[currencyISO].
                    decimalSeparator);

            // Apply the symbol.
            if (currencies[currencyISO].symbolIsPrefix) {
                strAmount = currencies[currencyISO].symbol + strAmount;
            } else {
                strAmount = strAmount + ' ' + currencies[currencyISO].symbol;
            }

            return strAmount;

        };
    });
```

5. Now that we've got our view completed and our filters ready, let's create the controller that will make our data available to the view. We're going to set an array of transaction objects on the $scope. Each transaction's properties will need to match our references in the view. (For example, if you call the investor name's property "investorName" in the view, you need to call the object property "investorName" here as well.) For the three amounts, we want to track specific data on each one (the amount and the currency code), so we'll create nested objects for each. The from property refers to the investor's side of the transaction, the to property refers to the investment's side of the transaction, and the transmit property refers to the amount/currency while the transaction was in flight:

```
// Controller that assigns three transactions. function ExampleCtrl($scope) {
$scope.transactions = [{
    investorName: "john doe",
    creationDate: "2015-03-01",
    submitDate: "2015-03-23",
    dueDate: "2015-04-01",
    from: {
        amount: 1234.56,
        currency: "EUR"
    },
    to: {
        amount: 1295.61,
        currency: "USD"
    },
    transmit: {
        amount: 11296.72,
        currency: "SEK"
    }
```

▼

```
    }, {
        investorName: "JAKE SMITH",
        creationDate: "2015-03-03",
        submitDate: "2015-03-05",
        dueDate: "2015-03-15",
        from: {
            amount: 567.89,
            currency: "EUR"
        },
        to: {
            amount: 623.03,
            currency: "USD"
        },
        transmit: {
            amount: 5286.38,
            currency: "SEK"
        }
    }, {
        investorName: "JaNe DoE",
        creationDate: "2015-03-17",
        submitDate: "2015-03-17",
        dueDate: "2015-04-06",
        from: {
            amount: 98765.43,
            currency: "EUR"
        },
        to: {
            amount: 108355.55,
            currency: "USD"
        },
        transmit: {
            amount: 919388.35,
            currency: "SEK"
        }
    }];
    }
```

6. Finally, let's give our user interface some CSS to make it pretty. We'll set the `<th>` column headers apart from the `<td>` data elements with colors and boldface. In addition, we'll apply some padding and wrapping to help present the data more clearly:

```
th, td {
    padding:0.6em;
    border: 1px solid;
}
```

```
th {
    background-color:#6699FF;
    font-weight:bold;
}
td {
    white-space: nowrap;
}
```

The preceding example yields what is shown in Figure 14.1.

Investor Name	Creation Date	Submit Date	Due Date	From Amount	To Amount	Transmit Amount
John Doe	3/1/15	3/23/15	4/1/15	€1.234,56	$1,295.61	11 296.72 kr
Jake Smith	3/3/15	3/5/15	3/15/15	€567,89	$623.03	5 286.38 kr
Jane Doe	3/17/15	3/17/15	4/6/15	€98.765,43	$108,355.55	919 388.35 kr

FIGURE 14.1
Transaction ledger.

Using a Filter to Search on ng-repeat

Up until this point, we've been using Angular filters for both simple and more complex formatting of data in our applications. Filters are also very powerful for actually filtering repeated data.

Now, let's apply some more advanced filtering logic to our transaction ledger. In the event that we had many transactions in this ledger, we'd want to give the user the ability to search for a specific transaction. Let's build a custom filter that we can use to search for the customer's name.

First, we add a search box to our view. We give it an ng-model of "searchInput". Then, just as we used the | character for formatting data, we'll use it again for filtering data. By adding it to our ng-repeat, we tell Angular that we want to run the transactions through this filter on each digest cycle and that we want to pass the "searchInput" variable into the filter.

In our new filter called transactionSearch, we first take in the searchString variable that we send as a parameter to the filter in the view. Next, we account for the default state when the user hasn't searched for anything (searchString is undefined). By returning true, we tell Angular that in this state we want to show all results. Then we account for capitalization issues between the raw data and the search string by making them all lowercase with JavaScript's

`.toLowerCase()`. Finally, we use some fancy ECMAScript 6 magic (the `.startsWith()` method) to do our filtering:

```
<!-- View to show data for three transactions -->
<div ng-app="app">
    <input type="text" ng-model="searchInput" placeholder="Search..." />
    <table ng-controller="ExampleCtrl">
        <tr>
            <th>Investor Name</th>
            <th>Creation Date</th>
            <th>Submit Date</th>
            <th>Due Date</th>
            <th>From Amount</th>
            <th>To Amount</th>
            <th>Transmit Amount</th>
        </tr>
        <tr ng-repeat="t in transactions | transactionSearch:searchInput">
            <td>{{ t.investorName | titlecase }}</td>
            <td>{{ t.creationDate | date:"shortDate" }}</td>
            <td>{{ t.submitDate | date:"shortDate" }}</td>
            <td>{{ t.dueDate | date:"shortDate" }}</td>
            <td>{{ t.from.amount | customcurrency:t.from.currency}}</td>
            <td>{{ t.to.amount | customcurrency:t.to.currency}}</td>
            <td>{{ t.transmit.amount | customcurrency:t.transmit.currency}}</td>
        </tr>
    </table>
</div>
.filter('transactionSearch', function () {
    return function (transactions, searchString) {
        return transactions.filter(function (transaction) {
            if (!searchString) return true;
            var name = transaction.investorName.toLowerCase();
            return name.startsWith(searchString.toLowerCase());
        });
    };
});
```

WATCH OUT!

.startsWith() May Not Work for You

Note, at the time of this writing, only Google Chrome's latest builds support the `.startsWith()` method; all versions of Internet Explorer, Firefox, and Opera do not support it. We included it here for brevity. If this isn't working in your browser, you can easily do some regular expression and substring work to get the job done.

When we search for J, the preceding example yields what is shown in Figure 14.2.

J							
Investor Name	Creation Date	Submit Date	Due Date	From Amount	To Amount	Transmit Amount
John Doe	3/1/15	3/23/15	4/1/15	€1.234,56	$1,295.61	11 296.72 kr
Jake Smith	3/3/15	3/5/15	3/15/15	€567,89	$623.03	5 286.38 kr
Jane Doe	3/17/15	3/17/15	4/6/15	€98.765,43	$108,355.55	919 388.35 kr

FIGURE 14.2
Transaction ledger filtered by J.

When we search for Ja, the example yields what is shown in Figure 14.3.

Ja							
Investor Name	Creation Date	Submit Date	Due Date	From Amount	To Amount	Transmit Amount
Jake Smith	3/3/15	3/5/15	3/15/15	€567,89	$623.03	5 286.38 kr
Jane Doe	3/17/15	3/17/15	4/6/15	€98.765,43	$108,355.55	919 388.35 kr

FIGURE 14.3
Transaction ledger filtered by Ja.

When we search for Jak, the example yields what is shown in Figure 14.4.

Jak							
Investor Name	Creation Date	Submit Date	Due Date	From Amount	To Amount	Transmit Amount
Jake Smith	3/3/15	3/5/15	3/15/15	€567,89	$623.03	5 286.38 kr

FIGURE 14.4
Transaction ledger filtered by Jak.

Summary

In this hour, we defined Angular filters and their uses for data formatting and for data searching/filtering. We looked at three built-in Angular filters: lowercase, date, and currency and how they apply in a few different situations. Then we took those situations one step further by adding some more stringent requirements that required us to write custom filters for each scenario. Finally, we consolidated our custom filters into a transaction ledger example and wrote a custom transactionSearch filter to do data searching/filtering.

Q&A

Q. How can filters help me manage the complexity of consistently formatting my data in my applications?

A. Just like many formatting features built in to the .NET framework, Angular's built-in filters cover many basic data formatting scenarios, which will lead to lower development time. In addition, just as you can build custom .NET extension methods to handle data formatting at a more global level through your application, custom Angular filters will also help you ensure that you are applying the same filtering logic in each instance.

Q. Can I use an Angular filter in code, or only in a view?

A. Angular filters can also be used in JavaScript. To do so, make sure you inject `$filter` into your service. Then use the following syntax:

```
// Factory that uses $filter.
function ExampleFactory($filter) {
    var name = $filter('lowercase')("JoHn DoE");
}
```

Q. Why should I use client-side filtering to search through my data when I can rely on my .NET Web API to do this searching for me?

A. It depends on the volume of data through which the user is searching. If your application presents hundreds or even thousands of rows of data, client-side filtering can be sluggish and cause a degraded user experience. In these situations, specifically where the cost of client-side filtering outweighs the cost of an extra HTTP request to your API for the filtered results, you should explore pushing off this work to the server. However, with smaller datasets, client-side filtering is a great way to provide a responsive interface to the user.

Q. If you've read Hour 11, "Depending on Dependency Injection," take a closer look at the section titled "A Better Currency Filter" earlier in this hour. What problem do you see with how we're managing our custom filter's dependency on `numberFilter`? How will minification affect this filter? How can we change our injection annotation appropriately?

A. Because we are relying on the Angular injector to inject the right dependency based solely on the variable's name, this will break if the variable's name changes (which will happen when this code is minified). Instead, we should be annotating our dependencies with one of the other methods listed in Hour 11.

Workshop

Quiz

1. What is the syntax for applying a filter in a view?

2. What is a built-in Angular filter you could use to format a date as M/D/YY? What about including the time as well?

3. When creating a custom filter, what Angular function do you use and how is it used?

Answers

1. To apply a filter in a view, use the pipe character after any data that you want to run through a filter. Then include the filter's name. If the filter has parameters, you can use a colon after the filter name and then the parameters (separated by colons). Example: `{{ myData | filter:"parameter" }}`

2. To format a date as M/D/YY, you can use `myDate | date:"shortDate"`. To also include the time, just remove "date" from the parameter to the `date` filter: `myDate | date:"short"`.

3. Creating a custom filter is accomplished by using the `.filter()` method on a reference to the Angular `app`. This method takes two parameters: a name for the filter to be used in your views and the function that will execute for each data element that uses this filter in the view.

Exercise

For the book management system mentioned in the Introduction, add an `ng-repeat` filter for searching your book list. Also, add the `customcurrency` filter from this chapter to format the price of the book.

Approaching Angular Patterns

What You'll Learn in This Hour:

▶ Design patterns

▶ Controller patterns and principles

▶ Service patterns and principles

▶ Angular architecture patterns

As with most languages and frameworks, there are generally accepted best practices on how things should be done. Angular is no different, and this chapter covers those practices, along with some other opinionated ways to do things. No one is going to force you to use these patterns, but many will make your code cleaner, easier to understand, and more maintainable. As a side note, a lot of this material should look familiar; you were introduced to these best practices learning about the individual Angular components earlier in this book. This hour provides a single location for these for quick reference.

Design Patterns

Angular has a few base design patterns and principles at its core that when followed will make your code much more maintainable. The big two are separation of concerns and modularity (both in code and file organization).

The first of these, separation of concerns, played a significant part in how Angular was developed. It follows the Model-View-* (MV*) pattern, which in practice is really more like Model-View-ViewModel (MVVM). The thing to remember is that no one component of your application should be doing too much. Everything should be kept lightweight and responsible for only one piece of functionality.

The second principle and design pattern is modularity. Angular modules provide a way to group independent functionality together and separate it from any one core functionality. You should group your application files by feature, not by component type, which will guide you in creating modules. Here is the example from Hour 4 of the proper way to organize your application files for easy modularity:

-Application

    -Login

        -LoginController.js

        -Login.js

        -Login.html

    -Song

        -SongController.js

        -Song.js

        -Song.html

    -Artist

        -ArtistController.js

        -Artist.js

        -Artist.html

GO TO ▶ For more on modules and modular applications, check out Hour 4, "Mastering Modules."

Controller Patterns and Principles

People new to Angular development tend to put a lot of logic into their controllers and abuse $scope. When you're first starting out, you might think that the controller is the best place for business logic, service calls, and error handling, but that is not the case.

The first principle that you want to keep in mind when writing controllers is that you want them as thin as possible. They should really only be providing the view with bindable properties and functions that call into other components to either get the data or process the event logic. By moving that logic out of your controller and into reusable components, you have simplified your controller, enabled code reuse, and are following the single responsibility principle.

GO TO ▶ For more on ControllerAs syntax, see Hour 5, "Covering Controllers."

The first controller pattern discussed here is the *ControllerAs* syntax. This feature was actually added in the 1.2 release of Angular, brings with it cleaner syntax in your views, and means that you no longer need to inject $scope into your controllers if you aren't using watchers or emitters.

Another useful controller pattern is to put your bindable members at the top of your controller. This allows you to quickly identify what is available to your view. This goes hand in hand with using functions to move implementation details to the bottom of your file. If you have a bindable property that is the result of a function, instead of placing the whole function at the top, assign your property to the named function and move the named function to the bottom of the file, like so:

```
app.controller('ArtistController', [artistController]);
function artistController() {
  var vm = this;
  vm.name = 'Foo Fighters'
  vm.search = search;
  function search(artist){
    vm.artist = artist
    return vm.artist;
  }
};
```

Another controller pattern made popular by John Papa is called the Activate pattern. Using the Activate pattern involves placing any startup logic inside a method called `activate`. This makes it easy to find when looking at the file, and allows you to call a single method if you need to do a refresh on your controller or view. An example of using the Activate pattern for a controller that needs data from an artist service is shown here:

```
function ArtistController(artistService) {
    var vm = this;
    vm.artists = [];
    activate();
    function activate() {
        return artistService.getArtists().then(function(data) {
            vm.artists = data;
            return vm.avengers;
        });
    }
}
```

Service Patterns and Principles

Angular patterns and principles that apply to services are the same or very similar to those of controllers. Services should always follow the single responsibility principle to ensure that they don't become bloated and unmaintainable. Like controllers, services should also put their "bindable" or callable members at the top and should utilize the revealing module pattern.

The revealing module pattern provides an interface for what functions on the service can be called externally. This is especially useful when placed at the top of the file because it provides a way to quickly view all callable methods that may need to be unit tested or mocked when testing other components. The revealing module pattern is shown here:

```
function artistService() {
    var service = {
        create: create,
        update: update,
    };
    return service;

    function create() {
        /*callable*/
    };

    function update() {
        /*callable*/
    };

    function remove(){
        /*not able to be called from outside the service*/
    };
}
```

Notice that we return an object that exposes the methods we want to be available outside of the service (public methods), but exclude the `remove` function, which we want to keep private.

WATCH OUT!
_____

Named Functions Only!

When using the revealing module pattern and placing your return object at the top, you must use named functions so that they are available after your return. If you use `var name = function() {}` syntax, your methods will be undefined.

_____

Angular Architecture Patterns

Angular provides all the components you need to create well-architected applications, as long as you keep in mind the single responsibility principle, modules, and organizing your application by feature. In our development of Angular applications, however, we really found the need for a parent or shell controller for our application (a Shell pattern). Although this is by no means absolutely necessary, it can provide a great way to handle application-wide events such as updating navigation UI and handling loading indicators.

The typical pattern, to take some application-wide action, is for a child controller to $emit an event that the shell controller is listening for using $on. This prevents your module-based controllers from having to worry about things that don't concern them.

Summary

This hour covered design patterns for Angular applications and best practices for both controllers and services. Then we wrapped up by introducing the Shell pattern for overall architecture. Although these topics may seem nitpicky or unnecessary when you start building large-scale applications with a team of developers, these little things will go a long way in ensuring maintainability and scalability.

Q&A

Q. Are these principles and practices the only way I should write my Angular application?

A. Yes and no. Some of these principles are at the very core of Angular, including modularity and single responsibility. Many consider the other principles and practices discussed here to be best practices, but we certainly don't discourage innovation or experimentation.

Workshop

Quiz

1. How do you separate public and private methods within a service?

2. Where should bindable members go in a controller?

3. Why use the activate pattern?

Answers

1. Implement the revealing module pattern.

2. At the top, for easy reference.

3. The activate pattern provides a single location for all initialization logic within a controller, along with the added benefit of making refreshing your controller and view possible by calling only one method again.

Exercise

For the book management system mentioned in the Introduction, ensure that your existing code (and all future code in other exercises) adheres to these best practices: controller activate patterns, bindable/actionable properties up top, revealing module, and named functions at the bottom.

Making Components Communicate

What You'll Learn in This Hour:

▶ Why components need to communicate

▶ What communication methods exist for different Angular components

▶ What a "watch" is

▶ How to use Angular's event system, including "broadcast" and "emit"

▶ How nested controllers can communicate using inherited scope

▶ How to use services to share data

Whether a component needs a piece of data to accomplish its job, or just a notification that it can start executing, communication between application components is super important.

In this hour, you'll learn why. This hour covers what methods exist to allow our Angular components to communicate and share data. Then you'll learn about Angular's "watch" feature, and its event bus system with "broadcast" and "emit." This hour wraps up by talking about nested controllers communicating through an inherited scope.

Communication Between Components

It's a common practice in Angular to have multiple controllers in one view. You might have one controller for a sidebar and another for the main content. Some Angular architectural patterns call for a "shell" or "parent" controller over the entire app. This is helpful if there is any logic that is applicable to the entire application, like routing or checking for authorization.

You may also have multiple directives in the same view. For instance, in a view with a long form, you might have a progress bar directive that keeps track of how many fields a user has completed, while another directive in that view might show users what section of the form they're currently on.

In any of these scenarios, it can be important for the components to be able to communicate with one another. A directive might need to know when a certain task another directive is responsible for has finished. Another scenario might include needing to send a piece of data from one controller to another.

Consider the following example (see Listing 16.1). We have a navigation bar at the top of the screen that contains a logout button. That navigation bar also has a directive that polls a service every 30 seconds to see whether there are any new notifications, such as a new message or comment. When the user clicks logout, we need to tell the polling directive to stop polling.

LISTING 16.1 Navigation Bar with Controller and `notifications-polling` Directive

```
1:   <-- navbar view -->
2:   <nav id="navbar" ng-controller="Navbar as vm">
3:       <ul class="nav navbar-nav">
4:         <li class="notifications">
5:           <a type="button" notifications-polling>
6:             <i class="fa fa-bell"></i>
7:           </a>
8:         </li>
9:         <li>
10:          <a ng-click="vm.logout()">
11:            <i class="fa fa-sign-out"></i>
12:            <span>Sign Out</span>
13:          </a>
14:        </li>
15:      </ul>
16:  </nav>
17:
18:  //navbar controller
19:  (function () {
20:      angular.module('app')
21:          .controller('Navbar', Navbar);
22:
23:      function Navbar() {
24:          var vm = this;
25:          vm.logout = logout;
26:
27:          function logout() {
28:              //clear current user
29:              //and
30:              //need to let polling know to stop!
31:          }
32:      }
33:  })();
34:
35:  //notificationsPolling directive
36:  (function () {
37:      angular.module('app')
```

```
38:            .directive('notificationsPolling', notificationsPolling);
39:
40:        function notificationsPolling($interval, NotificationsManager) {
41:            return {
42:                restrict: 'A',
43:                scope: false,
44:                link: function (scope, elem, attrs) {
45:                    var poll = $interval(function () {
46:                        NotificationsManager.fetchNotifications();
47:                    }, 30000);
48:                }
49:            }
50:        }
51:    })();
```

That's a lot of code and three different components! Don't worry, we've got this.

At the top you have the navbar view. It's got a notifications icon with a notifications-polling directive on it (line 5). There's also a logout button. When the user clicks the logout button, vm.logout runs. It's the job of vm.logout to clear all the logged-in user's information, which means that the notification call is going to fail. So, we need some way to tell the notifications-polling directive to stop polling! Lucky for us, Angular provides a couple of different ways to do that.

Eventually, we'll look at Angular's event system using $broadcast and $emit. That's analogous to .NET's events and delegates system. We'll also break down how to use a $watch to run a function when a particular value changes. But first we'll take a look at some more direct communication.

Calling Directive Functions from a Controller

It's relatively straightforward for a directive to call a function in a view's controller. We talked about it in the custom directives: Just pass in a controller function to the directive using the & symbol.

GO TO ▶ For a refresher on calling a controller function from a directive, head back to Hour 10, "Conquering Custom Directives."

But in our scenario with notifications-polling, we need to go the opposite way: calling a directive's function from the controller; remember, the Navbar controller needs to tell the directive to stop polling.

We could do this with shared scope (see Figure 16.1).

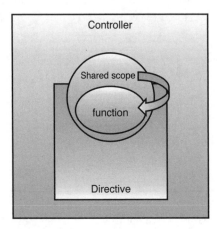

FIGURE 16.1
Controller calling a directive function with shared scope.

And in the case of the `notifications-polling` directive, that's definitely reasonable (see Listing 16.2). You're likely not going to have multiple copies of this directive, so it wouldn't be an issue to share scope. (Sharing scope across repeated directives means an update to one of the directive makes them all update.) So in that case, simply expose a function on the shared scope and call it from the controller. (The view remains unchanged.)

LISTING 16.2 Navbar and notifications-polling Directive Communicating via Shared Scope

```
 1:    //navbar controller
 2:    (function () {
 3:        angular.module('app')
 4:            .controller('Navbar', Navbar);
 5:
 6:        function Navbar($scope) {
 7:            var vm = this;
 8:            vm.logout = logout;
 9:
10:            function logout() {
11:                //clear current user
12:                //and
13:                //need to let polling know to stop!
14:                $scope.stopPolling();
15:            }
16:        }
17:    })();
18:
```

```
19:     //notificationsPolling directive
20:     (function () {
21:         angular.module('app')
22:             .directive('notificationsPolling', notificationsPolling);
23:
24:         function notificationsPolling($interval, NotificationsManager) {
25:             return {
26:                 restrict: 'A',
27:                 link: function (scope, elem, attrs) {
28:                     var poll = $interval(function () {
29:                         NotificationsManager.fetchNotifications();
30:                     }, 30000);
31:                     scope.stopPolling = function(){
32:                         $interval.cancel(poll);
33:                     }
34:                 }
35:             }
36:         }
37:     })();
```

The difference in this code and the first example is that here we define the `stopPolling` function on line 31 and assign it to `scope`. Because `scope` is shared between the directive and the controller, the controller is able to call that function on line 14. So in this example, and any scenario where using shared scope is okay, this works. But what if you can't use shared scope because your directive is inside a repeater or something? Then you can use isolate scope but share an object between the controller and the directive using the = symbol (see Listing 16.3). That object would contain the function you want to call (see Figure 16.2).

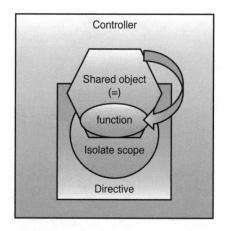

FIGURE 16.2
Controller calling a directive function with isolate scope.

LISTING 16.3 Navbar and notifications-polling Directive Communicating via Isolate Scope

```
1:   <-- navbar view -->
2:   <nav id="navbar" ng-controller="Navbar as vm">
3:       <ul class="nav navbar-nav">
4:         <li class="notifications">
5:           <a type="button" notifications-polling="vm.poll" >
6:             <i class="fa fa-bell"></i>
7:           </a>
8:         </li>
9:         <li>
10:          <a ng-click="vm.logout()">
11:            <i class="fa fa-sign-out"></i>
12:            <span>Sign Out</span>
13:          </a>
14:        </li>
15:      </ul>
16:  </nav>
17:
18:  //navbar controller
19:  (function () {
20:      angular.module('app')
21:          .controller('Navbar', Navbar);
22:
23:      function Navbar() {
24:          var vm = this;
25:          vm.logout = logout;
26:          vm.poll = {};
27:
28:          function logout() {
29:              //clear current user
30:              //and
31:              //need to let polling know to stop!
32:              vm.poll.stopPolling();
33:          }
34:      }
35:  })();
36:
37:  //notificationsPolling directive
38:  (function () {
39:      angular.module('app')
40:          .directive('notificationsPolling', notificationsPolling);
41:
42:      function notificationsPolling($interval, NotificationsManager) {
43:          return {
44:              restrict: 'A',
45:              scope: {
```

```
46:                         poll: '=notificationsPolling'
47:                     },
48:                 link: function (scope, elem, attrs) {
49:                     var poll = $interval(function () {
50:                         NotificationsManager.fetchNotifications();
51:                     }, 30000);
52:                     scope.poll.stopPolling = function(){
53:                         $interval.cancel(poll);
54:                     };
55:                 }
56:             }
57:         }
58:     })();
```

Here, just like in the previous example, the directive defines the function that the controller calls on the user's logout action. The difference is that instead of the entire scope being shared between the two components, only the `poll` object on scope is shared on line 46.

BY THE WAY

Just Like a .NET User Control

Both of these examples are analogous to a .NET controller invoking a method defined by a user control.

Unfortunately, in allowing the components to communicate like this, we are also coupling the components together. If we removed the directive from the view, the controller would try to call a function that doesn't exist. We also have that poll object on the scope. It would be nice to not have to create a controller object whose sole responsibility is to bind to the directive.

Because it's always a best practice to move logic to services, and it's much more natural for components to communicate with a service, it would be handy if the `notifications-polling` directive and our controller could just talk to a service that handles the communication. We'll look at that next.

Using $watch to Communicate

If we created a service in charge of polling, we could have the controller tell the manager when to stop polling. The manager would then be in charge of stopping the `notifications-polling` directive. But because services don't have access to the directive, how can it stop the directive? That's where $watch comes in (see Figure 16.3 and Listing 16.4).

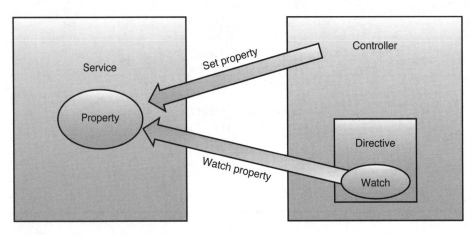

FIGURE 16.3
Watching a service property.

LISTING 16.4 Navbar Controller, `notifications-polling` Directive with a `$watch`, and Notifications Service

```
1:    //navbar controller
2:    (function () {
3:      angular.module('app', [])
4:        .controller('Navbar', Navbar);
5:
6:      function Navbar(NotificationsManager) {
7:        var vm = this;
8:        vm.logout = logout;
9:
10:       function logout() {
11:         //clear current user
12:         //and
13:         //need to let polling know to stop!
14:         console.log('stopping...');
15:         NotificationsManager.stopPolling();
16:       }
17:     }
18:   })();
19:
20:   //notificationPolling directive
21:   (function () {
22:     angular.module('app')
23:       .directive('notificationsPolling', notificationsPolling);
24:
25:     function notificationsPolling($interval, NotificationsManager) {
26:       return {
```

```
27:         restrict: 'A',
28:         scope: {},
29:         link: function (scope, elem, attrs) {
30:           var poll = $interval(function () {
31:             NotificationsManager.fetchNotifications();
32:           }, 1000);
33:           scope.$watch(function(){
34:             return NotificationsManager.isStopped;
35:           }, function(isStopped){
36:             if(isStopped){
37:               $interval.cancel(poll);
38:               console.log('stopped');
39:             }
40:           });
41:         }
42:       }
43:     }
44:   })();
45:
46:   // notifications service
47:   (function(){
48:     angular.module('app')
49:       .factory('NotificationsManager', NotificationsManager);
50:
51:     function NotificationsManager(){
52:       return {
53:         fetchNotifications: fetch,
54:         stopPolling: stopPolling,
55:         isStopped: false
56:       };
57:
58:       function fetch(){
59:         console.log('fetching...');
60:       }
61:
62:       function stopPolling(){
63:         this.isStopped = true;
64:       }
65:     }
66:   })();
```

This code really isn't so different from the previous example. We're still using isolate scope but aren't passing any scope properties in. We've also included the NotificationsManager factory that has a few properties on it. When the user logs out, our controller calls the NotificationsManager.stopPolling method. That method in turn sets the isStopped flag on the NotificationsManager. But the directive needs to know the flag is set to true. We set a $watch on that value on line 33.

Setting a $watch on a value lets Angular know that you want a particular function called when that value changes. This could be anything from a value a user inputs to a DOM element to a value inside a service.

WATCH OUT!

Watching a Function Return Value

You should have noticed that we aren't watching the NotificationsManager.isStopped property directly. Instead, we've wrapped it in a function and are watching the return value of that function. This is because a $watch typically only involves watching a property on $scope. We've used a more complex example here to show you the power of a $watch. To watch a $scope value, simply include the property name in quotes as the first parameter of the $watch function.

The second function in the $watch call on line 35 can actually take two parameters: the first is the new value of the property being watched, and the second one is the original value before it was changed. In our case, we're only interested in the new value, so we just pass that in.

We use the NotificationsManager as a third-party communicator between the controller and directive. Now those two components don't need to know about each other at all, and they become much more testable.

BY THE WAY

Did We Need a $watch Here?

You might be thinking that we could have just moved the $interval into the NotificationsManager, and we could have avoided the $watch altogether. And in this example, that's exactly right. Good catch! But in case you needed to do DOM manipulation in the $interval, that should be done in a directive. So we'll keep the $interval in the directive for now.

You can use a $watch any time your controller or directive needs to be notified of a property change. Be aware, however, that adding too many $watch calls can affect performance. The number of instances of $watch you can add before noticing performance issues is very high, but it's always a good practice to use a $watch only when necessary. In the next section, you'll see an example of how to tell the notifications-polling directive to stop polling without using a $watch.

BY THE WAY

Models and Binding Expressions Are Watches, Too!

We talked about data binding and models in Hour 6, "Understanding Views, Data Binding, and Event Handling," on views, but just a reminder, when you use ng-model or a binding expression with double curly braces, you're essentially using a $watch. The mechanism Angular uses to watch those properties is the same as when you use $watch explicitly like we've done in this. This is known as the *Angular digest cycle*.

Using Events to Communicate

In the .NET framework, you can use a delegate to tell a component to behave in a certain way, similarly to how we've set up communication with Angular. The following C# example is admittedly contrived, but if you understand how delegates work below, understanding Angular's event system will be a breeze (see Listing 16.5).

LISTING 16.5 C# Example of Delegates to Notify `Polling` Class to Stop

```
 1:  namespace app
 1:  {
 2:      public delegate void MyEventHandler();
 3:
 4:      public class Poll
 5:      {
 6:          public void startPolling()
 7:          {
 8:              //poll for notifications
 9:          }
10:
11:          public void stopPolling()
12:          {
13:              //stop polling for notifications
14:          }
15:      }
16:
17:      public class User
18:      {
19:
20:          //create the UserLogout event
21:          public event MyEventHandler OnUserLogout;
22:
23:          public void Logout()
24:          {
25:              OnUserLogout();
26:          }
27:
28:      }
29:
30:      public class NavBar
31:      {
32:
33:          Poll poll = new Poll();
34:          User currentUser = new User();
35:
36:          //When the user logs out, we want something to happen
37:          void HandleUserLogout()
38:          {
39:              //tell polling object to stop
```

```
40:                poll.stopPolling();
41:            }
42:
43:        public NavBar()
44:            {
45:                poll.startPolling();
46:                //create a delegate to handle a user logging out
47:                //and add it to OnUserLogout's event handlers
48:                currentUser.OnUserLogout += new MyEventHandler(HandleUserLogout);
49:            }
50:
51:        private void logout_btn_Click(object sender, EventArgs e)
52:            {
53:                currentUser.Logout();
54:            }
55:
56:        }
57:    }
```

Here, we're using a delegate in the `PollingManager` class to fire a `stopPolling` event to the `Polling` class after a user logs out in the `Navigation` class. If you're comfortable with how this C# code works, you'll see how similar the concepts in the next example are. We'll use events to stop polling, where before we used `$watch` (see Listing 16.6).

LISTING 16.6 Navbar Controller with a `polling` Directive, Using Angular Events

```
1:    //navbar controller
2:    (function () {
3:        angular.module('app', [])
4:            .controller('Navbar', Navbar);
5:
6:        function Navbar($scope) {
7:            var vm = this;
8:            vm.logout = logout;
9:            vm.currentUser = 'angularDev23';
10:
11:            function logout() {
12:                //clear current user
13:                //and
14:                //need to let polling know to stop!
15:                console.log('stopping...');
16:                $scope.$broadcast('stop-polling', vm.currentUser);
17:            }
18:        }
19:    })();
20:
21:    //notificationPolling directive
22:    (function () {
```

```
23:      angular.module('app')
24:          .directive('notificationsPolling', notificationsPolling);
25:
26:      function notificationsPolling($interval) {
27:          return {
28:              restrict: 'A',
29:              scope: {},
30:              link: function (scope, elem, attrs) {
31:                  var poll = $interval(function(){
32:                      console.log('fetching...');
33:                  }, 1000);
34:
35:                  scope.$on('stop-polling', function(event, data){
36:                      $interval.cancel(poll);
37:                      console.log(data + ' logged out');
38:                  });
39:              }
40:          }
41:      }
42: })();
```

From the previous example, we've replaced $watch in our directive with $on (line 35). This is telling the directive's scope that when a stop-polling event is caught, run the function defined as the second parameter.

We've replaced the call to the service with $broadcast (line 16). $broadcast fires the event "down: the chain to all scopes. The second parameter of the $broadcast call is any data you want to pass to the function catching the event. Here, we're passing a current user to the receiver of the event so that we can write to the console who logged out (see Figure 16.4).

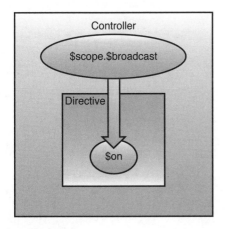

FIGURE 16.4
Using $scope.$broadcast to communicate.

BY THE WAY

Scope Chain

Because our directive has an isolate scope, and the directive is created inside the scope of our controller (check out the structure of our view a few pages back), the directive is considered to be "down" the chain of scopes.

If we need the directive to notify a parent controller of an event, we use $emit instead, and listen for the event in the controller using the same $on syntax (see Figure 16.5 and Listing 16.7).

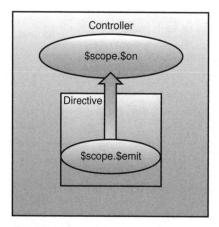

FIGURE 16.5
Using `$scope.$emit` to communicate.

LISTING 16.7 Navbar Controller with a `polling` Directive, Using Angular Events to Fire "Up" the Chain

```
 1:    //navbar controller
 2:    (function () {
 3:        angular.module('app', [])
 4:            .controller('Navbar', Navbar);
 5:
 6:        function Navbar($scope) {
 7:            var vm = this;
 8:            vm.pollCount = 0;
 9:
10:            $scope.$on('poll-count', function(){
11:              vm.pollCount++;
12:              console.log(vm.pollCount);
13:            });
14:        }
15:    })();
16:
17:    //notificationPolling directive
```

```
18:   (function () {
19:       angular.module('app')
20:           .directive('notificationsPolling', notificationsPolling);
21:
22:       function notificationsPolling($interval) {
23:           return {
24:               restrict: 'A',
25:               scope: {},
26:               link: function (scope, elem, attrs) {
27:                 var poll = $interval(function(){
28:                     console.log('fetching...');
29:                     scope.$emit('poll-count');
30:                 }, 1000);
31:               }
32:           }
33:       }
34:   })();
```

In this example, the directive "emits" a poll-count event every time the interval runs to fetch more data (line 29). The navbar controller catches the event to increment the pollCount property and writes the count to the console (line 10).

Nested Controller Communication

The last type of component communication we'll talk about is communication between a parent controller and a nested controller using inherited scope. This is similar to the concept discussed a few pages back when our polling directive shared the scope of the parent controller. The difference here is that the nested controller can directly access parent controller properties using $parent (see Figure 16.6 and Listing 16.8).

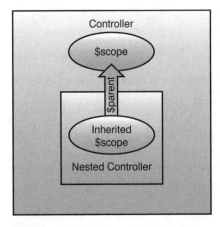

FIGURE 16.6
Nested controller communication with inherited $scope and $parent.

LISTING 16.8 Navbar Controller with a Nested `Polling` Controller, Communicating via `$parent`

```
 1:   //navbar controller
 2:   (function () {
 3:       angular.module('app', [])
 4:           .controller('Navbar', Navbar);
 5:
 6:       function Navbar($scope) {
 7:           var vm = this;
 8:           vm.pollCount = 0;
 9:       }
10:   })();
11:
12:   //Polling nested controller
13:   (function () {
14:       angular.module('app')
15:           .controller('Polling', polling);
16:
17:       function polling($scope, $interval) {
18:         var poll = $interval(function(){
19:           console.log('fetching...');
20:           console.log($scope.$parent.vm.pollCount++);
21:         }, 1000);
22:       }
23:   })();
```

We've turned our polling directive into a nested controller that is a child of our `navbar` controller. This new nested controller has access to the parent scope's properties using the `$parent` property on its `$scope`. In this way, the child scope is effectively communicating with the parent by grabbing data from the parent and incrementing that data.

You can make a controller a child (or "nested'") controller simply by creating it with the `ng-controller` directive in a view that already has a controller. The child controller just needs to be inside of the scope of the existing, or parent, controller (see Listing 16.9)

LISTING 16.9 Creating the Nested `polling` Controller as a Child of the `Navbar` Controller in the View

```
 1:   <-- navbar view -->
 2:     <nav id="navbar" ng-controller="Navbar as vm">
 3:         <ul class="nav navbar-nav">
 4:           <li class="notifications" ng-controller="Polling as pollingVM">
 5:             <a type="button">
 6:               <i class="fa fa-bell"></i>
 7:             </a>
 8:           </li>
```

```
 9:              <li>
10:                <a ng-click="vm.logout()">
11:                  <i class="fa fa-sign-out"></i>
12:                  <span>Sign Out</span>
13:                </a>
14:              </li>
15:            </ul>
16:         </nav>
```

Notice that the list element with the class of "notifications" now also has the ng-controller directive on it specifying that the element has a controller called Polling.

WATCH OUT!

Nested Controller Communication Is One Way!

We showed two-way communication using events, two-way binding with isolate scope in directives, and you could add a $watch to both the controller and directive for two-way communication. However, a parent scope does not have access to a child scope's properties. So a parent controller cannot directly communicate with a child controller in the same way.

Summary

This hour covered many different ways to allow your Angular components to communicate freely and why that's so important. Referencing your own .NET background knowledge of events and delegates and user controls, you learned in this hour about Angular's own event system. This hour also covered using services and scopes for communication.

Q&A

Q. **What about sibling component communication? If I have two controllers on the same page, but they aren't nested, can they communicate?**

A. Absolutely. Instead of using $scope to broadcast or emit an event, you can use $rootScope. Think of $rootScope as the parent scope for your entire application. Inject and use it just like $scope. There are a number of nuances to broadcasting and emitting events with $rootScope, but the most important thing to remember is that if you use $rootScope.$emit, only listeners created with $rootScope will catch that event ($rootScope.$on). Events created with $rootScope.$broadcast are broadcast to *all* scopes and can be caught with either a simple $scope.$on or a $rootScope.$on (see Figure 16.7).

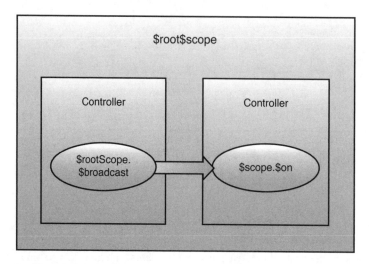

FIGURE 16.7
Events with $rootScope.

Q. **It seems like there are a lot of options for component communication. Is there one preferred method or best practice?**

A. Not really. Play around with the various options and see what you like best. We're partial to the event system because it avoids the complication of scope inheritance with scope communication, and it also avoids including a $watch if you're using the shared service method.

Workshop
Quiz

1. What is the difference between $broadcast and $emit?

2. What allows Angular to observe when an object changes?

3. How can you facilitate communication between two independent controllers on the same page?

Answers

1. $broadcast fires events "down" the scope chaining, whereas $emit fires events "up."

2. $scope.$watch

3. Use a shared service and a $watch, or use $rootScope to broadcast/emit events.

Exercise

For the book management system mentioned in the Introduction, implement a parent controller that will display the currently selected book title. On a user's selection of a book in the list, fire an event to this parent controller notifying it of the selected book so that it can display the title accordingly.

HOUR 17
Demonstrating Deployment

What You'll Learn in This Hour:

▶ Automating deployment tasks
▶ Writing production-ready Angular code
▶ Error-checking your Angular code
▶ Minifying and concatenating your Angular code
▶ Deploying Angular apps to Microsoft Azure

You've built your Angular app; now it's time to release it into the wild! This hour walks you through some preproduction build tasks using Gulp, a JavaScript task runner. Also, you'll learn about some strategies for ensuring that your code is ready for production release, including ways you can reduce the list of errors during development and automatically check your syntax for errors. Once we're clean of errors, we'll explore strategies for minifying and concatenating our JavaScript code (two activities that greatly improve performance of your application in production). Finally, after we've built our application, you'll learn how to actually push the code to Microsoft Azure.

Automating Deployment Tasks

As you've seen repeatedly throughout this book, JavaScript is no longer just some jQuery functions sprinkled among a few static HTML pages. We're now using frameworks, package management, preprocessors, dynamic file generation, and much more. With all of these technologies in play, we're no longer just making simple edits to these files and refreshing our browser to see changes. When we want to build our code, whether for local testing or for remote deployment, there is now a multitude of tasks that we need to run.

That's where tools like Gulp and Grunt come in. Both of these tools are useful for creating automated tasks. Developers who tend to like "code over configuration" will prefer Gulp because it is not only more verbose but also more explicit in what it is doing. Meanwhile, developers who tend to like "configuration over code" will prefer Grunt.

GO TO ▶ For more on Grunt, check out Hour 3, "Tinkering with Tools for Modern Front-End Development."

Later in this hour, we'll be using Gulp to illustrate various tasks that help prepare our application for deployment. But first, let's look at how we can get started with Gulp. If you haven't already, install NodeJS and npm in your development environment. Once you've got those, use this command to install Gulp globally: npm install gulp –g. Next, let's install a plug-in that will serve our app for us. Run the command npm install gulp-serve to install the plug-in used below.

BY THE WAY

Installing Gulp Globally

Adding the –g parameter to our Gulp installation command installs it globally so that you can use the gulp command in the command line. You'll still need to install it locally in your project by changing directory to your project's root directory and using npm install gulp.

Gulp uses a file called gulpfile.js to define all tasks. Let's look at an empty file that simply serves our application (see Listing 17.1). On line 1, we require() the npm package gulp and assign it to a variable called gulp. On line 2, we do the same for the gulp-serve npm package. Next, on line 4, we create a new Gulp task using the .task() method, give it a name of 'serve', and tell it to execute the serve() function, which comes from the gulp-serve plug-in.

Now, if you saved this file and opened a command line, you could use the gulp serve command to run this task. Because we'll be adding many tasks to this file, we define a 'default' task on lines 6–8 that allows us to chain other tasks. For now, this simply calls our lone 'serve' task, but we'll be adding more later. Adding this 'default' task allows us to simply run gulp on the command line without a task name. Over the course of this hour, we'll be adding other Gulp tasks to this file.

LISTING 17.1   An Empty gulpfile.js That Serves Your App

```
1:  var gulp = require('gulp'),
2:      serve = require('gulp-serve');
3:
4:  gulp.task('serve', serve('public'));
5:
6:  gulp.task('default', function() {
7:      gulp.start('serve');
8:  });
```

Writing Production-Ready Angular Code

Because we'll be using a Gulp task to check our code for errors on build (a process called *linting*, more on that later), let's first explore some strategies to minimize the number of errors that it finds.

IIFEs

An *immediately invoked function expression*, or IIFE, takes advantage of JavaScript's function closure to protect a JavaScript component's variables from polluting the global namespace. When your code is minified and concatenated for deployment (more on that later), the variables in your code could collide with variables in other code. An IIFE protects you against collisions by providing variable scope for each component that you build.

GO TO ▶ For more on IIFEs, check out Hour 2, "Presenting JavaScript Patterns."

Use Strict

JavaScript developers can use the `'use strict'` statement in their functions to force conformity to a stricter subset of the JavaScript language. Rather than JavaScript allowing certain things like global variables, duplicate object property names, and assignments that silently fail, errors will be thrown in the console instead. JavaScript is often typecast as a "loose" language, and this statement helps tighten things up a bit.

DID YOU KNOW?

How Is `'use strict'` Valid JavaScript?

You may be wondering how including the `'use strict'` string on a line without assignment to a variable is valid JavaScript. This is an example of an ECMAScript 5 directive (unrelated to Angular directives), which must appear as the first statement inside a function and must consist entirely of a string followed by a semicolon.

Let's look at some examples of `'use strict'` in action. For example, take the code below in Listing 17.2. We're using an IIFE here (lines 1 and 4) to keep our variable (line 2) out of the global namespace and logging that variable to the console (line 3).

LISTING 17.2 Logging a Variable Without `'use strict'`

```
1:  (function() {
2:      myName = "Chris";
3:      console.log(myName);
4:  })();
```

As you'd expect, this code yields "Chris" in the console. Now, let's add `'use strict'` to the top of our function before we declare our variable (Listing 17.3).

LISTING 17.3   Logging a Variable with `'use strict'`

```
1:  (function() {
2:      'use strict';
3:      myName = "Chris";
4:      console.log(myName);
5:  })();
```

Because strict mode doesn't allow for variable assignment to previously undeclared variables, this code throws an error in the console: "Uncaught ReferenceError: myName is not defined."

We can remedy this by using the `var` keyword to declare our variable (Listing 17.4).

LISTING 17.4   Logging a Variable with `'use strict'`

```
1:  (function() {
2:      'use strict';
3:      var myName = "Chris";
4:      console.log(myName);
5:  })();
```

This code will once again yield "Chris" in the console.

WATCH OUT!

Don't Get Carried Away with `'use strict'`

Using the `'use strict'` statement is a great way to enforce good code quality and consistency with your JavaScript and help eliminate errors; however, don't blindly add this statement to your existing applications. Because this statement causes the browser to throw errors, this may break existing parts of your codebase that depend on JavaScript's inherent flexibility. You would have to conduct detailed testing of your application in order to add this statement and be sure that it won't break existing functionality.

Error-Checking Your Angular Code

Now that we've discussed some strategies for writing production-ready code, let's look at how we can *lint* our code for errors. *Linting* your code is the process of using a tool to check that your code adheres to a defined syntax standard. Two tools that can help with linting JavaScript are JSLint and JSHint.

JSLint

Originally written by JavaScript guru Douglas Crockford in 2002, JSLint enforces its author's definition of what makes up JavaScript's good parts. Unfortunately, the software doesn't include a configuration file, meaning that if you don't agree with the rules that it uses, you're out of luck for changing them. In addition, the last stable release of JSLint dates back to 2011.

JSHint

In 2010, JavaScript developer Anton Kovalyov forked the JSLint project because he felt it was too rigid and needed to be configurable by those using it. As such, JSHint has extensive options for customization on which rules to include and exclude. Your team/company should decide as a group on which rules should be enforced, create a JSHint configuration file (.jshintrc), and include it in source control for all developers to use. This step isn't required; JSHint will still run with a default configuration if you don't provide overrides.

Let's modify our gulpfile.js from the first part of this hour to also lint our code (see Listing 17.5). First, use `npm install gulp-jshint` to install the Gulp plug-in that runs JSHint. Then, on line 3, reference it in your gulpfile.js using the `require()` method. On line 7, we add a new `'lint'` task, which will handle our linting for us. Unlike our `'serve'` task, where we simply wanted to run a function provided by the plug-in (`serve('public')`), we now want to run a few things, so we create an anonymous function that returns the gulp stream so it can be used by other tasks.

On line 8, we start by choosing our JavaScript files with the `.src()` method. This method takes an expression that can be used to match multiple files. In our example, we're matching any JavaScript files (/*.js) under any level of subfolders (/**) under the src/client/app folder. On line 10, we use the gulp `.pipe()` method to stream the selected files from `.src()` into the `jshint()` function, which is provided by the package we required on line 3. By default, JSHint uses the default configuration. If you want to override that configuration with your own that you share with your development team, pass the filename for that file into `jshint()` (like on line 9).

Next, on line 12, we define the reporter (the plug-in used to print JSHint results to the console) for JSHint to use. The default reporter doesn't highlight any part of the errors or color-code them in any way. If you want this, run `npm install jshint-stylish` and use line 11. Finally, we modify our `'default'` task to have a dependency on the `'lint'` task (line 15).

LISTING 17.5   Using JSHint in Gulp

```
1:  var gulp = require('gulp'),
2:      serve = require('gulp-serve'),
3:      jshint = require('gulp-jshint');
4:
5:  gulp.task('serve', serve('public'));
```

```
 6:
 7:  gulp.task('lint', function() {
 8:    return gulp.src('src/client/app/**/*.js')
 9:      //.pipe(jshint('.jshintrc'))
10:      .pipe(jshint())
11:      //.pipe(jshint.reporter('jshint-stylish'));
12:      .pipe(jshint.reporter('default'));
13:  });
14:
15:  gulp.task('default', ['lint'], function() {
16:      gulp.start('serve');
17:  });
```

In Figure 17.1, you can see a few errors generated by JSHint when we run `gulp lint` (I'm using `jshint-stylish` here.)

FIGURE 17.1
Running JSHint via Gulp.

Minifying and Concatenating Your Angular Code

We've now checked our code for errors; now it's time to start deploying! By this point in the book, it should be pretty apparent that one of the key tenets of good front-end architecture is breaking apart your source code into many files. This leaves us with files for directives, files for services, files for controllers, HTML files, and so on. Unfortunately, your app will experience a lot of extra overhead if it needs to fetch each of these files individually from the server; that's a lot of HTTP requests. A common best practice prior to deploying your app is to *minify* and *concatenate* your source code.

Minifying your JavaScript code reduces the size of your JavaScript files by removing whitespace and replacing all of your variable names with smaller names (for example, `function($http, $scope)` will become `function(a, b)`). In Angular, minifying your code may break your app if your dependency annotation strategy depends on parameter names (since minification renames parameters). Minifying will cut down on the overall size of our files, meaning that they can be transferred from server to client much faster. This equates to better performance in your app.

GO TO ▶ For more information on how minifying your code can affect your strategy for injecting Angular dependencies, check out Hour 11, "Depending on Dependency Injection."

Concatenating your JavaScript code bundles up all of your JavaScript code into one file, which is then served instead of the individual JavaScript files. This means that your browser only has to make one HTTP request to get all of the JavaScript for the entire app.

DID YOU KNOW?

Minifying and Concatenating in ASP.NET MVC

To accomplish the same minification and concatenation task in ASP.NET MVC, you can use bundles (specifically, the `ScriptBundle` object for concatenating JavaScript). Also, the `BundleTable.EnableOptimizations = true` statement will cause minification to occur.

Let's look at how we can modify our gulpfile.js to minify and concatenate our code (see Listing 17.6). First, run `npm install gulp-uglify gulp-concat` to install the two npm packages that we'll be using for minification and concatenation, respectively. Then, on lines 4 and 5 of gulpfile.js, reference those packages. On line 15, we create a new `'build'` task, which will use the same `.src()` and `.pipe()` methods as our `'lint'` task.

Similar to the `'lint'` task, we start by grabbing our JavaScript source files (line 16). We then use the `concat()` method from the `gulp-concat` package, which takes a parameter of the resulting filename. We want our single JavaScript file to be called app.js, so we pass that in as the name. Next, we tell `concat()` where to write this file using the `.dest()` method, which takes a directory structure as a parameter. These two commands in tandem will concatenate our JavaScript together into a file located at dist/js/app.js.

Next, let's minify that file. We pipe the output to `uglify()`, which will take care of the minification (line 19), and then use `.dest()` again to write the file to the file system (line 20). The last step is to include this in our `'default'` task. We want to first run the `'lint'` task and then run our new `'build'` task, so we pass that as the order in the array on line 23.

LISTING 17.6 Minifying and Concatenating in Gulp

```
 1:  var gulp = require('gulp'),
 2:      serve = require('gulp-serve'),
 3:      jshint = require('gulp-jshint'),
 4:      uglify = require('gulp-uglify'),
 5:      concat = require('gulp-concat');
 6:
 7:  gulp.task('serve', serve('public'));
 8:
 9:  gulp.task('lint', function() {
10:    return gulp.src('src/client/app/**/*.js')
11:       .pipe(jshint())
12:       .pipe(jshint.reporter('jshint-stylish'));
13:  });
14:
15:  gulp.task('build', function() {
16:    return gulp.src('src/client/app/**/*.js')
17:       .pipe(concat('app.js'))
18:       .pipe(gulp.dest('dist/js'))
19:       .pipe(uglify())
20:       .pipe(gulp.dest('dist/js'));
21:  });
22:
23:  gulp.task('default', ['lint', 'build'], function() {
24:      gulp.start('serve');
25:  });
```

If you run `gulp build` in the command line and navigate to the output directory (dist/js above), you should see an app.js file that contains all of your app's JavaScript files minified and concatenated together.

Deploying Your Angular Code to Microsoft Azure

You can use Gulp for more than just JavaScript. Gulp can process your LESS and SASS into CSS, combine your HTML templates, run tests, optimize images, and much more. As you saw near the end of the previous section, we created a new folder called dist for our final JavaScript file ready to be deployed. When performing other tasks with Gulp, make sure that your entire app's files end up in a folder like dist ready for distribution. For now, you can just copy your app's HTML, CSS, and images into the dist folder and manually link your new app.js in index.html (bonus points if you can get Gulp to do some of this lifting for you).

Once you are ready to deploy your dist folder, moving it out to a public-facing server is a breeze. If you're using Microsoft Azure, log in to the portal and choose Add in the bottom corner, choose Compute, and then Web App, and then Quick Create. Give it a URL and choose or create a service plan and you're off and running.

Once the Azure Web App is set up, you can publish your dist folder. There are a few methods for accomplishing this. First, you could use Git. Start by setting up a local Git repository on the Azure Web App by choosing Set Up Deployment from Source Control on the right side of your Azure Web App's Dashboard tab and choosing Local Git Repository. Then add a new remote for it locally (`git remote add azure https://yourusername@yourapp.scm.azurewebsites.net:443/yourapp.git` from the command line). Finally, use `git push azure master` to push your code into the repository. This will push your entire repo; if you want to just serve the dist folder, go to the Configure tab for your Azure Web App and scroll down to Virtual Applications and Directories. Append the folder structure you want to serve to site\wwwroot and restart the Azure Web App (for example, site\wwwroot\dist).

Not using Git? No problem! You could also use FTP to drop the files onto your Azure Web App. From your Azure Web App's Dashboard tab, locate FTP Host Name and Deployment / FTP User on the right side. You can use your favorite FTP client (we like FileZilla) to connect to your Azure Web App and copy the dist folder over.

Summary

This hour covered how tools like Gulp can help you automate tasks related to deployment of our Angular app. You also learned about how you can cut down on the number of errors that Gulp will find before you even get to deployment. We explored using JSHint via Gulp as a way to check our code for these errors before deployment. Once our code was error-free, we used Gulp to minify and concatenate our JavaScript into one file to be deployed. Finally, you learned two ways to deploy your apps to Microsoft Azure.

Q&A

Q. We used `gulp-concat` to concatenate our JavaScript files, but what about our HTML templates?

A. The purpose of concatenating our JavaScript was to cut down on the number of HTTP requests required by the browser to run our app. Some of these requests are for JavaScript files, but some of them are for HTML files. To concatenate HTML files, run `npm install gulp-angular-templatecache`, include it in your gulpfile.js, and write a new task that uses `.src()` to grab your HTML files, `.pipe()` them to `templateCache()`, and write them to dist with `.dest()`.

Q. Running all of this Gulp stuff is such a pain. Isn't there a way to also automate that?

A. Yes! You could set up a continuous integration server like JenkinsCI, either on-premises or in Azure, and configure it to fetch your code whenever you commit, run whatever Gulp commands you like, and publish the dist folder to Azure via FTP. If Jenkins isn't your thing, the latest version of Visual Studio Online includes support for running Gulp tasks as part of your app's build process. Woo automation!

Workshop

Quiz

1. What function do you use to include Node modules in your gulpfile,js?

2. What Gulp task do you use when you want to run `gulp` at the command line without specifying a specific task name?

3. What statement can you use to force your browser to evaluate JavaScript using a more rigid subset of the language?

4. When using the `gulp-jshint` package to run JSHint on your code, what method do you use to change the styling of the error report in the console?

5. What Gulp method do you use for reading files from the file system? How about for streaming data between Gulp functions? How about for writing files to the file system?

Answers

1. The `require()` method

2. The `'default'` task

3. The `'use strict'` statement

4. The `.reporter()` method

5. The `.src()` method for reading, the `.pipe()` method for streaming, and the `.dest()` method for writing

Exercise

For the book management system mentioned in the Introduction, run JSHint on your code, minify and concatenate your code, and deploy your app to Azure.

Unraveling Unit Tests

What You'll Learn in This Hour:

▶ Unit testing in Angular

▶ Karma and Jasmine

▶ Getting everything set up

▶ Testing controllers

▶ Testing services

▶ Testing directives

Most developers know that unit testing is important for ensuring your application functions as expected. However, many applications are written in a way that prevents proper unit testing because components are tightly coupled, which makes testing one without the other impossible. Because angular uses dependency injection, it allows you to mock all dependencies for a specific component you want to test, thus allowing you to focus entirely on that single component. This principle is the same as a .NET application, which uses dependency injection to ensure separation of concerns.

Unit Testing in Angular

Angular comes with dependency injection built in, which allows us to write testable code by ensuring separation of concerns. Throughout this book, we have talked about what does and doesn't belong within each of Angular's components. However, if you fail to heed these suggestions, your application may end up untestable because your component has too much responsibility.

Unit testing in Angular is not much different from unit testing a .NET application; however, you may be unfamiliar with the tools that we will be using. The most common tools for writing unit tests for your Angular application are Karma and Jasmine.

Karma and Jasmine

Karma is an easy-to-use and highly configurable unit test runner that was originally built by the Angular.js team; it is testing framework agnostic, and allows you to set up automatic monitoring of files, so your unit tests run automatically whenever a file changes.

Jasmine describes itself as a behavior-driven development framework for JavaScript. It has no dependencies and has an easy-to-understand syntax that makes describing and writing unit tests quite pleasant.

We will be using NPM and Bower to get everything set up for this hour. If you need a refresher on what those are or how to use them, see Hour 3, "Tinkering with Tools for Modern Front-End Development."

Getting Everything Set Up

To get started, create a folder called angular_tests somewhere easily accessible, as we are going to be using the command line for installing dependencies and running our unit tests.

After you have your folder created, go ahead and cd into your new folder. The first thing we are going to do is create a new package.json file by running the following command:

```
npm init
```

This is going to prompt you with a series of questions about your project; however, responses you provide it are of little consequence for our purposes. After you have finished the `init` questions, run the following commands to install Karma and require.js:

```
npm install karma --save-dev
npm install requirejs --save-dev
```

Next, we are going to initialize our Bower file by running the following:

```
bower init
```

Once again, this prompts you with about 10 or so questions, none of which will have any consequences. When you are done, run the following commands to install Angular and Angular Mocks:

```
bower install angular --save
bower install angular-mocks --save-dev
```

Now that you have Angular and Angular Mocks set up, we are on to our last step, which is to initialize Karma. Unlike the other two initializations, the answers to some of these prompts do matter, so be careful when responding. To initialize Karma, run the following command, making sure to choose the correct options, listed below:

```
karma init
```

Which testing framework do you want to use?

Press Tab to list possible options. Press Enter to move to the next question.

```
> jasmine
```

Do you want to use Require.js?

This will add the Require.js plug-in.

Press Tab to list possible options. Press Enter to move to the next question.

```
> no
```

Do you want to capture any browsers automatically?

Press Tab to list possible options. Enter an empty string to move to the next question.

```
> Chrome
>
```

What is the location of your source and test files?

You can use glob patterns (for example, js/*.js or test/**/*Spec.js).

Enter an empty string to move to the next question.

```
> bower_components/angular/angular.js
> bower_components/angular-mocks/angular-mocks.js
> app/**/*.js
WARN [init]: There is no file matching this pattern.

>
```

Should any of the files included by the previous patterns be excluded?

You can use glob patterns (for example, **/*.swp).

Enter an empty string to move to the next question.

```
>
```

Do you want Karma to watch all the files and run the tests on change?

Press Tab to list possible options.

```
> yes
```

The first thing you hopefully noticed is that we are telling Karma that we are using Jasmine as our testing framework. The second important thing is that we have listed three locations of files we are going to use in our tests. The first two are the locations where we installed Angular and Angular Mocks; the last one is a wildcard for all JavaScript files found under the app folder, which will include any subfolders within the app directory. This is where we will be creating both our application files, along with our test files. You will get a warning from Karma when you tell it to look for app/**.*.js because we haven't created that folder yet. Fear not, though; we will create that in just a few minutes.

The last thing we need to do before we start building out our application is to create an index.html file for our website. Create an empty index.html file and add the following lines of code to it:

```
1:  <!DOCTYPE html>
2:      <head>
3:          <title>Unit Testing Angular</title>
4:          <script src="bower_components/angular/angular.js"></script>
5:          <script src="app/app.js"></script>
6:      </head>
7:      <body>
8:          <div ng-app="myApp">
9:          </div>
10:     </body>
11: </html>
```

You should notice that we are adding a script for Angular and a script for our app.js file, which we are saying is located in a folder called app. Let's go ahead and create that folder now, and then within that folder create a .js file called app with the following code:

```
angular.module('myApp', [
  'myApp.EvenOrOdd'
]);
```

The previous code says we are going to define a module called myApp.EvenOrOdd, so let's go ahead and do that now. Within you app folder, create a new folder EvenOrOdd, and within that, create a new .js file called evenOrOdd.controller.js with the following content:

```
angular.module('myApp.EvenOrOdd', []).controller('EvenOddController', function () {
  var vm = this;
  vm.number;
  vm.result = 'Please Enter a Number';
  vm.evenOrOdd = function(number) {
    if (number % 2 === 0) {
      vm.result = 'Even';
    } else if (number % 2 === 1) {
      vm.result = 'Odd'
    } else {
      vm.result = 'Please Enter a Number'
    }
  };
});
```

This is a simple controller that has a method for determining whether a number is even or odd or neither based on the value that is passed in. Don't forget to add this script to your index file! Now that we have our application properly set up, it is time to write some tests.

Testing Controllers

Within the EvenOrOdd folder we created earlier, create a new file called `evenOrOdd.controller_tests.js`.

This is where we will be writing our unit tests using Jasmine. The first thing we are going to do is use the `describe` method, which can be thought of as a sort of test suite that describes what you are testing. Check out the following code to see it in action:

```
describe('myApp.EvenOrOdd module', function() {
        //Next block of code will go here
});
```

You'll notice that `describe` has two parameters; the first is a string that provides information on what is being tested. This is going to show up in the console if something doesn't pass so it's important to describe your suite appropriately. The next piece of code we're going to write within our `describe` block allows us to load the module we want to test before each test case and is as follows:

```
beforeEach(module('myApp.EvenOrOdd'));
```

This will ensure that our module is loaded before each of your tests is executed. You can have as many `beforeEach` calls as you need, and they are not limited to loading modules. The final block of code we need to write for our unit tests is actually another `describe` block, for a specific piece of functionality that we are going to test within our module, along with the initialization of that functionality, along with the results that we expect:

```
describe('EvenOddController controller', function(){
    it('should be defined', inject(function($controller) {
      //spec body
      var vm = $controller('EvenOrOddController');
      expect(vm).toBeDefined();
    }));
  });
```

You'll notice that we use Jasmine's `it()` method that takes a string and a function. The first parameter should describe what you expect from the test, and the second is a function to run your test. In our case, we are testing a controller, and because `$controller` doesn't exist in the global namespace, we use the inject function to inject `$controller` into our function so that we can use it to create our `EvenOrOddController`. In the spec body, we create a new instance of our `EvenOrOddController` and then say we expect that the variable we set to the instance of our controller to be defined. This is a good way to ensure that your controller exists and is named what you expect.

The following code is a whole suite for testing our `EvenOrOddController`, including testing our three possible scenarios for our `evenOrOdd` method:

```
describe('myApp.EvenOrOdd module', function() {
 beforeEach(module('myApp.EvenOdd'));

 describe('EvenOddController controller', function(){

   it('should be defined', inject(function($controller) {
     //spec body
     var vm = $controller('EvenOddController');
     expect(vm).toBeDefined();
   }));

 });

 describe('EvenOddController vm.evaluate', function(){

   it('should set result to even when number is divisible by 2',
 inject(function($controller) {
     //spec body
     var vm = $controller('EvenOddController');
     vm.evenOrOdd(4);
     expect(vm.result).toEqual('Even');
   }));

   it('should set result to odd when number is not divisible by 2',
 inject(function($controller) {
     //spec body
     var vm = $controller('EvenOddController');
     vm.evenOrOdd(7);
     expect(vm.result).toEqual('Odd');
   }));

   it('should set result to please enter a number when vm.number is not a number',
 inject(function($controller) {
     //spec body
     var vm = $controller('EvenOddController');
     vm.evenOrOdd('This is not a number');
     expect(vm.result).toEqual('Please Enter a Number');
   }));

 });

});
```

Now that we have covered the basics of testing controllers, we're going to take a look at testing Angular services.

Testing Services

Testing Angular services is, for the most part, very similar to how we tested controllers. So, to take our testing to the next level, we're also going to explore how to mock an HTTP request to return data.

First, let's create the following Angular factory that will make GET requests to a /user endpoint:

```
angular.module("myApp.User", [])
  .factory("UserFactory", ['$http', function($http){

    function getUsers(){
      return $http.get('/user')
        .success(function(data, status, headers, config){
          return data
        })
        .error(function(data, status, headers, config) {
          return status;
        });

    }

    return {
      getUsers: getUsers
    }
}]);
```

We have injected $http into our UserFactory, which has just one method, getUsers(), which will return the data from a successful HTTP request and return the status of a failed request. If you need a refresher on Angular services, they are discussed in Hour 7, "Discovering Services: Part I," and Hour 8, "Discovering Services: Part II."

Now that we have a service that we would like to test, go ahead and create a test file as we did for our controller tests earlier. After you have the file created, you can create a test suite using the describe function as we did before, along with beforeEach to set up our module:

```
describe('UserFactory factory', function() {
  var $httpBackend, UserFactory;

  // Set up the module
  beforeEach(function() {
    module('myApp.User');

    inject(function( _$httpBackend_, _UserFactory_) {
```

```
        $httpBackend = _$httpBackend_;
        UserFactory = _UserFactory_;

      });
    });
});
```

You'll notice that just inside our `describe` method we create two variables, which we then initialize in our `beforeEach`, where we set them to the result of their respective inject. At this point, you might be wondering how the inject function works and why we've put underscores before and after the names of the components we want to inject. Angular first strips off the underscores and then looks for components that match the name. Now you're probably thinking that if Angular removes the underscores anyway, what's the point in using them, and the answer is you don't always have to. However, because we named our variables at the top to the actual names of the components we wanted to inject, we do. This prevents naming collisions when Angular tries to inject your components.

Let's write our first unit test to make sure that we have injected our `UserFactory` properly and that it has a method called `getUser` that is a function:

```
describe('UserFactory: definition', function() {

    it('Should define methods', function () {
      expect(UserFactory.getUsers).toBeDefined()
      expect(UserFactory.getUsers).toEqual(jasmine.any(Function))
    });

  });
```

This is just a bit different from our controller tests, where we injected `$controller` and called its constructor function. Remember that all Angular services are singletons, so it is already instantiated when we inject it. Our first tests make sure that our `getUser` function is defined, and the second verifies that it is a function.

You may have noticed earlier that we aren't injecting `$http` into our test suite, which is what we used in our `UserFactory` to make the HTTP requests, but instead are injecting `$httpBackend`. This is a module that allows us to fake HTTP requests and return data to whatever method tried to use `$http`. The big difference is that `$http` is asynchronous, and writing asynchronous unit tests is terrible and a mess to maintain, so the Angular team decided to fake that as well. We'll cover how they did it in just a little bit, but for now, add the following lines of code just below your inject method:

```
afterEach(function() {
    $httpBackend.verifyNoOutstandingExpectation();
    $httpBackend.verifyNoOutstandingRequest();
  });
```

This afterEach() method makes sure that there are no outstanding expectations or requests when you reach the end of your test method, which is important as we dive into how they fake asynchronous calls. Now that we have some cleanup in place, let's write a couple of unit tests.

The first test will verify that if we receive a success response that we return the data that was returned from the service, and the second will verify that if we receive an error response that we return the status. We'll start off by creating a describe method for the tests we are going to run:

```
describe('UserFactory: getUser', function(){
        //Our test code will code inside here
 });
```

Next, let's replace the comment in our method with an it method that will mock our $http request and return us a 200 code that contains an array of users:

```
it('Should return user array', function() {
      var users = [{userName: 'User One'}, {userName: 'User Two'}];

      $httpBackend.expectGET('/user').respond(200, users);

      var result;

      UserFactory.getUsers()
        .success(function(data){
          result = data;
        }).error(function(reason){
          result = reason;
        });

      $httpBackend.flush();

      expect(result).toEqual(users);
  });
```

The first thing we do is create the array of user objects that we want to return from our service. Then we use the $httpBackend method to respond with a 200 code and our users array when a GET request is made to /user. This intercepts any request made to $http.get('/user') and returns 200 and our users array.

Next, we create a variable to hold the response of our getUsers method, and then we call UserFactory.getUsers. Because we call $http.get('/user') inside our getUsers method, we will be returned a 200 success code and the users array we defined earlier. However, this doesn't happen until we call $httpBacked.flush(), which triggers all fake requests made to $httpBackend to be returned with the response that was defined on the expect. This is how the Angular team handled synchronous testing of asynchronous code. Although it is a bit confusing at first, once you get the hang of it, it's not that bad. The final piece of code verifies that the result that was returned from getUsers is equal to the users array we defined.

Now that we understand how $httpBackend works, it's pretty easy to write our test case for when an error code is returned:

```
it('Should return status Not Found', function() {
    $httpBackend.expectGET('/user').respond(404, 'Not Found');

    var result = '';

    UserFactory.getUsers()
      .success(function(data){
        result = data;
      }).error(function(reason){
        result = reason;
      });

    $httpBackend.flush();

    expect(result).toEqual('Not Found');
  });
```

This uses almost the exact same code, but instead of returning a 200 and an array of users, we tell $httpBackend to return a 404 response with a Not Found message. This will trigger the error callback in our getUser() method, which we expect to return Not Found.

If you had trouble adding the code as we went along, here is what our entire testing file looks like when finished:

```
describe('MyController', function() {
  var $httpBackend, UserFactory;

  // Set up the module
  beforeEach(function() {
    module('myApp.User');

    inject(function( _$httpBackend_, _UserFactory_) {
      $httpBackend = _$httpBackend_;
      UserFactory = _UserFactory_;

    });
  });

  afterEach(function() {
    $httpBackend.verifyNoOutstandingExpectation();
    $httpBackend.verifyNoOutstandingRequest();
  });
```

```
describe('UserFactory: definition', function() {

  it('Should define methods', function () {
    expect(UserFactory.getUsers).toBeDefined()
    expect(UserFactory.getUsers).toEqual(jasmine.any(Function))
  });

});

describe('UserFactor: getUser', function(){
  it('Should return user array', function() {
    var users = [{userName: 'User One'}, {userName: 'User Two'}];

    $httpBackend.expectGET('/user').respond(200, users);

    var result;

    UserFactory.getUsers()
      .success(function(data){
        result = data;
      }).error(function(reason){
        result = reason;
      });

    $httpBackend.flush();

    expect(result).toEqual(users);
  });

  it('Should return status Not Found', function() {
    $httpBackend.expectGET('/user').respond(404, 'Not Found');

    var result = '';

    UserFactory.getUsers()
      .success(function(data){
        result = data;
      }).error(function(reason){
        result = reason;
      });

    $httpBackend.flush();

    expect(result).toEqual('Not Found');
  });
});
});
```

Now that we have covered how to test services, we'll wrap up our testing by covering directives.

Testing Directives

Directives are one of Angular's most powerful features, but they can also become very complex. In this section, we test a simple directive that replaces a special directive tag with some song lyrics that contain an expression. To get started, create a new file called `RedBalloons.directive.js` and write the following code:

```
angular.module('myApp.RedBalloons', [])
  .directive('redBalloons', function(){
    return {
      restrict: 'E',
      replace: true,
      template: '<h3> {{38 + 61}} Red Balloons Go By!</h3>'
    };
  });
```

We've defined a simple directive called `redBalloons` that will replace `<red-balloons></red-balloons>` tags with an `<h3>` with the text "99 Red Balloons Go By!"

Now that we have a directive, let's create our test suite just like we did for services, but instead of injecting `$httpBackend` and our `UserFactory`, we're going to inject `$compile` and `$rootScope`:

```
describe('RedBalloons: directive', function() {
  var $compile, $rootScope;

  beforeEach(module('myApp.RedBalloons'));

  beforeEach(inject(function(_$compile_, _$rootScope_){
    $compile = _$compile_;
    $rootScope = _$rootScope_;
  }));

});
```

`$compile` will allow us to compile our `<red-balloons></red-balloons>` tag, and `$rootScope` will allow us to trigger a digest cycle. Now let's write a unit test to ensure that our tag is replaced with "99 Red Balloons Go By!"

```
it('Replaces the element with the appropriate content', function() {
    var element = $compile("<red-balloons></red-balloons>"$rootScope);

    $rootScope.$digest();

    expect(element.html()).toContain("99 Red Balloons Go By!");
  });
```

You'll see that we use the constructor for $compile to replace the HTML and pass it the $rootScope as a scope. Then we call $rootScope.$digest() to trigger a digest cycle, which we need to evaluate any expression within our directive. In our case, that's {{38 + 61}}. Finally, we verify that our element contains HTML with the content "99 Red Balloons Go By!"

Here is what our entire suite for testing our directive looks like:

```
describe('RedBalloons: directive', function() {
  var $compile,
    $rootScope;

  beforeEach(module('myApp.RedBalloons'));

  beforeEach(inject(function(_$compile_, _$rootScope_){
    $compile = _$compile_;
    $rootScope = _$rootScope_;
  }));

  it('Replaces the element with the appropriate content', function() {
    var element = $compile("<red-balloons></red-balloons>"$rootScope);

    $rootScope.$digest();

    expect(element.html()).toContain("99 Red Balloons Go By!");
  });
});
```

Summary

We covered a lot of material in this hour, including how Angular was designed with testing in mind, how to install and set up Karma and Jasmine, along with unit testing controllers, services, and directives. Although we didn't cover testing every Angular component, the principles of injection and mocking carry over for testing all the rest.

Q&A

Q. What other testing frameworks can I use with Karma?

A. Mocha and QUnit are other popular choices, but Karma is framework agnostic, and if there is a different framework you want to use, Karma provides a plug-in API for writing your own integrations.

Q. Is it possible to write end-to-end tests for Angular?

A. Yes, although beyond the scope if this hour, end-to-end (E2E) tests can be written using Protractor, which runs on node.js.

Workshop

Quiz

1. How do we include our module in our test suite?

2. How do we trigger an expression to be evaluated when testing a directive?

3. Why do we sometimes use underscores when injecting modules?

Answers

1. `beforeEach(module('myApp.Module'));`

2. `$rootScope.$digest();`

3. Underscores are used to prevent naming collisions within your test suite.

Exercise

For the book management system mentioned in the Introduction, write tests against your controller, directive, and service.

HOUR 19
Destroying Debugging

What You'll Learn in This Hour:

► Strategies and tips for debugging an Angular application

► Tools for debugging

► Google Chrome Developer Tools

► Firefox Toolbox and Firefox Developer Edition

► Internet Explorer Developer Tools

► Batarang Chrome extension

Everyone makes mistakes. It's impossible to write software and have it work correctly the first time, every time. When running .NET apps locally in Visual Studio, we can set breakpoints, set watches on variables using the Watch window, and execute arbitrary statements using the Immediate window. Even if we're trying to debug apps running in Microsoft Azure, we can attach a local debugger and debug as if we were running it locally (so cool, by the way). Fortunately, there's a veritable "bat belt" of tools at our disposal for debugging front-end code as well; some tools are even specifically designed for debugging Angular apps.

This hour covers some generic debugging strategies and explores a few tools, including Google Chrome's Developer Tools, developer tools in other browsers, and the Google Chrome Batarang Extension.

Debugging Strategies and Tips

Let's start by discussing some basic debugging strategies. Note, these apply to JavaScript debugging in general, not just Angular.

► While you can always debug by including an `alert()` statement to show a value in your app, `alert()` can be problematic if left in a production application. Use `console.log()` for this purpose instead.

▶ You can use the `debugger` statement to programmatically set a breakpoint. If you're already in your IDE, this saves you the time of having to use your browser's developer tools (more on those later) to inspect the JavaScript source and find the line on which you want to set a breakpoint. Don't forget to remove these before you deploy your app to production!

▶ Just like in Visual Studio's Immediate window, you can use the console to execute arbitrary code. The Try It Yourself section later goes into more detail on this.

▶ Also, just like Visual Studio's ability to set watches on variables, you can usually use your browser's developer tools to do the same for your Angular app.

▶ If you recently created a new JavaScript file, did you forget to add it to your index.html? The best way to handle this is to use a build tool like Gulp to automatically inject `<script>` statements for you.

▶ If you're having an issue and need help from someone else or the community at large, it's best to reproduce your issue on a site like JSFiddle or Plunker, two sites that give you a browser-based sandbox for setting up small applications (with full HTML, CSS, and JavaScript support). Sometimes, the act of removing complexity as you use these sites will help you uncover the root problem.

▶ Sometimes it just helps to talk through what your code is doing with someone (or even alone). Google "rubber duck debugging" for more on this subject.

Now, let's look at some Angular-specific tips.

▶ If you're using custom directives, make sure to go from camelCase (for example, `notificationPolling`) in your JavaScript to snake-case (for example, `notification-polling`) in your HTML. It's easy when you're moving quickly to just copy and paste from JavaScript to HTML or vice versa.

▶ When you reference a module, make sure that you are including the empty array parameter once and only once per module. You should only do this statement once:

```
angular.module('app', []);
```

But you can use this line multiple times:

```
angular.module('app');
```

▶ If you're using the inline array or `$inject` options for annotating your dependencies, make sure that the string names of your components match up with your arguments (and make sure that the order is the same).

GO TO ▶ For more on Angular component dependencies, see Hour 11, "Depending on Dependency Injection."

Tools

When debugging ASP.NET apps, the best (and only) tool for the job is Visual Studio. Fortunately, when we debug Angular apps, we have a few tools available for us. If we're using the Google Chrome web browser, there is an excellent debugger built in to the browser called Google Chrome Developer Tools (DevTools, for short). Likewise, there's a similar tool built in to Firefox: the Firefox Toolbox. Both of these tools offer a multitude of features, including the following:

- DOM inspection

- Live HTML editing

- Live CSS editing

- Local data storage explorer (for example, IndexedDB, Local & Session Storage, WebSQL)

- Network request/response inspection

- Profiling for performance

- Debug console

In late 2014, the Firefox team took their developer tools to the next level by releasing a standalone version of Firefox (Firefox Developer Edition), which includes new themes, a built-in IDE called WebIDE, a responsive design view for viewing sites at standard sizes, and other tools. It's also worth noting that Chrome DevTools also includes in-browser editing and a similar responsive design view.

BY THE WAY

What About Firebug?

A few years ago, web developers typically used the Firebug extension to debug their JavaScript in Firefox, but the built-in Firefox tools have come a long way since then. As such, Firebug seems to be falling out of favor.

When debugging in Internet Explorer, your mileage may vary depending on what version of IE you are debugging. Later versions of IE (dubbed "new IE" by the web developer community) have decent dev tools, but older versions like 6 through 8 don't have the greatest tooling available.

Finally, we've also seen some independent browser extensions like Chrome's Batarang that help with Angular-specific debugging. Let's take a look at each of these tools in the context of debugging TodoMVC.

DID YOU KNOW?

TodoMVC

There are a lot of alternatives to Angular for managing your front-end code. Obviously, we're biased toward Angular, but if you want to explore other options, TodoMVC is a great site that implements a basic "To Do" application in many different frameworks so that you can compare. For this hour, we are referencing TodoMVC v1.3. If the code you see isn't following what's printed here, you can pull v1.3 from the TodoMVC GitHub repository: https://github.com/tastejs/todomvc/releases/tag/1.3.0.

Google Chrome Developer Tools

Let's start by looking at Google Chrome's Developer Tools.

▼ TRY IT YOURSELF

Debugging TodoMVC with Google Chrome Developer Tools

This section introduces various areas of Google Chrome Developer Tools by debugging TodoMVC. You'll learn how to set a breakpoint and inspect values when execution stops at that breakpoint. In addition, we'll look at two ways to inject arbitrary logic when debugging (see the example in Figure 19.1).

1. Open Google Chrome and navigate to http://todomvc.com/examples/angularjs.

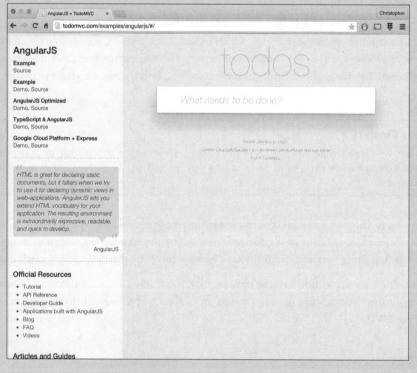

FIGURE 19.1
TodoMVC's Angular example.

2. Open the Developer Tools. The exact location and keystroke depend on your OS (on a Mac, View > Developer > Developer Tools, as shown in Figure 19.2).

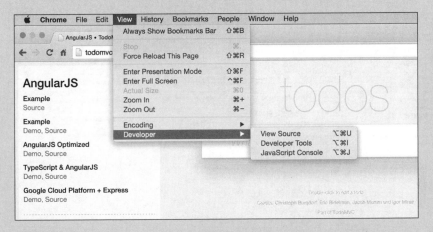

FIGURE 19.2
Navigating to Developer Tools in Google Chrome on Mac OS X.

3. You are presented with the default view of Chrome's Developer Tools: the Sources tab. Here you can see all the JavaScript source files organized by domain. In the tree view on the left side, the index.html file is selected by default. You can use this view to find specific source files. Find todoCtrl.js, shown in Figure 19.3.

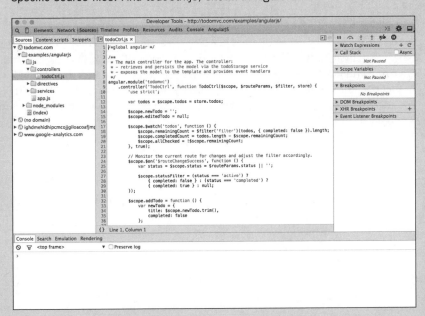

FIGURE 19.3
Navigating to todoCtrl.js.

4. Scroll down to line 33 and click the line number to add a breakpoint. We want to break when the user adds a new list item (see Figure 19.4).

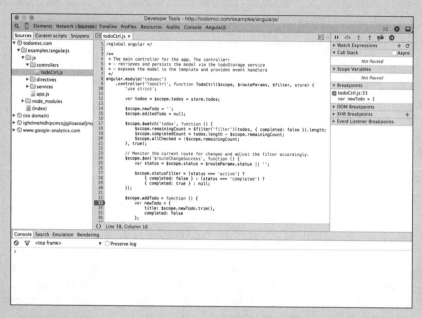

FIGURE 19.4
Adding a breakpoint.

5. Enter a new list item in TodoMVC and submit it (see Figure 19.5). The Chrome Developer Tools will reappear and will break at line 33. Just as you can hover over variables in Visual Studio at this point to see their values, you can do the same in Chrome Developer Tools. Hover over $scope.newTodo on line 34 (see Figure 19.6 and you'll see the list item text that you entered in the UI).

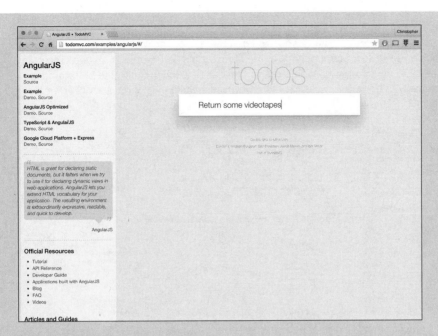

FIGURE 19.5
Submit a list item.

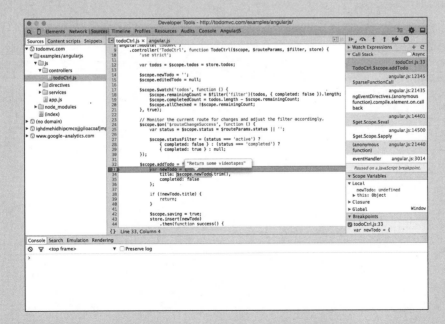

FIGURE 19.6
Inspect $scope.newTodo to see its value.

6. Another useful trick allows you to edit the JavaScript on-the-fly, similar to using the Immediate window in Visual Studio. You can use the console to arbitrarily assign values, or you can write JavaScript directly in the file right inside Chrome Developer Tools. In Figure 19.7, we use the console area of Chrome Developer Tools (the bottom pane) to manually set $scope.newTodo to a new value while execution is stopped at the breakpoint.

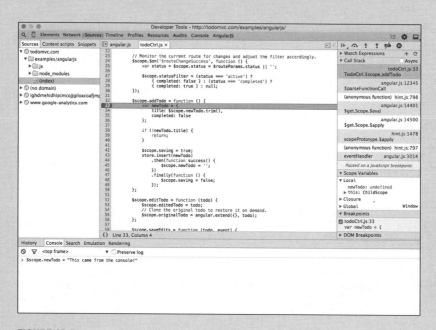

FIGURE 19.7
Using the console to set new values to variables.

Press Enter in the console area to submit your statement (shown in Figure 19.8). When you submit, the console echoes back the new value of the variable you updated, if any.

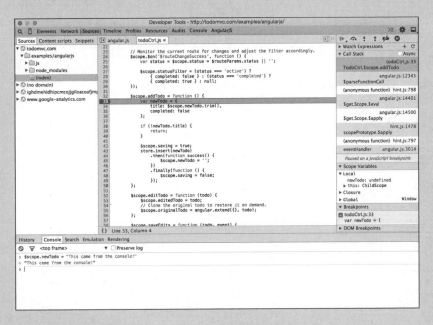

FIGURE 19.8
The console echoes back the new value.

Pressing Play through this breakpoint reveals that the list item's text was successfully set to "This came from the console!" (shown in Figure 19.9). Modifying things in this manner is great for debugging with different values versus making the changes in your IDE and refreshing the page.

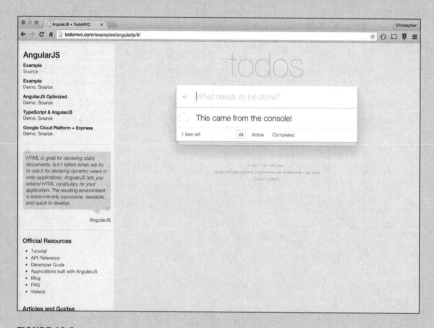

FIGURE 19.9
TodoMVC shows the updated list item text.

7. We can also include arbitrary JavaScript directly in the files within Chrome Developer Tools for rapidly testing code instead of making single changes in our IDE and refreshing the page each time. In Figure 19.10, we add the following code to line 38: `newTodo.title = "This came from code!";`

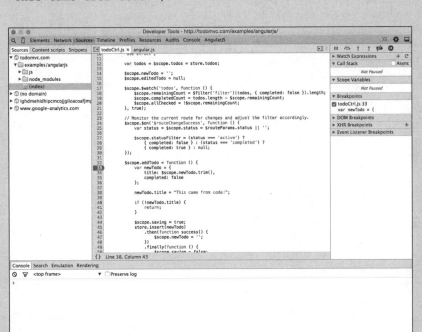

FIGURE 19.10
Adding arbitrary JavaScript to files.

Make sure to "save" the file to submit your change. If you are debugging locally, Chrome Developer Tools can actually save these changes right to the source files. (Chrome Developer Tools essentially becomes an IDE.) Because we're debugging on the server, Chrome Developer Tools gives you a yellow warning background with a message indicating that it can't save the file (see Figure 19.11).

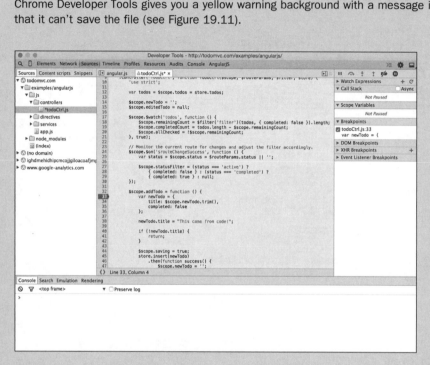

FIGURE 19.11
Saving changes to JavaScript files in Chrome Developer Tools.

Finally, enter a new list item with any text and step past the breakpoint and past our custom code. Your text will be replaced with "This came from code!" as we would expect (see Figure 19.12).

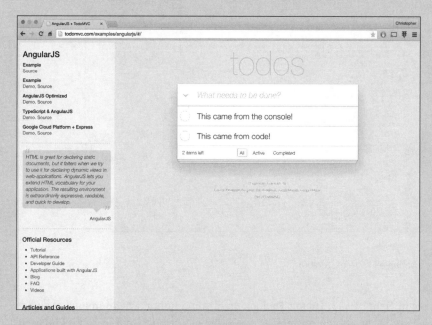

FIGURE 19.12
TodoMVC shows the updated list item text.

The team behind Google Chrome's Developer Tools is constantly adding new features for web developers. New features hit Chrome Canary before they are integrated into the main release of Chrome. If you're interested in being on the bleeding edge, check out Chrome Canary.

Firefox Toolbox and Firefox Developer Edition

Firefox Toolbox is similar to Google Chrome's Developer Tools in many ways. For example, breakpoints and variable inspection function exactly the same way (see Figure 19.13).

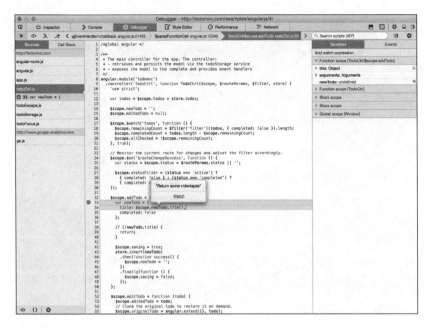

FIGURE 19.13
Hovering over a variable in Firefox Toolbox.

As you can see in Figure 19.13, Firefox Toolbox gives you a handy way to immediately add a watch for a variable when you hover over it. (Chrome Developer Tools requires you to first highlight the full variable name, right-click, and choose Add to Watch.) In addition, both Firefox Toolbox and Chrome Developer Tools display the call stack at the current execution point. (Firefox Toolbox puts this at the top in a horizontal bar, and Chrome Developer Tools devotes a full pane on the right side to the call stack.)

Late in 2014, the Firefox team announced Firefox Developer Edition, which is a version of Firefox targeted specifically at web developers. This browser runs independent of standard Firefox, with a separate profile so that you can use both applications side by side. Besides a dark theme, the browser puts the various tools that comprise Firefox Toolbox at your fingertips via a shortcut button (see Figure 19.14).

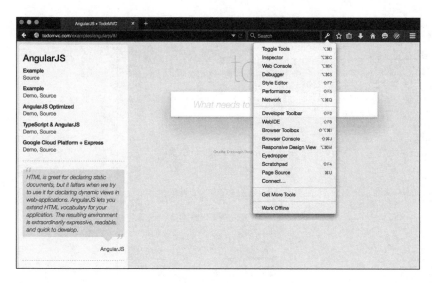

FIGURE 19.14
Firefox Developer Edition adds easy access to the Firefox Toolbox.

In addition, similar to Google Chrome Canary, this version of Firefox will receive new Firefox features at least 12 weeks before they reach the main Firefox release channel. The biggest benefit is definitely early access to experimental tools. One of these tools is Valence, a way to use the Firefox Toolbox to debug other browsers, including Chrome Desktop, Chrome for Android, and Apple's Mobile Safari for iOS 6 through 8 (and the iOS Simulator).

Internet Explorer Developer Tools

Depending on the version of Internet Explorer you are using, your mileage with developer tools may vary. IE11 handles many of the same features discussed earlier: breakpoints, variable inspection (see Figure 19.15), watches, and much more.

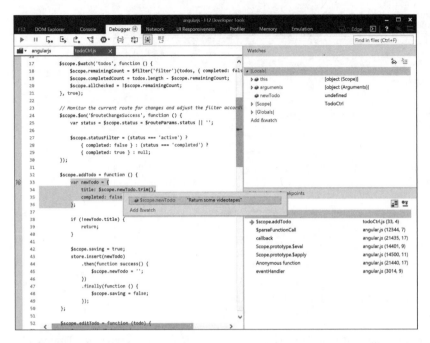

FIGURE 19.15
Hovering over a variable in Internet Explorer 11 developer tools.

However, in older versions of Internet Explorer, such as IE9, the developer tools are a different experience. When you open TodoMVC in IE9, click Start Debugging, which will refresh your page and allow you to open individual JavaScript files. In the file list, some files may appear more than once (see Figure 19.16). After guessing at which todoCtrl.js is right, you can add a breakpoint in the same location that we've been using, but it will not be hit when you enter a new item in the list in the UI.

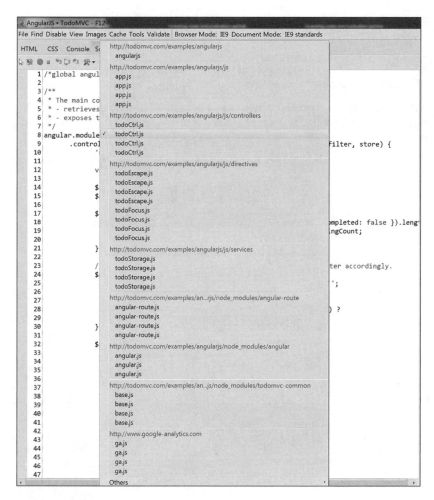

FIGURE 19.16
Internet Explorer 9 developer tools.

In IE8, the TodoMVC Angular demo that we've been using does not even load.

Batarang Chrome Extension

Rounding out our "bat belt" of tools for debugging Angular apps is Batarang, a Chrome extension developed specifically for debugging Angular apps. Let's go back to Chrome and explore Batarang.

Exploring Batarang

Let's use Batarang to inspect scopes and dependencies in the TodoMVC application.

1. Install Batarang. Be sure to use the version that includes "stable" in the name: https://chrome.google.com/webstore/detail/angularjs-batarang-stable/niopocochgahfkiccpjmmpchncjoapek?hl=en-US.

2. Once it's installed, open up Chrome Developer Tools and you'll see a new tab: AngularJS (see Figure 19.17).

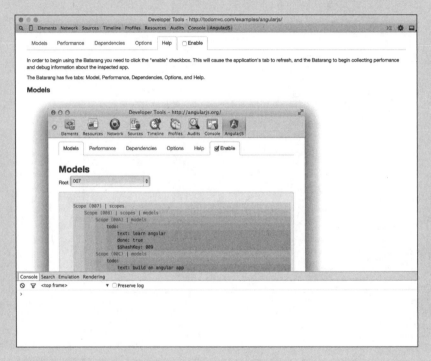

FIGURE 19.17
Batarang adds a new tab to Chrome Developer Tools.

3. On that tab, check the box for Enable, which will refresh the page and allow Batarang to begin collecting debug information (see Figure 19.18). This will automatically take you to the first Batarang tab: Models.

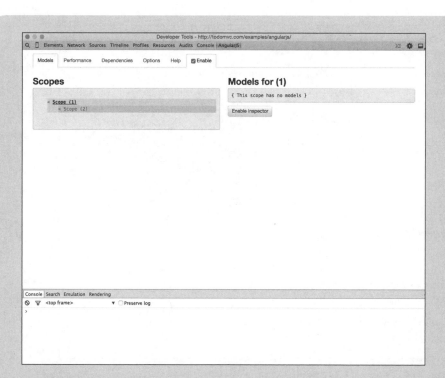

FIGURE 19.18
Enable Batarang.

4. The Batarang Models tab has two sections: Scopes and Models. The Scopes section enumerates all Angular scopes in the app. For TodoMVC, there are two scopes: the root scope on the `<body>` tag and an inner scope with all variables assigned to `$scope` in the `TodoCtrl` controller. Click the inner scope, and the Models section will update accordingly (see Figure 19.19).

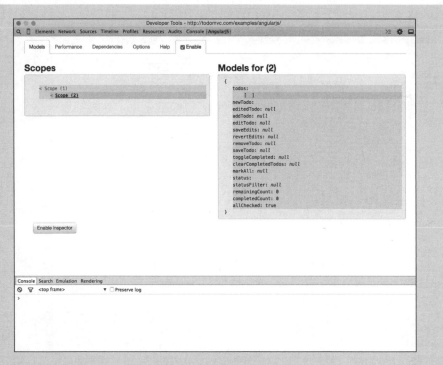

FIGURE 19.19
Viewing the inner scope on TodoMVC with Batarang.

5. Add a new list item in TodoMVC and watch the model change in real time as items are added to $scope (see Figure 19.20).

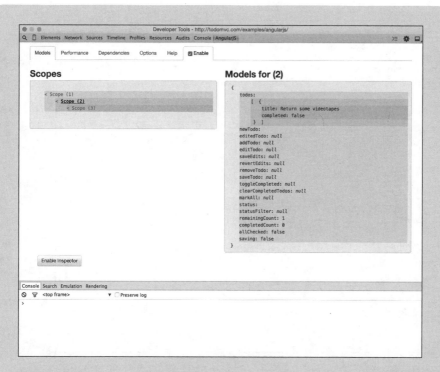

FIGURE 19.20
Viewing the inner scope on TodoMVC with Batarang after changing `$scope`.

6. Another valuable Batarang tab is the Dependencies tab. This tab illustrates the web of dependencies between custom components and built-in Angular components (see Figure 19.21).

GO TO ▶ For more on Angular component dependencies, see **HOUR 11**.

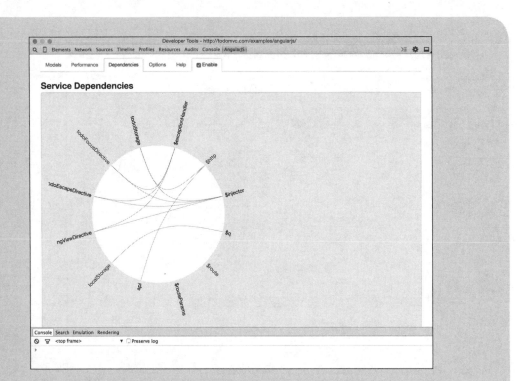

FIGURE 19.21
Batarang service dependency graph.

For TodoMVC, we can hover over `$http` and a line indicates that *it is depended on* by `todoStorage` and `api` (see Figure 19.22).

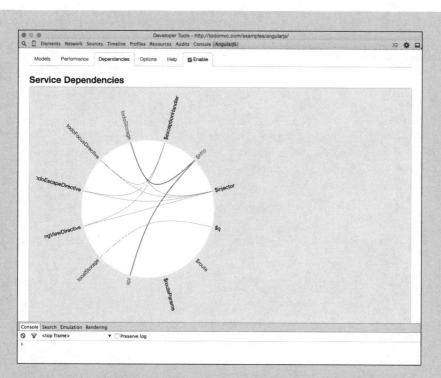

FIGURE 19.22
Batarang service dependency graph showing $http upstream dependencies.

Also, we can hover over `todoStorage` and see a line depicting that *it depends on* `$http` and `$injector` (see Figure 19.23).

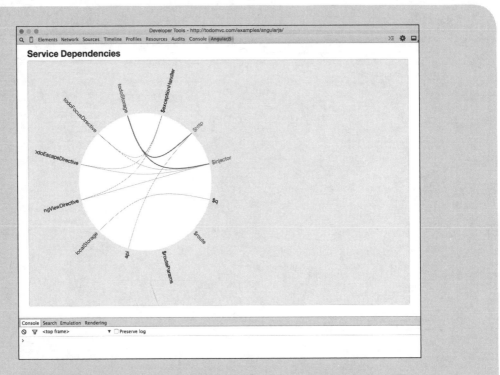

FIGURE 19.23
Batarang service dependency graph showing todoStorage downstream dependencies.

Summary

This hour started with some basic JavaScript debugging strategies and tips before exploring a few Angular-specific ones. Then we used Google Chrome's Developer Tools to debug the TodoMVC Angular application. We then looked at the broader landscape of developer tools in other browsers such as Firefox, Firefox Developer Edition, and Internet Explorer. Finally, we looked at Batarang, a Google Chrome extension built solely for debugging Angular apps.

Q&A

Q. I only develop in one browser. Why are you showing me how to debug in so many browsers?

A. We all prefer a modern browser when developing our apps, but the reality is that we need to support a wide array of browsers. When you're testing your app in other browsers, you will undoubtedly run into browser-specific issues. At that point, the only way to debug them is to use that browser's developer tools.

Q. **For any element in the DOM, how can I inspect the element's** $scope?

A. You can use Batarang for this, but otherwise, select the DOM element, and run this in the console: `element.angular($0).scope()`.

Workshop
Quiz

1. What JavaScript statement allows a developer to trigger a breakpoint programmatically?

2. What are two ways to execute arbitrary JavaScript code while execution is stopped at a breakpoint?

3. What advantage does Batarang give developers wanting to inspect $scope versus just using normal developer tools?

Answers

1. The `debugger` statement.

2. Use the console or (in some browsers only) edit the JavaScript source files directly in the browser's developer tools.

3. Essentially, Batarang automatically creates a watch for every variable of every $scope in the application. The developer doesn't need to open the source files in developer tools, find the line of code, place a breakpoint, and navigate the app to trigger the breakpoint; the developer can simply see changes to $scope as they occur.

Exercise

For the book management system mentioned in the Introduction, use the Dev Tools environment for your browser of choice to add a breakpoint to somewhere in your controller or service and inspect the variables that are in scope.

Applying Angular to ASP.NET Web Forms

What You'll Learn in This Hour:

▶ Strategies for modernizing web applications
▶ Translating Web Forms into Angular
▶ Augment Web Forms with Angular

Unfortunately, the reality of being a software development professional is that you don't always get to build applications from scratch (referred to as *green-field development*). At some point, you will undoubtedly need to maintain an existing application (referred to as *brown-field development*). Today, ASP.NET web developers faced with the latter typically are supporting ASP.NET Web Forms (a 15-year-old framework that was originally designed to augment the transition from desktop application development to web application development for Windows Forms developers). Although maintaining these applications tends to leave little room for making overarching technology changes, such as switching the entire app to Angular + ASP.NET Web API, developers can still implement modern technologies. In this hour, we start by discussing strategies for modernizing legacy web applications. Then we look at an existing legacy Web Forms application and how we can begin to use some of Angular's features to enhance the application.

Strategies for Modernizing Web Applications

Imagine you are a developer on a team with a few other developers and a technical lead or solution architect. You've inherited a legacy Web Forms application with about 25 different pages. Your task is to work through a list of bugs and small new features that have been collecting in the work management system over the past few months. Having just completed this book, you want to start using your newfound knowledge. "Let's start using Angular on these pages!" you exclaim to the technical lead on the project. She replies, "According to the project manager, there's a tight deadline and limited budget on this; I don't think we have time to start exploring new technologies right now."

Unfortunately, she's right. It would not make sense to spend the bulk of the project schedule on rewriting the existing application. Fortunately, there's a way for both parties to win: the team can still complete work, *and* you can start using Angular. It is likely that some of the new features to be added could benefit from Angular. When developing these features, you can include Angular and *only use it for these features*. Resist the temptation to rewrite the application. Starting small with subsets of functionality is a great way to introduce modern technologies into an old project, still complete your work on time, and (hopefully) make a lasting change on the technical direction of the project.

Translating Web Forms into Angular

In this section, we explore a few examples. First, we'll build out a small Web Forms app without using Angular. Then we'll make some larger changes to this app as we rewrite parts of it using Angular. Finally, we'll go back to our original Web Forms app without Angular and show how we can add functionality (using Angular) without modifying much of the existing Web Forms code.

Building Out a Web Forms Example

First, we will be building a Web Forms page that allows users to track the name and rating of their favorite music artists. For the purposes of explanation, we'll just be working with this one page; a real enterprise-level application would be much larger and would have many pages. After we implement the page, we'll include Angular and redo some of the user interface (UI) to enhance it a bit.

Let's start with a blank slate in Visual Studio. Create a new project and choose ASP.NET Web Application from the project template library. Give it a name and choose the Empty template. Tick the Add Folders and Core References For check box for Web Forms.

WATCH OUT!

Don't Include More Than You Need!

You can choose the Web Forms option here, but this will also include ASP.NET Identity and a lot of other stuff that we don't care about.

Once Visual Studio creates your solution, right-click your project and choose to Add New Item. From the menu that appears, choose Web Form as the item to add. Give it the name Default. aspx. You could call your page whatever you like, but by calling it Default.aspx, it will automatically be loaded as the first page (similar to how you don't need to type index.html in the URL of websites you visit).

If you expand the arrow next to Default.aspx in your Solution Explorer, you'll see a few files: the Default.aspx root file, which contains the markup; a Default.aspx.cs code-behind file, which contains the backing C# code for the page; and a Default.aspx.designer.cs file, which is autogenerated as you add Web Forms controls to the .aspx page.

Let's start with the markup (see Listing 20.1). We are going to create a table to show some data from the server. (We'll be doing this with data held in memory; a real application would read/write this data to a database.) We'll also build out a small form to add new data to the table. We start with the Web Forms declaration that ties this .aspx page to its code behind file. (This line should be autogenerated for you.)

Then we create a Web Form with `<form id="form1" runat="server">` (again, autogenerated for you). Inside that form, we set up three sections: an error message, a table, and a small form for adding new artists.

For our error message, a simple `<asp:Label>` will do just fine. In the table section, we set up an `<asp:Repeater>` with a `<HeaderTemplate>` for our `<table>` header row, `<ItemTemplate>` and `<AlternatingItemTemplate>` for data rows, and a `<FooterTemplate>` to close the `<table>`.

BY THE WAY

Data Binding Versus Code in Inline Server Tags

The ASP.NET Web Forms syntax for Inline Server tags is `<% %>`. Inside those tags, you can use a myriad of other symbols for specific purposes. To display string values or to call methods from the code behind file, use the *displaying expression* syntax, which uses an equals sign: `<%= DateTime.Now.ToString() %>`. For our example here, we want to use the *data-binding expression* syntax, which uses an octothorpe: `<%# Eval("Name") %>`. For more info, see this Microsoft documentation: https://support.microsoft.com/en-us/kb/976112.

The final section contains two `<asp:TextBox>` controls to capture input from the user (the artist's name and rating) and an `<asp:Button>` control to submit the new artist. Note the `OnClick="btnAdd_Click"` on the button; this ties the button to a method in our code behind file (more on that later).

LISTING 20.1   Artist Management Application: Web Form UI

```
1:   <%@ Page Language="C#" AutoEventWireup="true"
              CodeBehind="Default.aspx.cs" Inherits="Ch20.Default" %>
2:
3:   <!DOCTYPE html>
4:
5:   <html xmlns="http://www.w3.org/1999/xhtml">
6:   <head runat="server">
7:       <title>Artist Management</title>
```

```
 8:  </head>
 9:  <body>
10:      <form id="form1" runat="server">
11:          <section>
12:              <asp:Label runat="server" ID="lblError" ForeColor="Red" />
13:          </section>
14:          <br />
15:          <section>
16:              <asp:Repeater ID="rptArtists" runat="server">
17:                  <HeaderTemplate>
18:                      <table border="1">
19:                          <tr>
20:                              <th>Artist</th>
21:                              <th>Rating</th>
22:                          </tr>
23:                  </HeaderTemplate>
24:                  <ItemTemplate>
25:                      <tr style="background-color: palegoldenrod">
26:                          <td><%#Eval("Name") %></td>
27:                          <td><%#Eval("Rating") %></td>
28:                      </tr>
29:                  </ItemTemplate>
30:                  <AlternatingItemTemplate>
31:                      <tr style="background-color: white">
32:                          <td><%#Eval("Name") %></td>
33:                          <td><%#Eval("Rating") %></td>
34:                      </tr>
35:                  </AlternatingItemTemplate>
36:                  <FooterTemplate>
37:                      </table>
38:                  </FooterTemplate>
39:              </asp:Repeater>
40:          </section>
41:          <br />
42:          <section>
43:              Artist Name: <asp:TextBox runat="server" ID="txtName" />
44:              <br />
45:              Rating: <asp:TextBox runat="server" ID="txtRating" />
46:              <br />
47:              <asp:Button runat="server"
48:                  Text="Add Artist"
49:                  ID="btnAdd"
50:                  OnClick="btnAdd_Click" />
51:          </section>
52:      </form>
53:  </body>
54:  </html>
```

ASPX Designer Files

Once you save this .aspx page, Visual Studio will autogenerate the necessary backing properties in the Default.aspx.designer.cs file. Any Web Forms control in Default.aspx with the `runat="server"` attribute will require one of these properties so that they can be used in the Default.aspx.cs code behind file.

Next, let's look at Default.aspx.cs, our code behind file (see Listing 20.2). Actually persisting our artists to a database is beyond the scope of this hour, so we'll just use an in-memory cache to hold our artists (lines 11–15). In the `Page_Load()` method, we check whether the current request is a postback by using the `IsPostBack` variable available to us because we inherit from `Page`. If the current request is not a postback (that is, the first request), instantiate our list of artists to be cached. Regardless of whether this is the first request or not, we call a method called `BindArtistsRepeater()`, which we will create later.

What's a Postback?

When a user first requests a Web Forms page, like our Default.aspx that we've been building, the client browser issues an HTTP GET request to the server. The server responds with the assets needed for the client browser to render the page. When the user fills out the form and clicks submit, the entered form data is serialized into the body of an HTTP POST request and sent *back* to the server (a postback). Web Forms controls that are declared to run on the server (using `runat="server"`) can then be modified, and the page gets rerendered to the user with different data.

In our markup, we defined an event handler on our Add button called `btnAdd_Click()`. When the user clicks that button, the data in the form is posted back to the server, and this method is executed. In this method, we have access to our text boxes (`txtName` and `txtRating`), and we do some validation to make sure that the form is filled out correctly. If there's an error, we populate `lblError` and return control.

If everything looks good, we add a new `Artist` to the cache and blank out the text boxes. Finally, we call `BindArtistsRepeater()` so that our new `Artist` appears on the page, and we blank out the error message because our `Artist` creation was successful.

In the `BindArtistsRepeater()` method, we set the `DataSource` property of our Web Forms `<asp:Repeater>` control and set it to the `ArtistCache` object. Then we call the `.DataBind()` method on the repeater. This method enumerates the defined `DataSource` and renders the markup according to the repeater template we defined in the markup earlier.

LISTING 20.2   Artist Management Application: Web Form Code Behind

```
 1:  using Ch20.Models;
 2:  using System;
 3:  using System.Collections.Generic;
 4:  using System.Runtime.Caching;
 5:  using System.Web.UI;
 6:
 7:  namespace Ch20
 8:  {
 9:      public partial class Default : Page
10:      {
11:          public List<Artist> ArtistCache
12:          {
13:              get { return (List<Artist>)MemoryCache.Default.Get("artists"); }
14:              set { MemoryCache.Default.Set("artists", value,
                         ObjectCache.InfiniteAbsoluteExpiration); }
15:          }
16:
17:          protected void Page_Load(object sender, EventArgs e)
18:          {
19:              if (!IsPostBack)
20:              {
21:                  if (ArtistCache == null)
22:                  {
23:                      ArtistCache = new List<Artist>();
24:                  }
25:              }
26:
27:              BindArtistsRepeater();
28:          }
29:
30:          protected void btnAdd_Click(object sender, EventArgs e)
31:          {
32:              string artistName = txtName.Text;
33:              if (string.IsNullOrEmpty(artistName))
34:              {
35:                  lblError.Text = "Invalid artist name: cannot be empty.";
36:                  return;
37:              }
38:
39:              string rating = txtRating.Text;
40:              if (string.IsNullOrEmpty(rating))
41:              {
```

```
42:                    lblError.Text = "Invalid artist rating: cannot be empty.";
43:                    return;
44:                }
45:
46:                int ratingNum;
47:                if (!int.TryParse(rating, out ratingNum))
48:                {
49:                    lblError.Text = "Invalid artist rating: must be a number.";
50:                    return;
51:                }
52:
53:                ArtistCache.Add(new Artist {
54:                    Id = Guid.NewGuid(),
55:                    Name = artistName,
56:                    Rating = ratingNum
57:                });
58:
59:                txtName.Text = null;
60:                txtRating.Text = null;
61:
62:                BindArtistsRepeater();
63:                lblError.Text = null;
64:            }
65:
66:            private void BindArtistsRepeater()
67:            {
68:                rptArtists.DataSource = ArtistCache;
69:                rptArtists.DataBind();
70:            }
71:        }
72:    }
```

Run the solution in Visual Studio and add a few artists. Figure 20.1 shows what your UI should look like.

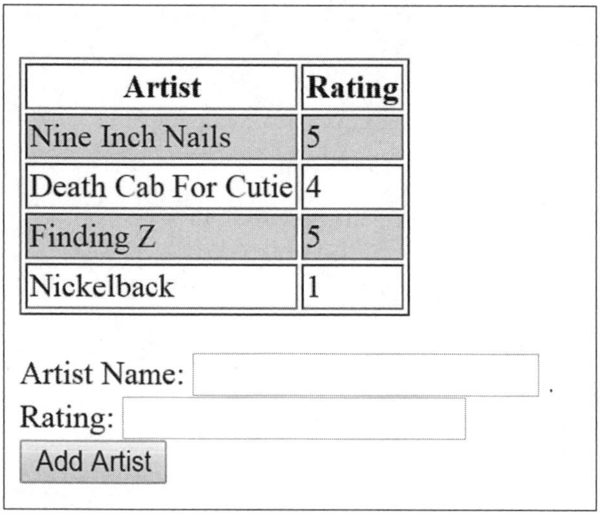

FIGURE 20.1
Artist Management Application UI using Web Forms.

Changing Web Forms Functionality to Angular

Now that we've built out our Artist Management application, let's redo it a bit to use Angular! We'll be revisiting the Web Forms page without Angular later, so keep it around; duplicate the page and call it DefaultAngular.aspx for this section of the hour.

Again, let's start with the markup (see Listing 20.3). Because we'll be using Angular for our UI, we won't need ASP.NET to prerender any of the markup before sending it to the user's browser, so we'll be removing all of the `runat="server"` attributes and all Web Forms controls. On lines 8–11, we include a reference to Angular and create three JavaScript files: app.js, artists.service.js, and artists.js. You'll notice by the path that we've put these in a new folder called Scripts within our solution. We'll discuss these files later. Next, on lines 12–16, we add a few styles that were previously defined with Web Forms control attributes. On lines 18 and 19, we declare the root for our Angular app and for our `ArtistsController`, respectively.

Modifying the first section of the UI, the error message, is easy. We simply replace our `<asp:Label>` with a simple `<div>` and bind it to a model property. In the second section, we replace the `<asp:Repeater>` control with a standard HTML `<table>` and use the `ng-repeat` directive to repeat the rows. To achieve the alternate styling that the previous `<ItemTemplate>` and `<AlternatingItemTemplate>` gave us, we use the `ng-class-odd` and `ng-class-even` directives to apply CSS classes that alternate based on the row's index. Finally, in the last section, we replace the `<asp:Textbox>` and `<asp:Button>` controls with `<input>` and `<button>`

elements. Because we won't be using the standard postback mechanism anymore, we won't be able to use the `OnClick="btnAdd_Click"` that we used earlier. Instead, we'll call a controller method called `vm.add()`.

LISTING 20.3 Artist Management Application: UI with Angular

```
1:   <%@ Page Language="C#" AutoEventWireup="true"
             CodeBehind="DefaultAngular.aspx.cs" Inherits="Ch20.DefaultAngular" %>
2:
3:   <!DOCTYPE html>
4:
5:   <html xmlns="http://www.w3.org/1999/xhtml">
6:   <head>
7:       <title>Artist Management</title>
8:       <script src="https://code.angularjs.org/1.3.15/angular.js"></script>
9:       <script src="Scripts/app.js"></script>
10:      <script src="Scripts/artists.service.js"></script>
11:      <script src="Scripts/artists.js"></script>
12:      <style>
13:          .error { color:red; }
14:          .odd { background-color:palegoldenrod; }
15:          .even { background-color:white; }
16:      </style>
17:  </head>
18:  <body ng-app="app">
19:      <div ng-controller="ArtistsController as vm">
20:          <section>
21:              <div class="error">{{vm.error}}</div>
22:          </section>
23:          <br />
24:          <section>
25:              <table border="1">
26:                  <tr>
27:                      <th>Artist</th>
28:                      <th>Rating</th>
29:                  </tr>
30:                  <tr ng-repeat="artist in vm.artists"
                         ng-class-odd="'odd'" ng-class-even="'even'">
31:                      <td>{{artist.Name}}</td>
32:                      <td>{{artist.Rating}}</td>
33:                  </tr>
34:              </table>
35:          </section>
36:          <br />
37:          <section>
```

```
38:             Artist Name: <input type="text" id="txtName"
                                 ng-model="vm.newArtistName" />
39:             <br />
40:             Rating: <input type="text" id="txtRating"
                             ng-model="vm.newArtistRating" />
41:             <br />
42:             <button ng-click="vm.add()">Add Artist</button>
43:         </section>
44:     </div>
45: </body>
46: </html>
```

Next, let's look at the changes to the code behind page (see Listing 20.4). Because we're stripping out the postback mechanism from our page, we are essentially translating the existing logic into a web service. Nothing changed with our `ArtistCache` or with the `Page_Load()` method except that we no longer call `BindArtistsRepeater()` because there is no repeater to bind; we removed all of the Web Forms controls.

Our `btnAdd_Click()` method has become a web method called `AddArtists()` with the usage of the `[WebMethod]` attribute. This attribute allows us to define methods that are available in a static context on our page (which is also why we added the `static` keyword to our method). Using this attribute on our `AddArtist()` and `GetArtists()` methods makes these methods available to Angular via AJAX requests. For the most part, Angular will interact with these methods just like any other server method that you may have seen with other server-side frameworks like ASP.NET MVC and ASP.NET Web API.

The `AddArtists()` method will be called by our Angular `ArtistManager` service. Because this method will no longer be called within the ASP.NET page lifecycle, we've replaced the `object` and `EventArgs` parameters standard for ASP.NET event handlers with new parameters: the `artistName` and `rating` that will be sent by Angular. If an error occurs, we return the error message for Angular to display; otherwise, we return `null` indicating success.

Finally, our `BindArtistsRepeater()` method becomes a `GetArtists()` method, which simply returns the `ArtistCache`.

DID YOU KNOW?

Making Web Forms **[WebMethod]**'s **RESTful**

In our example, rather than indicating success with a `null` response (and indicating error by returning a `string`), we should be using HTTP status codes. Unfortunately, because `[WebMethod]`s have to be declared as `static`, we don't have access to variables on the `Page` like the `Response` object. If this is a deal-breaker for your project, you might not be able to get away with just translating existing logic into `[WebMethod]`s as we've done here. Maybe it's time to implement a full Web API alongside your Web Forms app.

LISTING 20.4   Artist Management Application: Code Behind with Web Methods

```csharp
1:  using Ch20.Models;
2:  using System;
3:  using System.Collections.Generic;
4:  using System.Runtime.Caching;
5:  using System.Web.Services;
6:  using System.Web.UI;
7:
8:  namespace Ch20
9:  {
10:     public partial class DefaultAngular : Page
11:     {
12:         public static List<Artist> ArtistCache
13:         {
14:             get { return (List<Artist>)MemoryCache.Default.Get("artists"); }
15:             set { MemoryCache.Default. Set("artists", value,
                        ObjectCache.InfiniteAbsoluteExpiration);  }
16:         }
17:
18:         protected void Page_Load(object sender, EventArgs e)
19:         {
20:             if (!IsPostBack)
21:             {
22:                 if (ArtistCache == null)
23:                 {
24:                     ArtistCache = new List<Artist>();
25:                 }
26:             }
27:         }
28:
29:         [WebMethod]
30:         public static string AddArtist(string artistName, string rating)
31:         {
32:             if (string.IsNullOrEmpty(artistName))
33:             {
34:                 return "Invalid artist name: cannot be empty.";
35:             }
36:
37:             if (string.IsNullOrEmpty(rating))
38:             {
39:                 return "Invalid artist rating: cannot be empty.";
40:             }
41:
42:             int ratingNum;
43:             if (!int.TryParse(rating, out ratingNum))
44:             {
45:                 return "Invalid artist rating: must be a number.";
```

```
46:            }
47:
48:            ArtistCache.Add(new Artist {
49:                Id = Guid.NewGuid(),
50:                Name = artistName,
51:                Rating = ratingNum
52:            });
53:
54:            return null;
55:        }
56:
57:        [WebMethod]
58:        public static List<Artist> GetArtists()
59:        {
60:            return ArtistCache;
61:        }
62:    }
63: }
```

Now that we've explored the changes to our markup and to the code behind, let's look at the Angular code that wires the two together. Recall that in the markup, we defined three Angular files: app.js, artists.service.js, and artists.js. In app.js, all we need to do is create our Angular app reference with this:

```
angular.module('app', []);
```

Next, in artists.service.js, we'll be creating an Angular service that interacts with our two web methods in the code behind. We grab a reference to our app (defined earlier in app.js) and use the `.service()` method to create our `ArtistsManager`. We inject the $http service and create two functions that use it: `getArtists()` and `createArtist()`. Our web methods that we have defined in the code behind work over HTTP POST by default, so we use the `.post()` method on $http to send the request. Note the URLs in Listing 20.5. By default, all web methods are accessible in the following format: pageName.aspx/methodName.

WATCH OUT!

Read-Only Requests

Note the comment on line 7 of Listing 20.5. Although the `GetArtists` web method doesn't take any parameters (it's essentially read-only), we can't pass `null` as the request body because IIS6+ requires a Content-Length header (even if there is no content). Passing an empty object causes the browser to send a Content-Length header of 2, and the request will succeed.

LISTING 20.5   Artist Management Application: Artists Manager Angular Service

```
 1:   (function () {
 2:
 3:     angular.module('app')
 4:     .service('ArtistsManager', ['$http', function ($http) {
 5:
 6:       this.getArtists = function () {
 7:         //You have to pass an empty object here vs. null.
 8:         return $http.post("DefaultAngular.aspx/GetArtists", {});
 9:       };
10:
11:       this.createArtist = function (data) {
12:         return $http.post("DefaultAngular.aspx/AddArtist", data);
13:       };
14:
15:     }]);
16:
17:   })();
```

Finally, let's look at our controller in artists.js (see Listing 20.6). We grab a reference to
our app and use .controller() to create our ArtistsController. We then inject our
ArtistsManager service from earlier.

On line 10, we define a getArtists() method that will run initially (line 6) and will run
when a user successfully adds an artist (line 32). This method calls our service's getArtists()
method and includes a callback to execute when the request returns from the server. In that
callback, you'll see that we're accessing the response.data.d property and assigning that to
the artists collection on our view model. By default, web methods wrap their JSON responses
in an object with a single parameter of d.

DID YOU KNOW?

What's with This d Thing?

Having ASP.NET automatically wrap your response in an object with a parameter called d might initially
seem annoying, but it is actually a security feature. By doing this, ASP.NET is helping save you from
cross-site scripting (XSS) attacks. In JavaScript, the statement [] has meaning; it's how you create
a new array. If that alone was returned from the server, it could be executed under the right circumstances. Contrast that with { 'd': [] }, which is not a JavaScript statement that can be executed.
(Try it in your browser's console; you need something like var x = { 'd': [] } for it to work.)

Next, we define the add() function on our view model that is wired to our button. This function
creates a new artist object from the input boxes and sends it to the service's createArtist()
method. The success callback here checks if d on the response is not null (recall from earlier
that this meant an error message needed to be shown) or null (indicating success). If successful,
we blank out the input boxes, clear the error, and refresh the view with data from the server.

LISTING 20.6 Artist Management Application: Artists Controller

```
 1:  (function () {
 2:
 3:    angular.module('app')
 4:    .controller('ArtistsController', ['ArtistsManager', function (ArtistsManager) {
 5:      var vm = this;
 6:      getArtists();
 7:
 8:      /////////////////
 9:
10:      function getArtists() {
11:        ArtistsManager.getArtists().then(function (response) {
12:          vm.artists = response.data.d;
13:        });
14:      }
15:
16:      vm.add = function () {
17:
18:        var artist = {
19:          artistName: vm.newArtistName,
20:          rating: vm.newArtistRating
21:        };
22:
23:        ArtistsManager.createArtist(artist)
24:          .then(function (response) {
25:
26:          if (response.data.d !== null) {
27:            vm.error = response.data.d;
28:          } else {
29:            vm.newArtistName = null;
30:            vm.newArtistRating = null;
31:            vm.error = null;
32:            getArtists();
33:          }
34:
35:        }, function (response) {
36:          vm.error = response.statusText;
37:        });
38:      };
39:
40:    }]);
41:
42:  })();
```

Run the application in Visual Studio and it should function the same as the Web Forms app from earlier. Now that you're using Angular, you could add additional features to this page using things learned in other hours.

Augment Web Forms with Angular

In addition to using Angular as a way to change existing logic in your Web Forms application, you can also include Angular as a way to augment your application with additional functionality. You don't have to rewrite much of your Web Forms pages to start using Angular little by little. Let's revisit the first example in this hour (the Web Forms page without Angular), and let's add some Angular goodness without changing much of the existing page. Specifically, let's add a small directive on our artist table that allows users to favorite specific artists. We'll be saving a user's favorites to Local Storage.

First, duplicate your original Default.aspx into another page. (Let's call it DefaultLittleAngular. aspx because we're only using a little bit of Angular and keeping most of the Web Forms functionality.) Let's start with the markup (see Listing 20.7). On lines 8–12, we include Angular and add references to four JavaScript files: app.js, local-storage.service.js, favorites.js, and favorite-artists-directive.js. We define our Angular app on the `<body>` element and our controller root for our `FavoritesController` on the `<form>` element. That's really all we need to get up and running with Angular!

Section 1, the error message, remains the same: We want this to still be controlled by Web Forms. In Section 2, the list of artists, we'll add a third column called Actions (line 27) and a third cell to each of the rows in the `<asp:Repeater>`. In that cell, we'll use our `favoriteSelector` directive (more on that later) and pass in the artist's name as an attribute to that directive. Finally, we'll add a third section for listing our favorites. We use `ng-repeat` to list them all out and we give each one a button with an `ng-click` to a view model function for clearing that artist out of the favorites list.

LISTING 20.7 Artist Management Application: Markup with Favorites

```
 1:  <%@ Page Language="C#" AutoEventWireup="true"
             CodeBehind="DefaultLittleAngular.aspx.cs"
             Inherits="Ch20.DefaultLittleAngular" %>
 2:
 3:  <!DOCTYPE html>
 4:
 5:  <html xmlns="http://www.w3.org/1999/xhtml">
 6:  <head runat="server">
 7:      <title>Artist Management</title>
 8:      <script src="https://code.angularjs.org/1.3.15/angular.js"></script>
 9:      <script src="Scripts/app.js"></script>
10:      <script src="Scripts/local-storage.service.js"></script>
```

```
11:        <script src="Scripts/favorites.js"></script>
12:        <script src="Scripts/favorite-artists-directive.js"></script>
13:    </head>
14:    <body ng-app="app">
15:        <form id="form1" runat="server" ng-controller="FavoritesController as vm">
16:            <section>
17:                <asp:Label runat="server" ID="lblError" ForeColor="Red" />
18:            </section>
19:            <br />
20:            <section>
21:                <asp:Repeater ID="rptArtists" runat="server">
22:                    <HeaderTemplate>
23:                        <table border="1" ng-app="app">
24:                            <tr>
25:                                <th>Artist</th>
26:                                <th>Rating</th>
27:                                <th>Actions</th>
28:                            </tr>
29:                    </HeaderTemplate>
30:                    <ItemTemplate>
31:                        <tr style="background-color: palegoldenrod">
32:                            <td><%#Eval("Name") %></td>
33:                            <td><%#Eval("Rating") %></td>
34:                            <td favorite-selector artist="<%#Eval("Name") %>"></td>
35:                        </tr>
36:                    </ItemTemplate>
37:                    <AlternatingItemTemplate>
38:                        <tr style="background-color: white">
39:                            <td><%#Eval("Name") %></td>
40:                            <td><%#Eval("Rating") %></td>
41:                            <td favorite-selector artist="<%#Eval("Name") %>"></td>
42:                        </tr>
43:                    </AlternatingItemTemplate>
44:                    <FooterTemplate>
45:                        </table>
46:                    </FooterTemplate>
47:                </asp:Repeater>
48:            </section>
49:            <br />
50:            <section>
51:                Artist Name: <asp:TextBox runat="server" ID="txtName" />
52:                <br />
53:                Rating: <asp:TextBox runat="server" ID="txtRating" />
54:                <br />
55:                <asp:Button runat="server"
56:                    Text="Add Artist"
57:                    ID="btnAdd"
```

```
58:                    OnClick="btnAdd_Click" />
59:            </section>
60:            <br />
61:            <br />
62:            <section>
63:                <h1>Favorites</h1>
64:                <ul>
65:                    <li ng-repeat="favorite in vm.favorites">{{favorite}}
                       <button ng-click="vm.remove(favorite)">Remove Favorite</button></li>
66:                </ul>
67:            </section>
68:        </form>
69:    </body>
70:    </html>
```

Because we're only adding functionality to the page, we don't need to change anything in the Default.aspx.cs file! Next, let's look at the JavaScript files. If you completed the example in the second part of this hour, you've already got a file called app.js. We can reuse that file here, as well, so there's no need to re-create it. Now that we've got our markup ready and our app defined, let's explore the three other JavaScript files: local-storage.service.js, favorites.js, and favorite-artists-directive.js.

Because we'll be using Local Storage as a storage mechanism for our favorites list, let's create a separate factory for persisting data to Local Storage (see Listing 20.8). This component will offer three methods: a way to get data from Local Storage by key, a way to set data to Local Storage by key, and a way to remove data from Local Storage by key. Also, we're using Angular's `.toJson()` and `.fromJson()` to serialize and deserialize our objects. This way, the component that uses this factory doesn't have to worry about these details.

DID YOU KNOW?

Why Create a Factory for Local Storage Interaction?

We could just as easily interact with Local Storage from within our controller, but breaking this out not only helps us separate concerns and keep things light and testable, it also allows us to reuse this across controllers in the future and even swap out this implementation with a different storage mechanism without changing much of our controller. Yay, maintainability!

LISTING 20.8 Artist Management Application: Local Storage Manager

```
1:  (function () {
2:    angular.module('app')
3:      .factory('LocalStorageManager', LocalStorageManager);
4:
```

```
 5:     LocalStorageManager.$inject = [];
 6:
 7:     function LocalStorageManager() {
 8:       return {
 9:         Get: get,
10:         Set: set,
11:         Remove: remove,
12:       }
13:
14:       function get(key) {
15:         var storageItem = localStorage.getItem(key);
16:         if (isJson(storageItem)) {
17:           return angular.fromJson(storageItem);
18:         }
19:         return storageItem;
20:
21:       }
22:
23:       function set(key, value) {
24:         if (typeof value === 'string') {
25:           localStorage.setItem(key, value);
26:         } else {
27:           try {
28:             var stringVal = angular.toJson(value);
29:             localStorage.setItem(key, stringVal);
30:           } catch (error) {
31:             localStorage.setItem(key, error);
32:           }
33:         }
34:         return get(key);
35:       }
36:
37:       function remove(key) {
38:         localStorage.removeItem(key);
39:       }
40:
41:       //////
42:       function isJson(str) {
43:         try {
44:           JSON.parse(str);
45:         } catch (e) {
46:           return false;
47:         }
48:         return true;
49:       }
50:     }
51:
52:   })();
```

Next, let's look at our FavoritesController in favorites.js (see Listing 20.9). We grab a reference to our app and create the controller, injecting $scope (so that we can share scope with our directive) and the LocalStorageManager from earlier. On line 11, we define a getFavorites() method on $scope that will be called by our directive after an artist is successfully added to the favorites list. On line 15, we add a remove() method to our view model that will be called by the buttons rendered on each item in the favorites list. This method fetches the favorites list, removes the artist, sets the updated list back in Local Storage, and updates the collection of favorites on the view model. Finally, we call our $scope.getFavorites() method on line 26 so that the favorites list is fetched from Local Storage when the controller renders the first time (on page load).

LISTING 20.9 **Artist Management Application: Favorites Controller**

```
 1:  (function () {
 2:
 3:    angular.module('app')
 4:    .controller('FavoritesController', ['$scope', 'LocalStorageManager',
 5:      function ($scope, LocalStorageManager) {
 6:
 7:      var vm = this;
 8:
 9:      ////////////////
10:
11:      $scope.getFavorites = function () {
12:        vm.favorites = LocalStorageManager.Get('favoriteArtists');
13:      };
14:
15:      vm.remove = function (artist) {
16:        var favorites = LocalStorageManager.Get('favoriteArtists');
17:        var found = favorites.indexOf(artist);
18:        if (found !== -1) {
19:          favorites.splice(found, 1);
20:        }
21:
22:        LocalStorageManager.Set('favoriteArtists', favorites);
23:        vm.favorites = favorites;
24:      };
25:
26:      $scope.getFavorites();
27:
28:    }]);
29:
30:  })();
```

GO TO ▶ For more on custom directives, including more detail on scope, check out Hour 10, "Conquering Custom Directives."

Finally, let's look at our `favoriteSelector` directive: the directive that adds a button to each row of the `<asp:Repeater>` for adding the artist to the favorites list (see Listing 20.10). As with every component we write, we first grab a reference to our app. Then we use `.directive()` to create our `favoriteSelector` directive, injecting our `LocalStorageManager` from earlier. We restrict the usage of our directive to just attributes of elements with A on line 6. On line 7, we create the template for our directive. This HTML will be added as a child of the element on which we implement this directive (the third `<td>` in each row). On line 8, we indicate that our directive will have its own scope by including the `scope` property. This is necessary because we will have many instances of this directive on the page. If they all shared the same scope, it would be impossible to distinguish the artist's name. In addition, we set the value of `scope` to `true` so that Angular creates a new scope for each directive instance but will prototypically inherit this scope from the parent scope. This way, we can call `scope.getFavorites()`, a method on the parent's scope, from within our directive. Finally, on line 9, we define the `link` function. We create the `add()` method used by the button in our template on the scope. This method fetches the current list of favorites (or creates the list if this is the first favorite to be added), ensures that the artist is not already in the list, adds the artist to the list, and saves the list to Local Storage. Note that we access the artist using the `attrs` object. This object contains all data from other attributes on the directive's element. This is how we get the artist name. Finally, we call the controller's `getFavorites()` method so that the view refreshes.

LISTING 20.10   **Artist Management Application: Favorite Artists Directive**

```
 1:   (function () {
 2:
 3:     angular.module('app')
 4:     .directive('favoriteSelector', ['LocalStorageManager',
          function (LocalStorageManager) {
 5:       return {
 6:         restrict: 'A',
 7:         template: '<button type="button" ng-click="add();">Add Favorite</button>',
 8:         scope: true,
 9:         link: function (scope, element, attrs) {
10:           scope.add = function () {
11:             var favorites = LocalStorageManager.Get('favoriteArtists') || [];
12:             var found = favorites.indexOf(attrs.artist);
13:             if (found === -1) {
14:               favorites.push(attrs.artist);
15:               LocalStorageManager.Set('favoriteArtists', favorites);
16:             }
17:             scope.getFavorites();
18:           }
19:         }
20:       };
```

```
21:     }]);
22:
23:  })();
```

Let's see this all in action! Run the app in Visual Studio and populate a few artists. You should see the third column appear with the buttons to add an artist as a favorite. Click a few of those buttons and watch as the favorites list changes. Because the artists are held in memory on the server, you can restart the server (clearing out the artists list), and your favorites list should remain because it is persisted in Local Storage (see Figure 20.2).

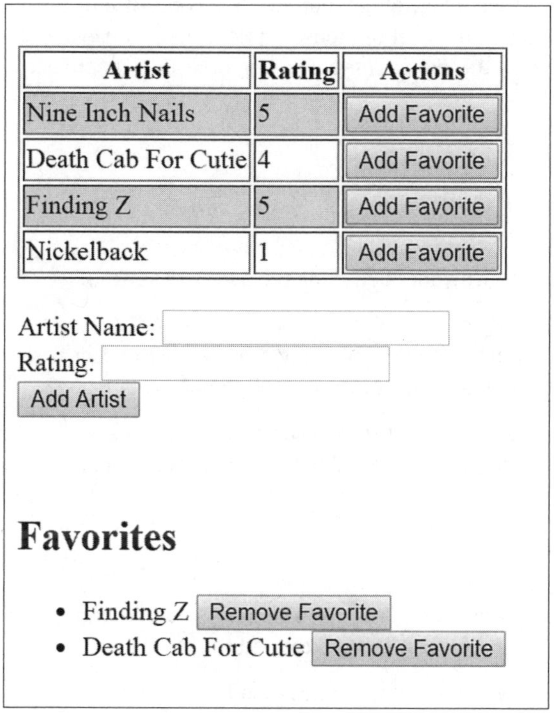

Artist	Rating	Actions
Nine Inch Nails	5	Add Favorite
Death Cab For Cutie	4	Add Favorite
Finding Z	5	Add Favorite
Nickelback	1	Add Favorite

Artist Name: [   ]
Rating: [   ]
[Add Artist]

Favorites

- Finding Z [Remove Favorite]
- Death Cab For Cutie [Remove Favorite]

FIGURE 20.2
Artist Management application UI using Web Forms and Angular.

Summary

In this hour, we explored strategies for modernizing applications. From rewriting entire pages in Angular to simply including small pieces of Angular on existing pages, there's a place for Angular in legacy Web Forms applications. We then built out a small Web Forms app and rewrote it using Angular. We then revisited the original Web Forms app and implemented new functionality with Angular but left the original logic intact.

Q&A

Q. **I want to start using Angular in my Web Forms app, but wouldn't it be hard to manage two UI technologies?**

A. If some pages use Web Forms UI controls and some pages use Angular, it could be confusing to new developers as they roll on to the project to decide which to use. There needs to be project documentation for the developer onboarding process that dictates what pages use Angular and why they use Angular. In addition, managing two UI technologies is much easier than managing five: pick a "modern" framework and stick with it. *Don't* add Angular to some pages, Knockout to a few more, Backbone to even more, and so on.

Including Angular is a way to fight against technology stagnation in the project. If the technical roadmap of the product doesn't include some level of modernization, newer developers will be increasingly less prepared to work on the project (see: working on a COBOL project).

Workshop

Quiz

1. In Web Forms, what attribute do you use to give your code behind class access to UI elements?

2. If you want to keep Web Forms logic intact in the code behind page but want to access the data from Angular, what attribute do you use to decorate your code behind function?

3. When moving a Web Forms `<asp:Repeater>` element to Angular, what directives can you use to achieve the alternating row styles supplied by `<ItemTemplate>` and `<AlternatingRowTemplate>`?

Answers

1. We use the `runat="server"` attribute on each element. If you're using Angular and you swap these out for standard HTML elements, you can remove this attribute.

2. We use the `[WebMethod]` attribute to allow a method to be accessed by Angular. Essentially, this allows you to transform an existing .aspx page into a web service.

3. We use the `ng-class-odd` and `ng-class-even` directives to achieve this.

Exercise

Given an ASP.NET Web Forms app that you've written or maintained (or, if you haven't done this, find one online), plan how you would begin to migrate functionality to Angular.

Applying Angular to ASP.NET MVC

What You'll Learn in This Hour:

▶ Building a sample ASP.NET MVC app

▶ Adding Angular to an ASP.NET MVC app

Contrasted with ASP.NET Web Forms, which we explored in the preceding hour, ASP.NET MVC is a much newer framework, with V1.0's release in 2009. ASP.NET MVC uses the Razor View Engine for composing dynamic web pages server-side before sending the finished HTML output to the user's web browser. Over Web Forms, the Razor syntax in ASP.NET MVC offers a cleaner bridge between markup and C# code.

Although there are many advantages to using MVC over Web Forms, all HTML is still rendered server-side. To provide a more responsive experience to the user (an experience without many round trips to the server), we can leverage Angular. If you haven't read the section "Strategies for Modernizing Web Applications" in Hour 20, "Applying Angular to ASP.NET Web Forms," go do so now. All of these same points are still valid for using Angular with ASP.NET MVC; you can use as little or as much of Angular as you like.

Over the course of this hour, we build a small sample app using ASP.NET MVC and Razor without Angular. Then this discussion turns to adding Angular to the app and enhancing it with additional functionality.

Building a Sample ASP.NET MVC App

Again, let's start with a blank slate in Visual Studio. Create a new project and choose ASP.NET Web Application from the project template library. Give it a name and choose the Empty template. Tick the Add Folders and Core References for MVC box.

WATCH OUT!

Don't Include More Than You Need!

You can choose the MVC option here, but this will also include ASP.NET Identity and a lot of other stuff that we don't care about for this app. In the future, if you're building out a full application with user accounts and a database, you'll want to go this route.

Once Visual Studio finishes scaffolding your project, you'll have a few folders in Solution Explorer. Let's create an `Artist` model (see Listing 21.1). Right-click the Models folder and choose Add, and then Class. We'll be tracking the artist's name and an optional rating from 1 to 5.

LISTING 21.1 Artist Management Application: Artist Model

```
 1:  using System;
 2:  using System.ComponentModel.DataAnnotations;
 3:
 4:  namespace Ch21.Models
 5:  {
 6:      public class Artist
 7:      {
 8:          public Guid Id { get; set; }
 9:
10:          [Required]
11:          public string Name { get; set; }
12:
13:          [Range(1, 5)]
14:          public int? Rating { get; set; }
15:      }
16:  }
```

Next, let's build our controller, `ArtistController` (see Listing 21.2). We'll keep track of our artists using the same in-memory cache as we used in Hour 20. Again, a real application would persist the artist data to a database. Right-click the Controllers folder and add a new controller called `ArtistController`. After we create the cache (lines 11–15) and the controller constructor that sets up the cache (lines 17–23), we have three controller actions. The first, `Index()`, simply renders the Index.cshtml view with the current `ArtistCache` as the view's model. The second, `Create()`, renders the Create.cshtml view. The third, `Create(Artist artist)`, is what receives the user input from the Create.cshtml form, creates the `Artist` in the `ArtistCache`, and redirects the user back to the `Index()` action, which renders the cache.

LISTING 21.2 Artist Management Application: Artist Controller

```
 1:  using System;
 2:  using System.Collections.Generic;
 3:  using System.Runtime.Caching;
 4:  using System.Web.Mvc;
 5:  using Ch21.Models;
 6:
 7:  namespace Ch21.Controllers
 8:  {
 9:      public class ArtistController : Controller
10:      {
11:          public List<Artist> ArtistCache
12:          {
```

```
13:             get { return (List<Artist>)MemoryCache.Default.Get("artists"); }
14:             set { MemoryCache.Default.Set("artists", value,
                    ObjectCache.InfiniteAbsoluteExpiration); }
15:         }
16:
17:         public ArtistController()
18:         {
19:             if (ArtistCache == null)
20:             {
21:                 ArtistCache = new List<Artist>();
22:             }
23:         }
24:
25:         public ActionResult Index()
26:         {
27:             return View(ArtistCache);
28:         }
29:
30:         public ActionResult Create()
31:         {
32:             return View();
33:         }
34:
35:         [HttpPost]
36:         [ValidateAntiForgeryToken]
37:         public ActionResult Create(Artist artist)
38:         {
39:             artist.Id = Guid.NewGuid();
40:             ArtistCache.Add(artist);
41:             return RedirectToAction("Index");
42:         }
43:     }
44: }
```

Now that we have our model and our controller, let's look at our two views. Right-click the Views folder and create a new view. First, we'll create our Index.cshtml view, so give your view a name of Index in the Add View dialog. Under template, you can choose Empty and copy the code from below, or you can choose List and Visual Studio will automatically generate the view for you. Choose our Artist class as the model class and click the Add button.

BY THE WAY

Autogenerated Front-End Files

Doing this will create many more folders and files automatically, including all sorts of front-end stuff like fonts, JavaScript files, Cascading Style Sheets (CSS) files, and so on. Don't worry too much about this yet; we'll be changing some of this over to Angular later.

Let's explore our Index.cshtml view that lists our artists (see Listing 21.3). On line 1, we declare the model for this view: an enumerable collection of `Artist` objects. On lines 3–5, we set the page title in the `ViewBag`. On line 10, we add a link to the `Create()` action on our controller (which renders the Create.cshtml view). On lines 16 and 19, we display the name of each property (which can be overridden on the `Artist` model with the `[DisplayName]` attribute). Finally, on lines 23–33, we have a `@foreach` block that repeats each artist in the `Model` and displays the name and rating properties of each.

LISTING 21.3   Artist Management Application: Artist List View

```
 1:   @model IEnumerable<Ch21.Models.Artist>
 2:
 3:   @{
 4:       ViewBag.Title = "Index";
 5:   }
 6:
 7:   <h2>Artists</h2>
 8:
 9:   <p>
10:       @Html.ActionLink("Create New", "Create")
11:   </p>
12:
13:   <table class="table">
14:       <tr>
15:           <th>
16:               @Html.DisplayNameFor(model => model.Name)
17:           </th>
18:           <th>
19:               @Html.DisplayNameFor(model => model.Rating)
20:           </th>
21:       </tr>
22:
23:       @foreach (var item in Model)
24:       {
25:           <tr>
26:               <td>
27:                   @Html.DisplayFor(modelItem => item.Name)
28:               </td>
29:               <td>
30:                   @Html.DisplayFor(modelItem => item.Rating)
31:               </td>
32:           </tr>
33:       }
34:
35:   </table>
```

Next, let's build out the Create.cshtml view (see Listing 21.4) that we linked to from Index.cshtml. Right-click the Views folder and create a new view called `Create`. Again, you can use the Empty template and copy the code from below, or you can use `Create` as the template. Choose our `Artist` model as the model class and click the Add button.

We start the same way as the previous view: declaring our model on line 1 and the title on line 4. On line 10, we use the `HtmlHelper` method `BeginForm()` to create our form. On line 12, we use the `HtmlHelper` method `AntiForgeryToken()` to generate a hidden form field (with the value set to an anti-forgery token) that is validated when the form is submitted.

DID YOU KNOW?

MVC Anti-Forgery Tokens

ASP.NET helps protect your application against cross-site request forgery (CSRF/XSRF) by rendering a signed token to the page when the view is processed. This token must be included when the form is submitted back to the server. Without this, someone could create a form on a different site and post it back to your server.

In our form, we have three `<div>` elements: one for the artist name, one for the artist rating, and one for the submit button. For the first two, we use some more `HtmlHelper` methods to generate the label, the editor, and the validation message. For the submit button, we don't need to do anything out of the ordinary: just adding `type="submit"` will submit the form for us. Finally, we add an `ActionLink` to the `Index()` controller action, which renders the Index.cshtml view from earlier.

LISTING 21.4   Artist Management Application: Create Artist View

```
 1:  @model Ch21.Models.Artist
 2:
 3:  @{
 4:      ViewBag.Title = "Create";
 5:  }
 6:
 7:  <h2>Create Artist</h2>
 8:
 9:
10:  @using (Html.BeginForm())
11:  {
12:      @Html.AntiForgeryToken()
13:
14:      <div class="form-horizontal">
15:          <h4>Artist</h4>
16:          <hr />
17:          @Html.ValidationSummary(true, "", new { @class = "text-danger" })
18:          <div class="form-group">
```

```
19:                 @Html.LabelFor(model => model.Name, htmlAttributes: new {
                        @class = "control-label col-md-2" })
20:             <div class="col-md-10">
21:                 @Html.EditorFor(model => model.Name, new {
                        htmlAttributes = new { @class = "form-control" } })
22:                 @Html.ValidationMessageFor(model => model.Name, "", new {
                        @class = "text-danger" })
23:             </div>
24:         </div>
25:
26:         <div class="form-group">
27:             @Html.LabelFor(model => model.Rating, htmlAttributes: new {
                        @class = "control-label col-md-2" })
28:             <div class="col-md-10">
29:                 @Html.EditorFor(model => model.Rating, new {
                        htmlAttributes = new { @class = "form-control" } })
30:                 @Html.ValidationMessageFor(model => model.Rating, "", new {
                        @class = "text-danger" })
31:             </div>
32:         </div>
33:
34:         <div class="form-group">
35:             <div class="col-md-offset-2 col-md-10">
36:                 <input type="submit" value="Create" class="btn btn-default" />
37:             </div>
38:         </div>
39:     </div>
40: }
41:
42: <div>
43:     @Html.ActionLink("Back to List", "Index")
44: </div>
45:
46: <script src="~/Scripts/jquery-1.10.2.min.js"></script>
47: <script src="~/Scripts/jquery.validate.min.js"></script>
48: <script src="~/Scripts/jquery.validate.unobtrusive.min.js"></script>
```

When Visual Studio generated our first view, you might have noticed that views are grouped into subfolders by controller name under the Views folder (see Figure 21.1). In addition, another folder named Shared appeared with one file in it: _Layout.cshtml. If you come from a Web Forms background, this file is similar in concept to a master page. This is essentially the "shell" in which our views from earlier are rendered. The code in Listing 21.5 was only modified from what was generated to change the name of the application (lines 6 and 33) and to update the ActionLink (line 20).

FIGURE 21.1
Views folder structure in Visual Studio.

LISTING 21.5   Artist Management Application: _Layout.cshtml

```
 1:  <!DOCTYPE html>
 2:  <html>
 3:  <head>
 4:      <meta charset="utf-8" />
 5:      <meta name="viewport" content="width=device-width, initial-scale=1.0">
 6:      <title>@ViewBag.Title - Artist Management</title>
 7:      <link href="~/Content/Site.css" rel="stylesheet" type="text/css" />
 8:      <link href="~/Content/bootstrap.min.css" rel="stylesheet" type="text/css" />
 9:      <script src="~/Scripts/modernizr-2.6.2.js"></script>
10:  </head>
11:  <body>
12:      <div class="navbar navbar-inverse navbar-fixed-top">
13:          <div class="container">
14:              <div class="navbar-header">
15:                  <button type="button" class="navbar-toggle"
                          data-toggle="collapse" data-target=".navbar-collapse">
16:                      <span class="icon-bar"></span>
17:                      <span class="icon-bar"></span>
18:                      <span class="icon-bar"></span>
19:                  </button>
20:                  @Html.ActionLink("Artist Management", "Index", "Artist", new {
                          area = "" }, new { @class = "navbar-brand" })
21:              </div>
22:              <div class="navbar-collapse collapse">
23:                  <ul class="nav navbar-nav">
24:                  </ul>
25:              </div>
26:          </div>
27:      </div>
28:
```

```
29:        <div class="container body-content">
30:            @RenderBody()
31:            <hr />
32:            <footer>
33:                <p>&copy; @DateTime.Now.Year - Artist Management</p>
34:            </footer>
35:        </div>
36:
37:        <script src="~/Scripts/jquery-1.10.2.min.js"></script>
38:        <script src="~/Scripts/bootstrap.min.js"></script>
39:    </body>
40: </html>
```

Finally, we can run our application. Run it in Visual Studio and your browser will open. Uh oh, you get an error: 404 Not Found! This is because we need to update our default request so that ASP.NET knows how to route requests to the application root. In the Web Forms world, this is akin to setting the startup page. In the App_Start folder, there is a file called RouteConfig.cs. All we need to update is the default route on line 15 to point to the Index action on our ArtistController, as shown in Listing 21.6.

LISTING 21.6 Artist Management Application: Updated Default Route

```
 1: using System.Web.Mvc;
 2: using System.Web.Routing;
 3:
 4: namespace Ch21
 5: {
 6:     public class RouteConfig
 7:     {
 8:         public static void RegisterRoutes(RouteCollection routes)
 9:         {
10:             routes.IgnoreRoute("{resource}.axd/{*pathInfo}");
11:
12:             routes.MapRoute(
13:                 name: "Default",
14:                 url: "{controller}/{action}/{id}",
15:                 defaults: new { controller = "Artist", action = "Index",
                                    id = UrlParameter.Optional }
16:             );
17:         }
18:     }
19: }
```

Now, rerun your application and you should be presented with the artist list view (see Figure 21.2). Click the Create New link and you'll see the create form where you can add an artist (see Figure 21.3). After adding an artist, you'll be redirected back to the artist list view, and you should see your artist (see Figure 21.4).

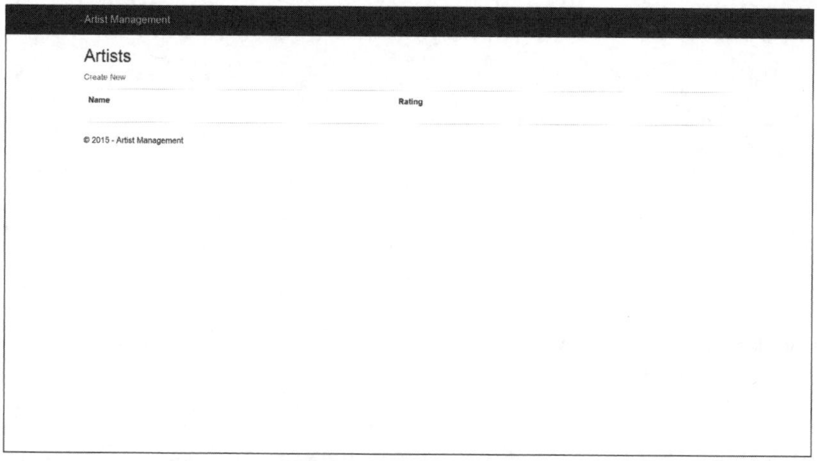

FIGURE 21.2
Artist Management application: artist list view (empty).

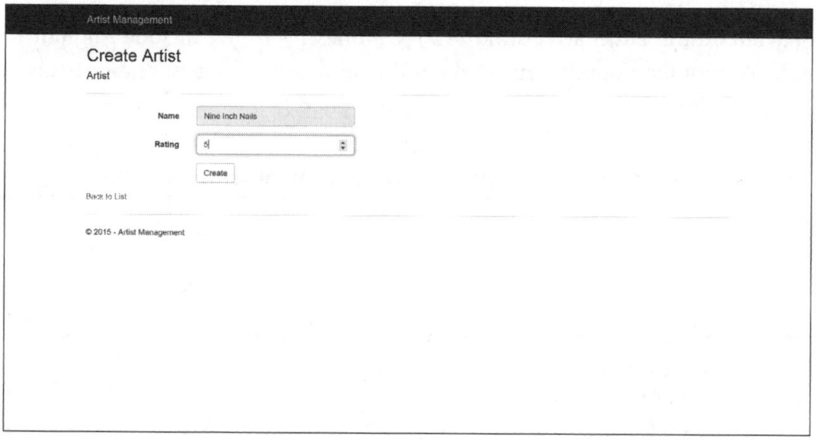

FIGURE 21.3
Artist Management application: create artist view.

FIGURE 21.4
Artist Management application: artist list view (populated).

Adding Angular to an ASP.NET MVC App

Now that we've built out our MVC app, let's start adding in Angular. In this section, we'll be including Angular in our app, using it to fetch the artist list via AJAX, and implementing a search box on our list.

Let's start with our _Layout.cshtml page (see Listing 21.7). On lines 10–14, we include Angular and create four more JavaScript files: app.js, artist-search-filter.js, artists.service.js, and artists.js. On line 16, we use ng-app to declare our app. That's it for this page.

LISTING 21.7   **Artist Management Application: _Layout.cshtml with Angular**

```
 1:   <!DOCTYPE html>
 2:   <html>
 3:   <head>
 4:       <meta charset="utf-8" />
 5:       <meta name="viewport" content="width=device-width, initial-scale=1.0">
 6:       <title>@ViewBag.Title - Artist Management</title>
 7:       <link href="~/Content/Site.css" rel="stylesheet" type="text/css" />
 8:       <link href="~/Content/ bootstrap.min.css" rel="stylesheet" type="text/css" />
 9:       <script src="~/Scripts/modernizr-2.6.2.js"></script>
10:       <script src="https://code.angularjs.org/1.3.15/angular.js"></script>
11:       <script src="~/Scripts/app.js"></script>
12:       <script src="~/Scripts/artist-search-filter.js"></script>
```

```
13:        <script src="~/Scripts/artists.service.js"></script>
14:        <script src="~/Scripts/artists.js"></script>
15:    </head>
16:    <body ng-app="app">
17:        <div class="navbar navbar-inverse navbar-fixed-top">
18:            <div class="container">
19:                <div class="navbar-header">
20:                    <button type="button" class="navbar-toggle" data-toggle="collapse"
                                data-target=".navbar-collapse">
21:                        <span class="icon-bar"></span>
22:                        <span class="icon-bar"></span>
23:                        <span class="icon-bar"></span>
24:                    </button>
25:                    @Html.ActionLink("Artist Management", "Index", "Artist", new {
                                area = "" }, new { @class = "navbar-brand" })
26:                </div>
27:                <div class="navbar-collapse collapse">
28:                    <ul class="nav navbar-nav">
29:                    </ul>
30:                </div>
31:            </div>
32:        </div>
33:
34:        <div class="container body-content">
35:            @RenderBody()
36:            <hr />
37:            <footer>
38:                <p>&copy; @DateTime.Now.Year - Artist Management</p>
39:            </footer>
40:        </div>
41:
42:        <script src="~/Scripts/jquery-1.10.2.min.js"></script>
43:        <script src="~/Scripts/bootstrap.min.js"></script>
44:    </body>
45:    </html>
```

Next, let's look at our Index.cshtml page (see Listing 21.8). On lines 13 and 35, we wrap our table in a `<div>` element so that we can mount our `ArtistsController` there with the `ng-controller` directive. On line 14, we add an input box to capture the user's search criteria and tie it to the `searchInput` property of the view model. (This should look familiar if you read Hour 14, "Figuring Out Filters"; we are using the same search mechanism here.) On line 25, we take out the Razor `@foreach` and use the `ng-repeat` directive with our `artistSearch` filter, which receives the `searchInput` as a parameter. Finally, we remove Razor's data bindings and add in Angular ones on lines 27 and 30.

LISTING 21.8 Artist Management Application: Index.cshtml with Angular

```
 1:  @model IEnumerable<Ch21.Models.Artist>
 2:
 3:  @{
 4:      ViewBag.Title = "Index";
 5:  }
 6:
 7:  <h2>Artists</h2>
 8:
 9:  <p>
10:      @Html.ActionLink("Create New", "Create")
11:  </p>
12:
13:  <div ng-controller="ArtistsController as vm">
14:      <input type="text" ng-model="vm.searchInput" placeholder="Search..." />
15:      <table class="table">
16:          <tr>
17:              <th>
18:                  @Html.DisplayNameFor(model => model.Name)
19:              </th>
20:              <th>
21:                  @Html.DisplayNameFor(model => model.Rating)
22:              </th>
23:          </tr>
24:
25:          <tr ng-repeat="artist in vm.artists | artistSearch:vm.searchInput">
26:              <td>
27:                  {{artist.Name}}
28:              </td>
29:              <td>
30:                  {{artist.Rating}}
31:              </td>
32:          </tr>
33:
34:      </table>
35:  </div>
```

When we were using Razor and MVC to render our artists list, we simply passed the
ArtistCache to the View() method in our ArtistController (C#, not Angular) controller
action (see Listing 21.9). We still want to keep that so the view renders on page load, though
we can remove the ArtistCache parameter (line 27) because Angular will be fetching that
for us; however, we want to add an additional action that serializes the ArtistCache to JSON
(lines 30–33). This is the endpoint that we'll use in Angular to get our artists.

LISTING 21.9   Artist Management Application: Artist Controller with a JSON Action

```
1:  using System;
2:  using System.Collections.Generic;
3:  using System.Runtime.Caching;
4:  using System.Web.Mvc;
5:  using Ch21.Models;
6:
7:  namespace Ch21.Controllers
8:  {
9:      public class ArtistController : Controller
10:     {
11:         public List<Artist> ArtistCache
12:         {
13:             get { return (List<Artist>)MemoryCache.Default.Get("artists"); }
14:             set { MemoryCache.Default.Set("artists", value,
                       ObjectCache.InfiniteAbsoluteExpiration); }
15:         }
16:
17:         public ArtistController()
18:         {
19:             if (ArtistCache == null)
20:             {
21:                 ArtistCache = new List<Artist>();
22:             }
23:         }
24:
25:         public ActionResult Index()
26:         {
27:             return View();
28:         }
29:
30:         public JsonResult All()
31:         {
32:             return Json(ArtistCache, JsonRequestBehavior.AllowGet);
33:         }
34:
35:         public ActionResult Create()
36:         {
37:             return View();
38:         }
39:
40:         [HttpPost]
41:         [ValidateAntiForgeryToken]
42:         public ActionResult Create(Artist artist)
43:         {
44:             artist.Id = Guid.NewGuid();
45:             ArtistCache.Add(artist);
46:             return RedirectToAction("Index");
```

```
47:           }
48:       }
49:   }
```

We included a few more JavaScript files: app.js, artists.js, artists.service.js, and artist-search-filter.js. Let's explore each of them.

App.js is the same as the previous hours: `angular.module('app', []);`

Our `ArtistsController` (artists.js; see Listing 21.10) is also similar to the one we used in Hour 20. We actually just need to remove some code because we aren't handling artist creation via Angular. (If you want to do that, see the following By the Way.) On line 13 of this file in Hour 20, we were using `response.data.d` because of the way Web Forms [WebMethod] wraps responses in an object with a single `'d'` parameter. Fortunately, that is no longer the case in MVC; the serializer gives you the JSON exactly as you'd expect it, so we simply use `response.data` here.

BY THE WAY

Angular Routing Versus MVC Routing

If you decide to move the Create Artist page to Angular and want to make that a separate Angular view instead of an entirely separate MVC view/page, be cautious of how you handle routing. If you use an Angular route that removes the hash from the URL, your routes will interfere with MVC's routes. One way to deal with this is to update your MVC `RouteConfig` with a "catchall" route that routes the user back to the initial view where Angular is loaded.

LISTING 21.10   Artist Management Application: Artist Controller

```
1:   (function () {
2:
3:     angular.module('app')
4:     .controller('ArtistsController', ['ArtistsManager', function (ArtistsManager) {
5:
6:       var vm = this;
7:       getArtists();
8:
9:       ////////////////
10:
11:       function getArtists() {
12:         ArtistsManager.getArtists().then(function (response) {
13:           vm.artists = response.data;
14:         });
15:       }
16:
17:     }]);
18:
19:   })();
```

Following the same trend, our Angular service for fetching artist data (see Listing 21.11) is also very similar to the one used in Hour 20. Again, we'll just remove the second method since Angular isn't adding artists for us this time. Also, on line 7, we switch the $http method to a GET and direct the request at "/Artist/All" because we are using our new All() action on the ArtistController.

LISTING 21.11   Artist Management Application: Artist Angular Service

```
 1:  (function () {
 2:
 3:    angular.module('app')
 4:    .service('ArtistsManager', ['$http', function ($http) {
 5:
 6:      this.getArtists = function () {
 7:        return $http.get("/Artist/All");
 8:      };
 9:
10:    }]);
11:
12:  })();
```

Finally, let's discuss the new functionality that we're able to add now that Angular is handling our artist list data: searching. We accomplish this by filtering our list of artists with a custom filter: artistSearch (see Listing 21.12). As mentioned before, this is very similar to the custom filter we created during Hour 14, save for the addition of line 6 for handling an empty list of artists.

LISTING 21.12   Artist Management Application: Artist Search Filter

```
 1:  (function() {
 2:
 3:    angular.module('app')
 4:      .filter('artistSearch', function() {
 5:        return function(artists, searchString) {
 6:          if (!artists) return;
 7:          return artists.filter(function(artist) {
 8:            if (!searchString) return true;
 9:            var name = artist.Name.toLowerCase();
10:            return name.startsWith(searchString.toLowerCase());
11:          });
12:        }
13:      });
14:
15:  })();
```

That wasn't so bad, was it? Now that we've wired up Angular, let's play with our new feature. Click Run in Visual Studio and add a few artists (see Figure 21.5). Then use the search box (see Figure 21.6). Instant searching!

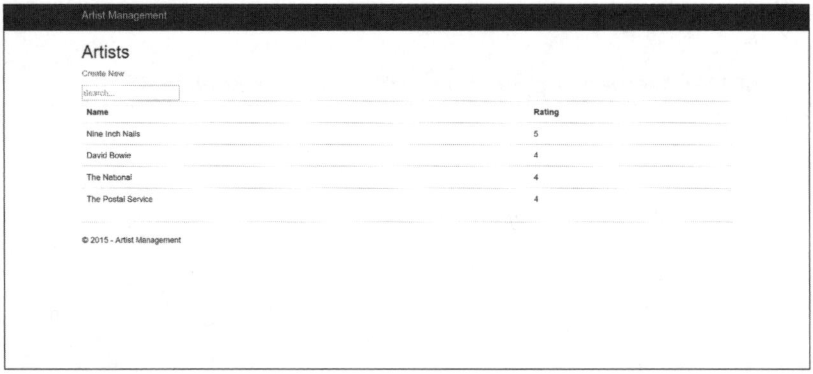

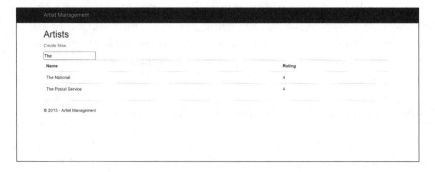

FIGURE 21.5
Artist Management application: artist list view fetching artists via Angular.

FIGURE 21.6
Artist Management application: searching the artist list view.

Summary

In this chapter, we rebuilt our Artist Management application using ASP.NET MVC and Razor views. Then we migrated some of the functionality to Angular and added a new feature: client-side searching.

Q&A

Q. I noticed we used the `@Html.AntiForgeryToken()` method to help protect against CSRF. How can I protect against CSRF when using Angular with Web API?

A. If we had implemented authentication, such as Forms Authentication, in our MVC app, we would have been using *cookie-based authentication,* which is susceptible to CSRF attacks. However, if you're using Angular with Web API and you are using *token-based authentication*, by which a token is obtained from the server and passed with every subsequent request as the `Authorization` header, the browser won't automatically send the token along like it will with cookies, which is a key vulnerability exploited in CSRF attacks.

Q. In this hour, we included Angular in our MVC project so that we could implement searching on our Artist list. I can do this in MVC with a few extra actions. Why do I need Angular?

A. Using Angular to fetch our list of artists gave us the ability to create our search feature. This is easily done in MVC without Angular; however, we are now handling this *client-side,* whereas it would be handled *server-side* if you strictly used MVC. By handling this client-side, we can increase responsiveness and decrease chattiness of our app because every search keystroke will not fire an HTTP request to the server and the user remains on one page (no postbacks) throughout the entire experience. Note, however, that there is a point of diminishing returns. With large datasets, the browser would need to pull all the data in the initial load to handle searching client-side. This could be a long-running request. For these datasets, consider a paginated or "chunked" approach.

Workshop

Quiz

1. In ASP.NET MVC, what object do you return when you want to return a view? What about JSON?

2. In Web Forms we used the `<asp:Repeater>` element to repeat HTML for each item in a list. How do you do this in Razor? How about in Angular?

3. When returning JSON via a `JsonResult` in an ASP.NET MVC controller, what extra code do you have to use to allow `GET` requests?

Answers

1. To return a view, return an `ActionResult` object. For JSON, return a `JsonResult` object.

2. In Razor, we use the `@foreach` statement in conjunction with setting something enumerable as the `Model`. In Angular we use `ng-repeat` in conjunction with something enumerable on the view model.

3. The `Json()` method takes a second parameter: `JsonRequestBehavior.AllowGet`. MVC blocks `GET` requests by default, so developers have to opt in to using them due to the security risk of exposing sensitive data when using `GET` requests.

Exercise

Given an ASP.NET MVC app that you've written or maintained (or, if you haven't done this, find one online), plan how you would begin to migrate functionality to Angular.

Using Angular with ASP.NET Web API

What You'll Learn in This Hour:

▶ Single-page apps with Angular and Web API

▶ Creating a simple Web API

▶ Consuming the Web API in Angular

▶ Consuming third-party APIs in Angular

This hour covers the preferred way of integrating AngularJS and .NET: Web API. We'll start by understanding the role Web API plays in implementing a single-page app. Also, this hour covers the basics on setting up a Web API project, including setting up the project, building a controller, testing the application programming interface (API), and deploying the project to Microsoft Azure. After that, you'll learn how to interact with this API via Angular. This hour concludes with how to use Angular in conjunction with third-party APIs.

Single-Page Apps with Angular and Web API

Most .NET developers are quite familiar with the standard .NET approach to application user interface (UI) development: server-rendered UI via Web Forms or MVC. We used to write our UI logic in .aspx pages or .cshtml pages and intersperse them with server logic. On each request, these pages are rendered into HTML on the server, sent to the client, and entirely repainted in the user's browser.

As developers began migrating standard desktop applications to web applications, a need for better performance arose. This is what the ASP.NET UpdatePanel in Web Forms set out to accomplish. With Web Forms UpdatePanels, it was possible to execute the partial update of a page. This allowed for better performance because it wouldn't cause a full postback to the server. Fortunately, we can take this a step further with the Angular + Web API combination: We can dynamically update whatever parts of the UI that we like and only pass lightweight requests to (and receive lightweight JSON responses from) the server. With Web API, we can completely separate our UI from the server by simply serving all data as JSON that is then interpreted by our Angular front-end and rendered into HTML in the user's browser.

Serving JSON from ASP.NET Without Web API

In Web Forms, you can use an `HttpHandler` (the file extension is .ashx) to handle requests and return JSON easily. These actually run outside of the standard page lifecycle, so they're much faster. Also, you can use Windows Communication Foundation (WCF) services (the file extension is .svc) as another way to serve up JSON. WCF services are mainly used when implementing service-oriented architecture (apps talk to each other) and when communication needs to occur over non-HTTP protocols like TCP. You can use it to serve JSON, but it requires extensive configuration. Finally, as you're aware from Hour 21, "Applying Angular to ASP.NET MVC," we can use ASP.NET MVC to serve JSON by using the `JsonResult` class.

All of these cases differ from Web API in that Web API will automatically map requests to controller functions by using the HTTP verb of the request. (For example, `GET` requests will map to functions that start with "Get..." by convention.) With these other technologies, you must explicitly define the allowed HTTP verbs using attributes on your methods or other configuration.

This allows us to rethink our UI architecture. What was once a collection of independent web pages can now exist on one page with logical boundaries between functions. We can drive more performance out of our apps by only loading things such as the initial Hypertext Markup Language (HTML), images, fonts, and so on once for the duration of the user's session, regardless of how many "pages" they navigate to.

This also allows us to rethink our project structure and tools. Consider that you are working on a team with dedicated front-end and back-end/API developers. By developing both the front end and the back end of the application independently (that is, separate projects, separate repositories), deployment of changes can occur independently. Also, by developing the application in this manner, each team can use the tools that they desire. In an ASP.NET Web Forms or MVC application with server-rendered HTML, front-end developers are forced to use Visual Studio. But in a segregated application that separates UI and API into separate projects, the front-end developers are free to use whatever text editor they want; all they are building is HTML, Cascading Style Sheets (CSS), and JavaScript.

Does all of this have you excited about building performant apps with Angular and Web API? Let's get started!

Creating a Simple Web API

In this section, we build a simple Web API that tracks a list of a user's favorite music artists. For brevity, we'll just be maintaining these as a list in memory on the server. Obviously, in a real application, you'd want to persist these to a database.

WATCH OUT!

In-Memory Caches Versus Persistence

Building out a data persistence layer in our Web API is beyond the scope of this hour. (That is, you don't need to know Entity Framework to understand Angular.) However, in a real application, we wouldn't want to share the artist cache across users, and we wouldn't want the cache to disappear when the app restarts (which happens by default on Azure App Service after 20 minutes of inactivity).

Let's start with a blank slate in Visual Studio. Create a new project and choose ASP.NET Web Application from the project template library. Give it a name and choose the Empty template. Tick the Add Folders and Core References For check box for Web API.

WATCH OUT!

Don't Include More Than You Need!

You can choose the Web API option here, but this will also include MVC and a lot of view-specific stuff that we don't care about; we'll be building the UI later with Angular, so we don't need these things.

Once your solution is created, you'll see a few folders including Controllers and Models. Right-click the Controllers folder and add a controller called `ArtistController`. Also, right-click the Models folder and add a class called Artist.cs.

For our `Artist` class, let's track two data points: the artist's name and a 1–5 rating. In addition, let's enforce that the name is required and that the rating is between 1 and 5 (see Listing 22.1).

LISTING 22.1   Artist Model

```
 1:   using System;
 2:   using System.ComponentModel.DataAnnotations;
 3:
 4:   namespace Ch22.Models
 5:   {
 6:       public class Artist
 7:       {
 8:           public Guid Id { get; set; }
 9:
10:           [Required]
11:           public string Name { get; set; }
12:           [Range(1, 5)]
13:           public int? Rating { get; set; }
14:       }
15:   }
```

For our controller, we're going to build out simple create, read, update, and delete actions (see Listing 22.2). On line 10, we use Web API's attribute-based routing via the [RoutePrefix] attribute to set the root route for this controller to api/artists. Next, on line 11, we declare this controller as `ArtistController` and inherit from `ApiController`. As mentioned earlier, we'll just store the submitted artists in memory on the server. On lines 13 through 17, we set up a property called `ArtistCache` that wraps some calls to `System.Runtime.Caching`'s `MemoryCache` object for storing a collection of artists. Then, on lines 19 through 25, we set up a constructor for this controller that will seed the cache with a blank list of artists.

GO TO ▶ How does this compare to routing in Angular? For more on Angular routing, check out Hour 12, "Rationalizing Routing."

The rest of this class shows the implementations for five actions:

1. A GET HTTP request to api/artist to get the list of artists from the cache

2. Another GET HTTP request to api/artists/{id} that gets a specific artist by ID (a GUID in this example) from the cache

3. A POST HTTP request to api/artists to create an artist in the cache

4. A PUT HTTP request to api/artists/{id} to update an artist in the cache

5. A DELETE HTTP request to api/artists/{id} to delete an artist from the cache

All five of these methods declare their route using the `[Route]` attribute. The real route value for each method at runtime will be set to the `[RoutePrefix]` defined earlier plus the value on this attribute. In addition, all five of these methods return an `IHttpActionResult`, even if the method itself doesn't return an object (like the `Delete()` method, for example). There are many Web API methods available on the inherited `ApiController` that implement this interface. Table 22.1 describes the ones used in this example.

TABLE 22.1 Web API `IHttpActionResults` Used in `ArtistsController.cs`

Method	HTTP Status Code	Description	Parameters
Ok()	HTTP 200	The request was successful.	This method can take an optional object to be serialized and returned to the client.
Created()	HTTP 201	The request was successful and a resource has been created.	This method takes a `Uri` or `string` URL that indicates the location at which the newly created resource is now accessible and the object itself.
BadRequest()	HTTP 400	The request was not successful due to an issue with the request (for example, bad input from the client).	This method takes the `ModelState` object from the current controller context.

Method	HTTP Status Code	Description	Parameters
NotFound()	HTTP 404	The request was not successful because the server couldn't find the requested resource.	This method doesn't take any parameters.

LISTING 22.2 `ArtistsController` with Create, Read, Update and Delete Actions

```
 1:  using System;
 2:  using System.Collections.Generic;
 3:  using System.Linq;
 4:  using System.Runtime.Caching;
 5:  using System.Web.Http;
 6:  using Ch22.Models;
 7:
 8:  namespace Ch22.Controllers
 9:  {
10:      [RoutePrefix("api/artists")]
11:      public class ArtistController : ApiController
12:      {
13:          public List<Artist> ArtistCache
14:          {
15:              get { return (List<Artist>)MemoryCache.Default.Get("artists"); }
16:              set { MemoryCache.Default.Set("artists", value,
                        ObjectCache.InfiniteAbsoluteExpiration); }
17:          }
18:
19:          public ArtistController()
20:          {
21:              if (ArtistCache == null)
22:              {
23:                  ArtistCache = new List<Artist>();
24:              }
25:          }
26:
27:          // GET api/artists
28:          // Gets the artists
29:          [Route("")]
30:          public IHttpActionResult Get()
31:          {
32:              return Ok(ArtistCache);
33:          }
34:
35:          // GET api/artists/{id}
36:          // Gets the artist
37:          [Route("{id}")]
```

```
38:        public IHttpActionResult Get(Guid id)
39:        {
40:            var artist = ArtistCache.FirstOrDefault(a => a.Id == id);
41:            if (artist == null)
42:                return NotFound();
43:
44:            return Ok(artist);
45:        }
46:
47:        // POST api/artists
48:        // Creates an artist.
49:        [Route("")]
50:        public IHttpActionResult Post(Artist artist)
51:        {
52:            if (!ModelState.IsValid)
53:                return BadRequest(ModelState);
54:
55:            artist.Id = Guid.NewGuid();
56:            ArtistCache.Add(artist);
57:            return Created("api/artists/" + artist.Id, artist);
58:        }
59:
60:        // PUT api/artists/{id}
61:        // Updates an artist.
62:        [Route("{id}")]
63:        public IHttpActionResult Put(Guid id, [FromBody] Artist newArtist)
64:        {
65:            if (!ModelState.IsValid)
66:                return BadRequest(ModelState);
67:
68:            var artist = ArtistCache.FirstOrDefault(a => a.Id == id);
69:            if (artist == null)
70:                return NotFound();
71:
72:            artist.Name = newArtist.Name;
73:            artist.Rating = newArtist.Rating;
74:            return Ok();
75:        }
76:
77:        // DELETE api/artists/{id}
78:        // Deletes an artist.
79:        [Route("{id}")]
80:        public IHttpActionResult Delete(Guid id)
81:        {
82:            var artist = ArtistCache.FirstOrDefault(a => a.Id == id);
83:            if (artist == null)
84:                return NotFound();
85:
```

```
86:                 ArtistCache.Remove(artist);
87:                 return Ok();
88:             }
89:         }
90:     }
```

Testing Your API

Now that we've set up our controller, we can run our code and start interacting with it. Before we dive into the Angular side of this, let's just test the controller methods to ensure that things are working correctly. By default, Visual Studio will run your solution on a random port. Run the solution and you'll be presented with a blank browser window with the URL set to localhost plus this random port. For example, if you have Google Chrome set as your browser in Visual Studio, a blank page in Google Chrome will open with the URL set to http://localhost:6789.

Because this project is strictly an API and doesn't contain any views, we'll have to interact with our application using another tool. Any API testing tool will work, but we're quite fond of Postman, a Google Chrome plug-in for "supercharging your API workflow" (their words).

DID YOU KNOW?

Other Options for Testing Your API

Aside from Postman that was mentioned earlier (link to install: https://www.getpostman.com), you can also use tools like Fiddler or SoapUI. Another approach is Swagger; your Web API can dynamically serve a self-documenting client that allows users to not only learn how they can interact with your Web API but also allows them to actually interact with the API right in their browser. You can find more info on Swagger at http://swagger.io/.

In Figure 22.1, we've created a new request to test the creation of artists (the POST request). Grab the URL with the randomized port number from the blank browser window that appeared when you ran the solution in Visual Studio and plug it into the Enter Request URL Here area in Postman. Switch the HTTP method from GET to POST and choose x-www-form-urlencoded to edit the key/value pairs that will be sent with the request. Recall that our Artist class has two properties that we want to set from the UI: the artist's name and the rating from 1–5. Enter both of those for your favorite artist and click the Save button to save your changes to this request in Postman (so that we can test it again later). Click the Send button and you should get back the artist object that you sent with the ID property populated. Continue setting up Postman requests for the other four requests. Don't forget that for the requests that take an ID, the URL is /api/artists/ plus the ID. You should be able to create a few artists, get the entire collection, get an artist by itself, edit the artist's name or rating (or both), and delete an artist.

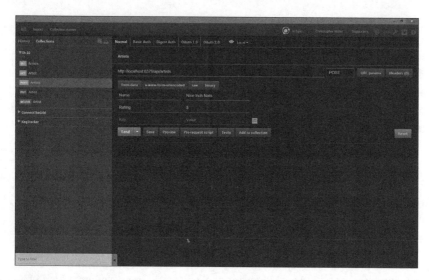

FIGURE 22.1
Crafting a POST request using Postman.

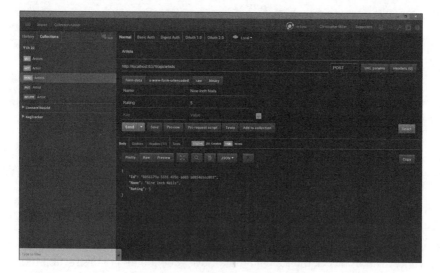

FIGURE 22.2
The response from a POST request using Postman.

Deploying Your API

Throughout this hour, we'll be using Plunker, an online Hypertext Markup Language (HTML), Cascading Style Sheets (CSS), and JavaScript editor to build our Angular app. You could just as easily create a new Angular project in Visual Studio like you've done in previous hours, but

Plunker (and other tools like it) is a great tool to have, especially for debugging and building small test applications. Because later we'll be building our Angular UI using Plunker, we'll need to deploy our app to a public-facing server. For ease, let's use Microsoft Azure, though you could deploy to a variety of places including Heroku, Amazon Web Services, or your own Internet Information Services (IIS) server. At the time of this writing, if you have a Microsoft Live account (free to create), you can enroll in a free one-month trial of Microsoft Azure here: http://azure.microsoft.com/en-us/pricing/free-trial. After you've activated your trial, log in to your Live account through Visual Studio. Then right-click your API project and click Publish to launch an interactive dialog that allows you to create a new Azure website. Step through the dialog and give your application a name (will also become the URL: your-app-name. azurewebsites.net). Finally, Visual Studio will open your browser when the deployment has completed, and you'll see the standard Azure new website screen. To test your API, simply update the URL in your Postman requests to point to your API running on Azure and continue to test as we did earlier.

Consuming the Web API in Angular

Now that we've created a basic Web API, tested it with Postman, and deployed it to Azure, let's start interacting with it in Angular. We'll be building a simple UI that lists all the artists, allows the user to add more, allows the user to edit an artist, and allows the user to delete an artist.

CORS

Unfortunately, before we can even start accessing our API from Angular, we need to think about *cross-origin resource sharing*, or CORS. CORS is a mechanism that will allow our Angular app to access our API app although they live on separate machines, and thus separate origins. The *same-origin security policy* of web browsers defines that scripts on one page can access data on another page only if both pages have the same origin. An origin is the scheme (for example, HTTP or HTTPS), the domain name, and the port number.

For example, if you had an API hosted at www.myawesomemusicapi.com, you would be unable to access it from another site, say www.myawesomemusicui.com, without CORS.

DID YOU KNOW?

Further Reading on CORS

To learn more about how CORS works, specifically in the context of ASP.NET Web API, check out Microsoft's article on enabling CORS in Web API: http://www.asp.net/web-api/overview/security/enabling-cross-origin-requests-in-web-api#how-it-works.

Fortunately, setting up CORS is a breeze in Web API. First, install the Microsoft.AspNet.WebApi.Cors package from NuGet. Then open your WebApiConfig.cs class (under the App_Start folder) and add in this line:

```
config.EnableCors();
```

After adding that, we'll also add in some simple JSON formatting (lines 23 and 24 in Listing 22.3). This isn't related to CORS, but is the last config-related change we need to make. Listing 22.3 shows the full WebApiConfig.cs.

LISTING 22.3   Web API Config Class

```
 1:  using System.Web.Http;
 2:  using Newtonsoft.Json;
 3:  using Newtonsoft.Json.Serialization;
 4:
 5:  namespace Ch22
 6:  {
 7:      public static class WebApiConfig
 8:      {
 9:          public static void Register(HttpConfiguration config)
10:          {
11:              // Web API configuration and services
12:              config.EnableCors();
13:
14:              // Web API routes
15:              config.MapHttpAttributeRoutes();
16:
17:              config.Routes.MapHttpRoute(
18:                  name: "DefaultApi",
19:                  routeTemplate: "api/{controller}/{id}",
20:                  defaults: new { id = RouteParameter.Optional }
21:              );
22:
23:              config.Formatters.JsonFormatter
                        .SerializerSettings.Formatting = Formatting.Indented;
24:              config.Formatters.JsonFormatter
                        .SerializerSettings.ContractResolver
                        = new CamelCasePropertyNamesContractResolver();
25:          }
26:      }
27:  }
```

Finally, we must decorate our controller with an attribute that tells Web API to include CORS functionality for all methods on that controller. We will do that with this line. (Include this on Line 10 of ArtistsController.cs right above the controller declaration.)

```
[EnableCors(origins: "", headers: "", methods: "*")]
```

Specifically, this attribute is telling Web API to send the `Access-Control-Allow-Origin` response header with the wildcard value of `"*"`. After these two changes are in place, redeploy your application to Azure.

Writing Services

Now that we've addressed the CORS issue, let's start writing the Angular UI to interact with our API. As a reminder, we'll be building a simple UI that allows the user to add an artist (name and an optional rating), view saved artists, edit an artist, and delete an artist.

Let's start by building out the HTML for our UI. Using Plunker, create an index.html file (or overwrite the one that Plunker provides). First, we'll set up our `ng-app` on the `<body>` tag, and we'll use the *ControllerAs* syntax to define our controller on the `<div>` element below the `<body>` element. Later, we'll define our `ArtistsController` in JavaScript. The meat of the application lies in three distinct `<section>` elements: one for the list of artists, one for adding a new artist, and one for editing an artist.

Section 1: Viewing Artists

We'll use the `ng-if` directive to only show this section if there are artists to show. That way, we won't be showing a header without content. Next, we use the `ng-repeat` directive to repeat a `<div>` element for each artist in the `vm.artists` collection. In this `<div>`, we show a `<span>` with the artist's name, another `<span>` with the artist's rating (constrained with an `ng-if` directive that only shows it if the artist has a rating), and two `<button>` elements: one for enabling edit mode for this artist and the other for deleting this artist.

Section 2: Adding a New Artist

In this section, we have two `<input>` elements for capturing a new artist's name and rating as entered by the user. We establish a `newArtist` object on the view model and assign the name and rating to the models, respectively. Finally, a `<button>` to add the artist.

Section 3: Editing an Artist

If the user clicks the Edit button in Section 1, the controller will populate this section with the details for the artist. We show a read-only view of the artists's ID (generated by the server) and two `<input>` elements for the artist's name and rating (modeled the same way as in Section 2). Finally, we add a `<button>` to submit the changes.

Listing 22.4 shows the full code for the HTML.

LISTING 22.4 HTML View for the Artist Management Angular App

```
1:  <!DOCTYPE html>
2:  <html>
3:
```

```
 4:      <head>
 5:        <script data-require="angular.js@*" data-semver="1.3.15"
 6:                 src="https://code.angularjs.org/1.3.15/angular.js"></script>
 7:        <script src="app.js"></script>
 8:        <script src="artists.service.js"></script>
 9:        <script src="artists.js"></script>
10:      </head>
11:
12:      <body ng-app="app">
13:        <div ng-controller="ArtistsController as vm">
14:          <h1>Artist Management</h1>
15:          <section ng-if="vm.artists.length > 0">
16:            <h2>Saved Artists</h2>
17:            <div ng-repeat="artist in vm.artists">
18:              <span>{{::artist.name}}</span>
19:              <span ng-if="artist.rating > 0">{{::artist.rating}} stars</span>
20:              <button ng-click="vm.editMode(artist)">Edit</button>
21:              <button ng-click="vm.delete(artist.id)">Delete</button>
22:            </div>
23:          </section>
24:          <section>
25:            <hr />
26:            <h2>Add New Artist</h2>
27:            <label for="addName">Name: </label>
28:            <input type="text" id="addName"
29:                   ng-model="vm.newArtist.name" placeholder="Artist Name" />
30:            <br />
31:            <label for="addRating">Rating: </label>
32:            <input type="range" id="addRating" ng-model="vm.newArtist.rating"
33:                   min="0" max="5" step="1" value="0" />
34:            <br />
35:            <button ng-click="vm.add()">Add</button>
36:          </section>
37:          <section ng-if="vm.editArtist != null">
38:            <hr />
39:            <h2>Edit Artist</h2>
40:            <div>ID: {{vm.editArtist.id}}</div>
41:            <label for="editName">Name: </label>
42:            <input type="text" id="editName" ng-model="vm.editArtist.name"
43:                   placeholder="Artist Name" /><br />
44:            <label for="editRating">Rating: </label>
45:            <input type="range" id="editRating" ng-model="vm.editArtist.rating"
46:                   min="0" max="5" step="1" value="0" /><br />
47:            <button ng-click="vm.edit()">Submit Edit</button>
48:          </section>
49:        </div>
50:      </body>
51:
52:    </html>
```

Next, let's explore the JavaScript. We'll create three files in Plunker: app.js, artists.js, and artists. service.js. In app.js, we just create our app module with one line of code:

```
angular.module('app', []);
```

Next, in artists.js, we create our controller (see Listing 22.5). We start by wrapping our code in an immediately invoked function expression (IIFE) and grabbing a reference to our app. We use the .controller() syntax to create the controller and pass in a reference to our yet-to-be-built Angular service called ArtistsManager. We set up our view model variable and immediately execute the getArtists() function because we want to get artists when the view renders. That function uses the ArtistManager service to get the list of artists and registers a callback function that will execute when the AJAX request to the server completes. We use the .then() method to define this (because our service returns a promise and makes the response from the server available to any registered callback functions).

GO TO ▶ For more on IIFEs, go to Hour 2, "Presenting JavaScript Patterns."

GO TO ▶ For more on deferred objects and promises, take a look at Hour 8, "Discovering Services: Part 2."

Through the rest of the controller, we define the four functions that do the entire work of the application. First, we have vm.add(), which creates a new artist using ArtistManager's .createArtist() method. We create a new artist object, making sure to set the rating only if the user has selected a value of 1–5 (not zero), and pass it to the method. We also register a callback that will null out the model for newArtist and re-fetch the list of artists. Next, we have vm.editMode(), which simply sets the selected artist in the list to the editArtist, which populates Section 3 of the UI. Then we have vm.edit(), which performs the same functionality as vm.add() but just uses a different method on the ArtistsManager:.updateArtist(). This method also takes the artist's ID as its first parameter. Finally, we have vm.delete(), which simply calls the .deleteArtist() method on ArtistsManager and passes in the selected artist's ID. On the callback, we make sure to refresh the list of artists.

LISTING 22.5   Angular Controller for the Artist Management Angular App

```
 1:  (function() {
 2:
 3:  angular.module('app')
 4:  .controller('ArtistsController', ['ArtistsManager',
 5:  function(ArtistsManager){
 6:
 7:    var vm = this;
 8:    getArtists();
 9:
10:    //////////////
11:
12:    function getArtists() {
```

```
13:        ArtistsManager.getArtists().then(function(response) {
14:          vm.artists = response.data;
15:        });
16:    }
17:
18:    vm.add = function() {
19:      ArtistsManager.createArtist({
20:        name: vm.newArtist.name,
21:        rating: vm.newArtist.rating > 0
22:          ? vm.newArtist.rating
23:          : null
24:      }).then(function() {
25:        vm.newArtist = null;
26:        getArtists();
27:      });
28:    };
29:
30:    vm.editMode = function(artist) {
31:      vm.editArtist = artist;
32:    };
33:
34:    vm.edit = function() {
35:      ArtistsManager.updateArtist(
36:        vm.editArtist.id,
37:        {
38:          name: vm.editArtist.name,
39:          rating: vm.editArtist.rating > 0
40:            ? vm.editArtist.rating
41:            : null
42:      }).then(function() {
43:        vm.editArtist = null;
44:        getArtists();
45:      });
46:    };
47:
48:    vm.delete = function(id) {
49:      ArtistsManager.deleteArtist(id)
50:        .then(getArtists);
51:    };
52:
53:  }]);
54:
55:  })();
```

In the preceding section, we mentioned `ArtistsManager` quite a bit; let's take a look at how to build that component. In the artists.service.js file, we start off with an IIFE and the reference to our app before using the `.service()` method to define a custom service that depends on Angular's $http service.

GO TO ▶ For more on the `$http` service, go to Hour 8.

The actual logic here is pretty straightforward: We just provide four methods for our controller to use to interact with the server. Because our Web API is RESTful, we use the proper HTTP verbs to indicate the intended functionality of each method (for example, GET requests for getting artists, DELETE requests for deleting an artist). Conveniently, the `$http` service provides methods for us to use for each of these verbs. Table 22.2 describes this in more detail.

TABLE 22.2   Angular `$http` Service Methods

`$http` Method	HTTP Verb	Parameters
`.get()`	GET	This method takes the URL.
`.post()`	POST	This method takes the URL and the JSON object to send as the request body.
`.put()`	PUT	This method takes the URL (which should include the resource's ID that you are editing) and the updated JSON object to send as the request body.
`.delete()`	DELETE	This method takes the URL (which should include the resource's ID that you are editing).

Listing 22.6 shows the full service.

LISTING 22.6   Angular Service for the Artist Management Angular App

```
 1:  (function() {
 2:
 3:   angular.module('app')
 4:   .service('ArtistsManager', ['$http', function($http) {
 5:
 6:     var apiUrl = "http://angularwebapich22.azurewebsites.net/";
 7:
 8:     this.getArtists = function() {
 9:       return $http.get(apiUrl + "api/artists");
10:     };
11:
```

```
12:     this.createArtist = function(data) {
13:        return $http.post(apiUrl + "api/artists", data);
14:     };
15:
16:     this.updateArtist = function(id, data) {
17:        return $http.put(apiUrl + "api/artists/" + id, data);
18:     };
19:
20:     this.deleteArtist = function(id) {
21:        return $http.delete(apiUrl + "api/artists/" + id);
22:     };
23:
24:  }]);
25:
26:  })();
```

After you've got it all wired up, you should be able to immediately start interacting with your API hosted on Azure because we already fixed the CORS issue. See Figures 22.3 through 22.9 for some screenshots of our app in action.

WATCH OUT!

In line 6 of artists.service.js, don't forget to update the apiUrl variable with the location of your API running in Azure (or wherever).

FIGURE 22.3
Default view of the Artist Management Angular App without any artists.

Artist Management

Add New Artist

Name: `Nine Inch Nails`
Rating: ────────○
`Add`

FIGURE 22.4
Adding an artist and rating it 5.

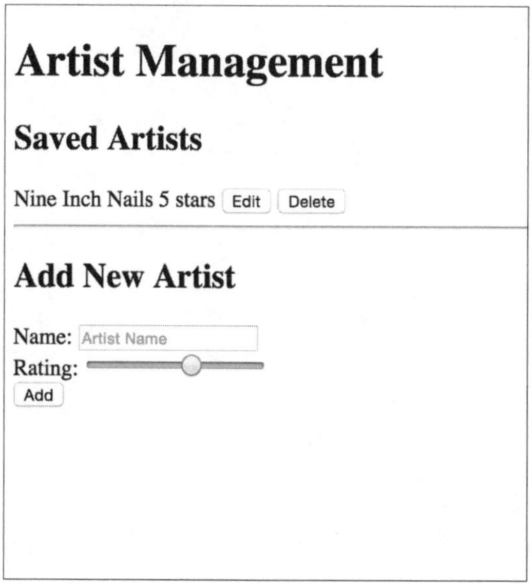

Artist Management

Saved Artists

Nine Inch Nails 5 stars `Edit` `Delete`

Add New Artist

Name: `Artist Name`
Rating: ─────○───
`Add`

FIGURE 22.5
Submitting a new artist saves it on the server and triggers a refresh.

Artist Management

Saved Artists

Nine Inch Nails 5 stars [Edit] [Delete]
Death Cab For Cutie 4 stars [Edit] [Delete]

Add New Artist

Name: [Artist Name]
Rating: ═══════○────────
[Add]

Edit Artist

ID: 8af41d93-54a3-46d3-a27a-8f80cb08154f
Name: [Death Cab For Cutie]
Rating: ════════○──────
[Submit Edit]

FIGURE 22.6
Editing an artist populates the edit section.

Artist Management

Saved Artists

Nine Inch Nails 5 stars [Edit] [Delete]
Death Cab For Cutie 4 stars [Edit] [Delete]

Add New Artist

Name: [Artist Name]
Rating: ═══════○───────────
[Add]

Edit Artist

ID: 8af41d93-54a3-46d3-a27a-8f80cb08154f
Name: [Death Cab For Cutie]
Rating: ══════════════════○──
[Submit Edit]

FIGURE 22.7
While editing an artist, changing the rating.

Artist Management

Saved Artists

Nine Inch Nails 5 stars [Edit] [Delete]
Death Cab For Cutie 5 stars [Edit] [Delete]

Add New Artist

Name: [Artist Name]
Rating: ═══════○════════
[Add]

FIGURE 22.8
Submitting the changes closes the edit section and triggers a refresh.

Artist Management

Saved Artists

Nine Inch Nails 5 stars [Edit] [Delete]

Add New Artist

Name: [Artist Name]
Rating: ═══════○════════
[Add]

FIGURE 22.9
Deleting an artist removes it and triggers a refresh.

Consuming Other APIs with Angular

Now that we've consumed our custom API with Angular, let's explore consuming other APIs as well. We've spent this entire hour building a simple app for managing users' favorite music artists, but we're not giving them the ability to listen to any music! Let's use the Spotify API to change that. Spotify is a music streaming service that offers free, ad-supported music to 60+ million listeners around the world. The Spotify API allows developers to search for artists, songs, albums, and genres; play music samples; and much more. Typically, the Spotify API requires authentication with an API key; however, the endpoints we are using are publicly available at https://api.spotify.com/v1. Therefore, we won't need any additional keys or files to make this work — just plain HTTP requests.

Specifically, we'll be using the Spotify API to find the selected artist's Spotify ID, use that ID to get the artist's top track, and use an HTML5 <audio> element to display a streaming music player for the 30-second preview of the top track. Sound good? Let's get to it!

Let's start by updating our HTML. First, let's add a <script> reference to our yet-to-be-built Angular service for interacting with Spotify: spotify.service.js (see line 7 in Listing 22.7). In Section 1, let's add a third action that allows the user to play the top track for the selected artist. This button's ng-click will be a controller method called .play() that takes the artist's name as a parameter. Also, we'll add a fourth section titled Now Playing. Here, we add an <audio> element and give it two attributes: autoplay because we want the player to start playing as soon as the user clicks the Play button that we built earlier, and controls because we want the embedded player to have a control set available to the user for pausing, skipping ahead, and so on. We also add an ng-src directive with a controller method that fetches the audio URL. Finally, we add a button for closing the player. This entire section is constrained with an ng-if directive so that it appears only when vm.playUrl is set (more on that later).

Listing 22.7 shows the updated HTML.

LISTING 22.7 Updated View Including Spotify Integration

```
 1:   <!DOCTYPE html>
 2:   <html>
 3:
 4:     <head>
 5:       <script data-require="angular.js@*" data-semver="1.3.15"
 6:               src="https://code.angularjs.org/1.3.15/angular.js"></script>
 7:       <script src="app.js"></script>
 8:       <script src="spotify.service.js"></script>
 9:       <script src="artists.service.js"></script>
10:       <script src="artists.js"></script>
11:     </head>
12:
13:     <body ng-app="app">
```

```
14:        <div ng-controller="ArtistsController as vm">
15:          <h1>Artist Management</h1>
16:
17:          <section ng-if="vm.artists.length > 0">
18:            <h2>Saved Artists</h2>
19:            <div ng-repeat="artist in vm.artists">
20:              <span>{{::artist.name}}</span>
21:              <span ng-if="artist.rating > 0">{{::artist.rating}} stars</span>
22:              <button ng-click="vm.editMode(artist)">Edit</button>
23:              <button ng-click="vm.delete(artist.id)">Delete</button>
24:              <button ng-click="vm.play(artist.name)">Play (using Spotify)</button>
25:            </div>
26:          </section>
27:
28:          <section>
29:            <hr />
30:            <h2>Add New Artist</h2>
31:            <label for="addName">Name: </label>
32:            <input type="text" id="addName"
33:                   ng-model="vm.newArtist.name" placeholder="Artist Name" />
34:            <br />
35:            <label for="addRating">Rating: </label>
36:            <input type="range" id="addRating" ng-model="vm.newArtist.rating"
37:                   min="0" max="5" step="1" value="0" />
38:            <br />
39:            <button ng-click="vm.add()">Add</button>
40:          </section>
41:
42:          <section ng-if="vm.editArtist != null">
43:            <hr />
44:            <h2>Edit Artist</h2>
45:            <div>ID: {{vm.editArtist.id}}</div>
46:            <label for="editName">Name: </label>
47:            <input type="text" id="editName" ng-model="vm.editArtist.name"
48:                   placeholder="Artist Name" /><br />
49:            <label for="editRating">Rating: </label>
50:            <input type="range" id="editRating" ng-model="vm.editArtist.rating"
51:                   min="0" max="5" step="1" value="0" /><br />
52:            <button ng-click="vm.edit()">Submit Edit</button>
53:          </section>
54:
55:          <section ng-if="vm.playUrl != null">
56:            <hr />
57:            <h2>Now Playing</h2>
58:            <audio autoplay controls ng-src="{{vm.getAudioUrl()}}"></audio>
59:            <br />
60:            <button ng-click="vm.closePlayer()">Close Player</button>
61:          </section>
```

```
62:
63:        </div>
64:      </body>
65:
66:  </html>
```

Next, let's build an Angular service that hits the Spotify API; we'll call this file spotify.service.js.

Just as with our custom `ArtistsManager` from earlier, we'll grab a reference to our app and use `.service()` to create an Angular service that depends on the `$http` service. Fortunately, Spotify provides a version of its API that doesn't require authentication or an API key, so we'll use that for demo purposes.

Third-Party API Authentication

If you want to use a third-party API that does require authentication or an API key, the third party will typically host all sorts of documentation around how to get a key and how to send the key with each request.

Our service has two methods: one for searching the artist's name to find its Spotify ID, and another for using that ID to get the audio preview URL for the artist's top track. Just as in `ArtistsManager`, we use `$http` to fire off get requests against the API URL, and we register a callback that digs through the response data to get the two pieces of data that we need.

Listing 22.8 shows the full code.

LISTING 22.8   Angular Service for Interacting with the Spotify API

```
 1:  (function() {
 2:
 3:  angular.module('app')
 4:  .service('SpotifyService', ['$http', function($http) {
 5:
 6:    var apiUrl = "https://api.spotify.com/v1/";
 7:
 8:    this.getSpotifyArtistIdByName = function(name) {
 9:      return $http.get(apiUrl + "search?q=" + name + "&type=artist")
10:      .then(function(response) {
11:        return response.data.artists.items[0].id;
12:      });
13:    };
14:
15:    this.getTopTrackURLForArtist = function(spotifyArtistId) {
16:      var url = apiUrl + "artists/" + spotifyArtistId + "/top-tracks?country=US";
```

```
17:        return $http.get(url)
18:          .then(function(response) {
19:            return response.data.tracks[0].preview_url;
20:          });
21:      };
22:
23:   }]);
24:
25:   })();
```

Finally, let's wire this all up in our controller. We need to inject two more dependencies: an Angular provider called $sce (more on that later) and our new SpotifyService. We'll also add three new methods: vm.play(), vm.closePlayer(), and vm.getAudioUrl(). For our play method, we pass in the selected artist's name. (This is tied to the Play button in Section 1 of the HTML.) In this method, we use our SpotifyService to get the artist's ID and use that to get the preview URL, which we set to vm.playUrl. Setting this value on the view model will trigger Section 4 to appear because of our ng-if directive on the section. Our vm.closePlayer() method simply nulls out this playUrl property on the view model, which in turn causes Section 4 to disappear. Finally, our vm.getAudioUrl() method uses the Strict Contextual Escaping service (the $sce service that we injected earlier) to trust our preview URL.

DID YOU KNOW?

Why Do We Need $sce?

Straight from the Angular API documentation: "By default, Angular only loads templates from the same domain and protocol as the application document." This means that Angular will throw an error if we try to use our playUrl directly. We have to pass it through the $sce service's .trustAsResourceUrl() method to use it on our <audio> element.

Listing 22.9 shows the full code for our updated controller.

LISTING 22.9 Updated Controller with Spotify Integration

```
1:   (function() {
2:
3:   angular.module('app')
4:   .controller('ArtistsController', ['$sce', 'ArtistsManager', 'SpotifyService',
             function($sce, ArtistsManager, SpotifyService) {
5:      var vm = this;
6:      getArtists();
7:
8:      /////////////////
9:
10:     function getArtists() {
```

```
11:        ArtistsManager.getArtists().then(function(response) {
12:          vm.artists = response.data;
13:        });
14:      }
15:
16:      vm.add = function() {
17:        ArtistsManager.createArtist({
18:          name: vm.newArtist.name,
19:          rating: vm.newArtist.rating > 0
20:            ? vm.newArtist.rating
21:            : null
22:        }).then(function() {
23:          vm.newArtist = null;
24:          getArtists();
25:        });
26:      };
27:
28:      vm.editMode = function(artist) {
29:        vm.editArtist = artist;
30:      };
31:
32:      vm.edit = function() {
33:        ArtistsManager.updateArtist(
34:        vm.editArtist.id,
35:        {
36:          name: vm.editArtist.name,
37:          rating: vm.editArtist.rating > 0
38:            ? vm.editArtist.rating
39:            : null
40:        }).then(function() {
41:          vm.editArtist = null;
42:          getArtists();
43:        });
44:      };
45:
46:      vm.delete = function(id) {
47:        ArtistsManager.deleteArtist(id)
48:          .then(getArtists);
49:      };
50:
51:      vm.play = function(name) {
52:        SpotifyService.getSpotifyArtistIdByName(name).then(function(id) {
53:          SpotifyService.getTopTrackURLForArtist(id).then(function(url) {
54:            vm.playUrl = url;
55:          });
56:        });
57:      };
58:
```

```
59:     vm.closePlayer = function() {
60:       vm.playUrl = null;
61:     };
62:
63:     vm.getAudioUrl = function() {
64:       return $sce.trustAsResourceUrl(vm.playUrl);
65:     };
66:
67:   }]);
68:
69:  })();
```

After you've got these updates in place, we can start playing some music! Figure 22.10 and Figure 22.11 show some screenshots of our app in action.

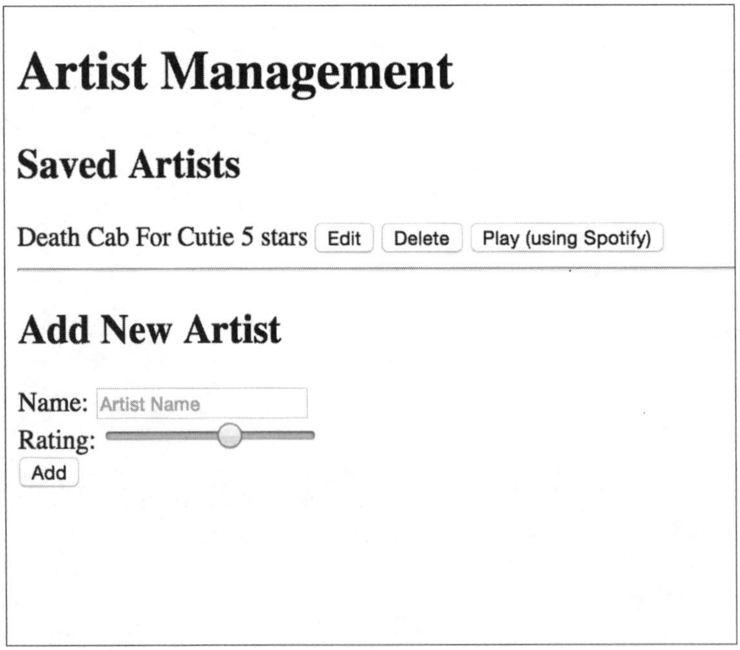

Artist Management

Saved Artists

Death Cab For Cutie 5 stars [Edit] [Delete] [Play (using Spotify)]

Add New Artist

Name: [Artist Name]
Rating: ━━━━━━○━━━━━━
[Add]

FIGURE 22.10
Default view with a saved artist (new option to Play).

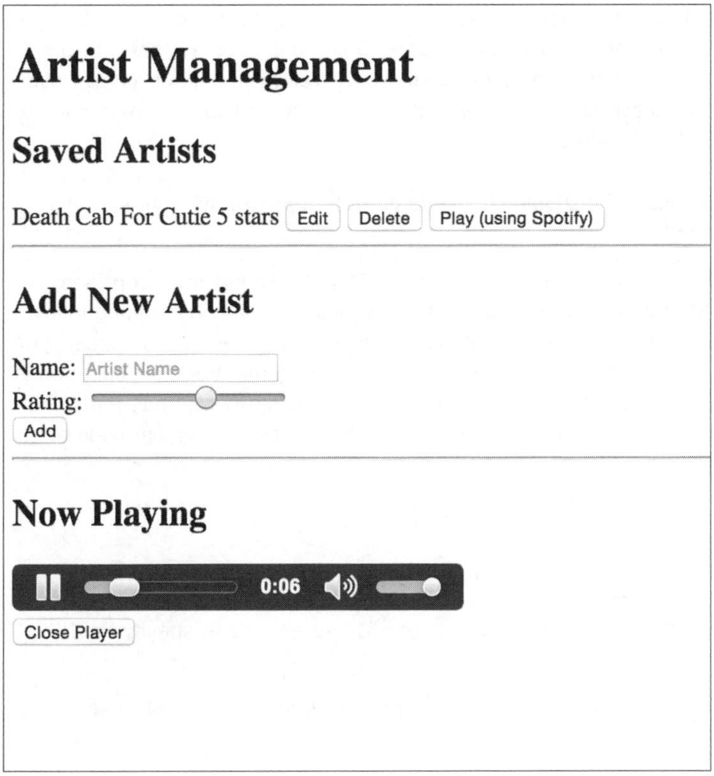

FIGURE 22.11
Clicking Play shows the Now Playing section and plays music.

Summary

In this hour, we first looked at the progression from independent, server-rendered pages to partial page updates to single-page apps. We introduced the preferred way of interacting with .NET from Angular: Web API. We built a sample API, tested it, and deployed it to Azure, taking special care to implement CORS correctly. We also built a small Angular app that uses that API and tied it to a third-party API as well.

Q&A

Q. When we built our custom Angular services that interact with the Web API and the Spotify API, why did we create them separately? Why not just inject `$http` into the controller and do everything there?

A. Although this would certainly work, it isn't a best practice. The key to maintainable Angular code is keeping controllers as free of logic as possible. Doing this ensures that they are testable. By separating our Angular code that interacts with Web API from our Angular code that interacts with Spotify via two separate services, we have created two reusable components that multiple controllers could use.

Q. **What are some other reasons why I should choose to entirely separate my front end and back end in my application?**

A. By building your UI as one project that simply includes HTML, CSS, and JavaScript and building your API as a separate project with the two communicating over a common interface like JSON, you could later decide to change technologies on either end. Consider if we no longer wanted to use ASP.NET as our API for the Artist Management app we built in this hour. We could easily swap in a Ruby or Python API and, so long as the API has the same endpoints and returns the same JSON, we wouldn't have to change our Angular code at all!

Workshop

Quiz

1. In Web API, what attribute do we use on our `ApiController` actions to specify the URL for the action?

2. Why is CORS support an issue when our Angular UI and Web API are deployed to separate servers?

3. What Angular service allows us to execute requests against our Web API?

Answers

1. We use the `[Route]` attribute on each action. These are appended to the value set on the controller with the `[RoutePrefix]` attribute.

2. Browsers implement a security policy called the *same-origin security policy*, which dictates that scripts on one page can access data on another page only if both pages have the same origin. In our case, the Web API requires special configuration to allow JSON to be sent across origins.

3. We use the `$http` service to execute HTTP requests against the API.

Exercise

For the book management system mentioned in the Introduction, integrate with the included Web API project. This Web API offers user account registration, login, and full create/read/update/delete for the book list. First, implement accounts/authentication, fetching a book list, and adding to the book list. For bonus points, implement updating list items and deleting list items.

Using Angular with ASP.NET SignalR

What You'll Learn in This Hour:

▶ When should you use SignalR?

▶ How to configure SignalR

▶ How to send messages from your API

▶ How to receive messages in Angular

SignalR is a .NET library for building web apps that support real-time data. The server tracks all clients using something called a *hub* object, which acts as a central point for pushing data to all clients in real time. The hub can also call JavaScript in a connected client's browser. SignalR uses a variety of technologies for cross-browser support, including the HTML5 WebSockets application programming interface (API). It's smart enough to choose the best technology available for the browser, resorting to long polling if WebSockets is unavailable.

This hour discusses creating real-time web applications using ASP.NET's SignalR library and AngularJS. Over the course of this hour, you enhance the Artist Management application from Hour 22, "Using Angular with ASP.NET Web API," so that whenever any user adds a new artist, edits an artist, or deletes an artist, all users' list of artists automatically refresh in real time. Specifically, we start by configuring SignalR. (Note that this will also include a primer on OWIN.) Then we delve into how to use it within our API. Finally, you'll learn about interacting with SignalR from Angular.

When Should You Use SignalR?

Real-time technologies like SignalR can fundamentally change how users interact with web apps. Years ago, if users wanted new information, they were limited to simply refreshing the entire page. Later, developers started writing client-side code that would poll the server for new data at a regular interval. Now, clients can receive new data from the server as it becomes available and can send data to the server via the same stream.

As new emails automatically arrive in your Gmail inbox or new stories appear in your Facebook feed, real-time technologies like SignalR are at work. These technologies are perfect for apps that use quickly changing data sets such as stock monitoring dashboards or collaborative authoring tools (for example, Google Docs). Instead of checking for out-of-band changes when a user tries to save a document, for instance, users can be notified in real time if the data they are working on is being updated by other users and always have access to the latest information.

Let's now turn our attention to adding SignalR to our Artist Management application developed in Hour 22. Users of the application will now know in real time when the list of artists changes, without having to refresh the page.

Configuring SignalR

Let's start by adding a SignalR hub class to our project. Right-click on your project in Visual Studio, choose Add, and then choose New Item. Search for SignalR and choose SignalR Hub Class (v2). Call your hub ArtistHub.

WATCH OUT!

Missing Project Template

If you can't find that project template, use NuGet to install this package: Microsoft.AspNet.SignalR. If you go this route, just add a normal class that looks like the one shown in Listing 23.1.

LISTING 23.1   Artist SignalR Hub

```
1:   using Microsoft.AspNet.SignalR;
2:
3:   namespace Ch23
4:   {
5:       public class ArtistHub : Hub
6:       {
7:       }
8:   }
```

Adding SignalR to the OWIN Pipeline

Because we are using SignalR v2, we must register our SignalR hub using OWIN middleware. Let's take a quick tangent to discuss OWIN and how it relates to our project. Then we'll map SignalR and get to work using it!

The Open Web Interface for .NET (OWIN) is a community-driven specification for how to build .NET apps that are decoupled from Internet Information Services (IIS) and the System.Web namespace. If you've been building ASP.NET apps for some time, you've undoubtedly used components from the `System.Web` namespace. This namespace is huge and contains many components (for example, Web Forms and URL Authorization) that you might not need; some of these components run on each request, which limits performance if you don't need them. Because of this, the need arose for a lighter, more nimble framework over the past few years.

Remember, OWIN is a *specification*, not a *framework* — an interface, not an implementation. Microsoft Katana is a framework that bridges the gap between current ASP.NET frameworks, like Web API and SignalR, and OWIN. When you add references to the `Microsoft.Owin` namespace, you are adding Katana components to your project.

The OWIN specification decouples ASP.NET applications from IIS and `System.Web` by breaking `System.Web`'s components into small, standalone components called *OWIN middleware*. These middleware components are passthrough components that form a pipeline between a server and application to inspect, route, or modify request and response messages. This pipeline is configured at app startup by using the `IAppBuilder` interface.

Let's create an OWIN startup class and instruct the OWIN pipeline to map our SignalR hub. Again, right-click on the project, choose Add, and then choose New Item. Search for OWIN, and choose OWIN Startup Class. Create a class called `Startup.cs`, and move it into your App_Start folder (see Listing 23.2).

The resulting class adds an `OwinStartup` assembly attribute that identifies our `Startup` class as the class Katana will use when bootstrapping the application at runtime.

DID YOU KNOW?

Another Way to Specify the Startup Class

The `OwinStartup` assembly attribute method of identifying the OWIN startup class is used by many developers and occurs automatically when creating the class (as you saw earlier), but it isn't actually necessary. Before looking for this attribute, Katana first looks for a class named `Startup` anywhere in the namespace.

Our class has one method, `Configuration()`, which takes an `IAppBuilder` parameter. Katana executes this function when your application starts up. To make cross-origin requests against SignalR, install the Microsoft.Owin.Cors package from NuGet and use the `app.UseCors()` middleware allowing all domains.

WATCH OUT!

OWIN and CORS

Make sure that the `app.UseCors()` method is the first middleware that you configure in your pipeline. Requests are passed from middleware to middleware according to the order in which the middleware components are configured.

Because we're now using OWIN, we want to instruct the pipeline to use our Web API. We configure our Web API using the same method as before (`WebApiConfig.Register(config)`), but now we pass the configuration object to another OWIN middleware: `app.UseWebApi()`. Install the `Microsoft.AspNet.WebApi.Owin` package to enable this middleware. Because we're now using OWIN, we can delete our Global.asax file.

Finally, we use the `app.MapSignalR()` method on the `Owin.OwinExtensions` namespace to map our SignalR hub.

BY THE WAY

Changing the SignalR Endpoint

By default, the `app.MapSignalR()` method mounts SignalR at `"/signalr"`. If you want to change this, simply pass in your desired URL string to this method.

LISTING 23.2   OWIN Startup Class with SignalR Configuration

```
 1:  using System.Web.Http;
 2:  using Microsoft.Owin;
 3:  using Microsoft.Owin.Cors;
 4:  using Owin;
 5:
 6:  [assembly: OwinStartup(typeof(Ch23.Startup))]
 7:
 8:  namespace Ch23
 9:  {
10:      public class Startup
11:      {
12:          public void Configuration(IAppBuilder app)
13:          {
14:              var config = new HttpConfiguration();
15:
16:              app.UseCors(CorsOptions.AllowAll);
17:              app.MapSignalR();
18:              WebApiConfig.Register(config);
19:              app.UseWebApi(config);
20:          }
21:      }
22:  }
```

We've now configured our SignalR hub using OWIN. Let's start interacting with it in our API and in Angular.

Sending SignalR Messages in Your API

Let's use our `ArtistHub` in our controller (see Listing 23.3). We start by creating a private variable of type `IHubContext` called _artistHub. We populate this in the constructor by using the `GlobalHost.ConnectionManager` class, which has a `GetHubContext<>()` method that takes a type parameter of the hub you want to get. In our case, this is our `ArtistHub`. Once we have a reference to our hub, we simply use it throughout our controller whenever we want all clients to refresh their list of artists. Specifically, we do this after any artist creation, update, or deletion (lines 63, 81, and 95) in Listing 23.3 using `Clients.All.getArtists()`. The `Clients.All` object is a dynamic object that allows us to write whatever method we like on it. When this `getArtists()` method is called, SignalR translates the call into a message (with the same name as the method, `getArtists`) and sends the message to each client currently connected to our `ArtistHub`. The client can interpret this message however it sees fit. In our instance, we listen for this message and run our method that fetches the artist list (see Listing 23.8 later).

LISTING 23.3 Updated ArtistController for SignalR Interaction

```
 1:  using System;
 2:  using System.Collections.Generic;
 3:  using System.Linq;
 4:  using System.Runtime.Caching;
 5:  using System.Web.Http;
 6:  using System.Web.Http.Cors;
 7:  using Ch23.Models;
 8:  using Microsoft.AspNet.SignalR;
 9:
10:  namespace Ch23.Controllers
11:  {
12:      [RoutePrefix("api/artists")]
13:      [EnableCors(origins: "*", headers: "*", methods: "*")]
14:      public class ArtistController : ApiController
15:      {
16:          private readonly IHubContext _artistHub;
17:
18:          public List<Artist> ArtistCache
19:          {
20:              get { return (List<Artist>)MemoryCache.Default.Get("artists"); }
21:              set { MemoryCache.Default.Set("artists", value,
                        ObjectCache.InfiniteAbsoluteExpiration); }
22:          }
23:
24:          public ArtistController()
25:          {
26:              _artistHub = GlobalHost.ConnectionManager
                          .GetHubContext<ArtistHub>();
```

```
27:              if (ArtistCache == null)
28:              {
29:                  ArtistCache = new List<Artist>();
30:              }
31:          }
32:
33:          // GET api/artists
34:          // Gets the artists
35:          [Route("")]
36:          public IHttpActionResult Get()
37:          {
38:              return Ok(ArtistCache);
39:          }
40:
41:          // GET api/artists/{id}
42:          // Gets the artist
43:          [Route("{id}")]
44:          public IHttpActionResult Get(Guid id)
45:          {
46:              var artist = ArtistCache.FirstOrDefault(a => a.Id == id);
47:              if (artist == null)
48:                  return NotFound();
49:
50:              return Ok(artist);
51:          }
52:
53:          // POST api/artists
54:          // Creates an artist.
55:          [Route("")]
56:          public IHttpActionResult Post(Artist artist)
57:          {
58:              if (!ModelState.IsValid)
59:                  return BadRequest(ModelState);
60:
61:              artist.Id = Guid.NewGuid();
62:              ArtistCache.Add(artist);
63:              _artistHub.Clients.All.getArtists();
64:              return Created("api/artists/" + artist.Id, artist);
65:          }
66:
67:          // PUT api/artists/{id}
68:          // Updates an artist.
69:          [Route("{id}")]
70:          public IHttpActionResult Put(Guid id, [FromBody] Artist newArtist)
71:          {
72:              if (!ModelState.IsValid)
```

```
73:                    return BadRequest(ModelState);
74:
75:            var artist = ArtistCache.FirstOrDefault(a => a.Id == id);
76:            if (artist == null)
77:                return NotFound();
78:
79:            artist.Name = newArtist.Name;
80:            artist.Rating = newArtist.Rating;
81:            _artistHub.Clients.All.getArtists();
82:            return Ok();
83:        }
84:
85:        // DELETE api/artists/{id}
86:        // Deletes an artist.
87:        [Route("{id}")]
88:        public IHttpActionResult Delete(Guid id)
89:        {
90:            var artist = ArtistCache.FirstOrDefault(a => a.Id == id);
91:            if (artist == null)
92:                return NotFound();
93:
94:            ArtistCache.Remove(artist);
95:            _artistHub.Clients.All.getArtists();
96:            return Ok();
97:        }
98:    }
99: }
```

Receiving SignalR Messages in Angular

Now that we've got our Web API all wired up with SignalR, let's explore how to interact with SignalR in Angular. We will be building an Angular factory called `SignalRHub` that takes a hub name as a parameter and exposes an `.on()` method (think publish/subscribe pattern).

GO TO ▶ For more on pub/sub, go to Hour 2, "Presenting JavaScript Patterns."

Let's start with including some additional libraries in our HTML. Microsoft provides a client-side library for working with SignalR called jquery.signal.lr. (Yes, it depends on jQuery.) When we created our SignalR hub on the API, you may have noticed the addition of a Scripts folder and the inclusion of a few JavaScript files. Microsoft's jQuery SignalR library is included by default here and is served by the API so that we can access it from Angular. The rest of our view remains the same as in Hour 22.

LISTING 23.4   Updated Script References in HTML

```
 1:   <head>
 2:        <script data-require="jquery@2.1.3" data-semver="2.1.3"
                    src=" http://code.jquery.com/jquery-2.1.3.min.js"></script>
 3:        <script src="http://localhost:8080/Scripts/jquery.signalR-2.2.0.min.
                    js"></script>
 4:        <script data-require="angular.js@*" data-semver="1.3.15"
                    src="https://code.angularjs.org/1.3.15/angular.js"></script>
 5:        <script src="app.js"></script>
 6:        <script src="signalrhub.factory.js"></script>
 7:        <script src="spotify.service.js"></script>
 8:        <script src="artists.service.js"></script>
 9:        <script src="artists.js"></script>
10:   </head>
```

WATCH OUT!

Serving jquery.signalr from your API

On line 3 of Listing 23.4, we reference a JavaScript file called jquery.signalr that is served from your API. Since you're developing this API locally, you'll need to update the URL to the default URL and port that Visual Studio uses to run your API. In Listing 23.5, you'll need to update the URL as well.

Let's create our new Angular factory that will proxy all messages between SignalR and the rest of our Angular app. Create a new file called `signalrhub.factory.js`. Because we will now be using our API URL in two places (the `artists.service.js` Angular Service and our new signalrhub.factory.js), let's refactor our app a bit and set up the API URL as a constant when we start our app (in app.js):

LISTING 23.5   Updated app.js for API URL Injection

```
 1:   angular.module('app', [])
 2:       .constant('apiUrl', 'http://localhost:8080');
```

Let's inject this `apiUrl` into our `ArtistsManager` service (see Listing 23.6). Note that the base URL doesn't have a trailing slash, so we added these to each call in the service.

LISTING 23.6   Updated ArtistsManager for API URL Injection

```
 1:   (function() {
 2:
 3:   angular.module('app')
```

```
 4:      .service('ArtistsManager', ['$http', 'apiUrl', function($http, apiUrl) {
 5:
 6:        this.getArtists = function() {
 7:          return $http.get(apiUrl + "/api/artists");
 8:        };
 9:
10:        this.createArtist = function(data) {
11:          return $http.post(apiUrl + "/api/artists", data);
12:        };
13:
14:        this.updateArtist = function(id, data) {
15:          return $http.put(apiUrl + "/api/artists/" + id, data);
16:        };
17:
18:        this.deleteArtist = function(id) {
19:          return $http.delete(apiUrl + "/api/artists/" + id);
20:        };
21:
22:    }]);
23:
24:    })();
```

Now, let's build our `SignalRHub` factory (see Listing 23.7), injecting `apiUrl` in the same way. We start with an immediately invoked function expression (IIFE) and by grabbing a reference to our app module. We'll be using `.factory()` here instead of `.service()` because we'll be doing some work outside of the public functions that we expose (specifically, the connection management work). This factory depends on `$rootScope`, so we can run a digest cycle on the root-most scope and on `apiUrl` as discussed earlier. We expose a function that takes a hub name as a parameter. This will allow the component that uses this factory to indicate the hub name that should be used. (This is useful if you have multiple SignalR hubs in one app.)

Inside this function, we start by creating a connection using the Microsoft jQuery SignalR library's `$.hubConnection()` method and creating a proxy on that connection with the given hubName via `connection.createHubProxy()`. Next, we start the connection with `connection.start()` and log a message when the connection is started. Finally, we expose a method called `.on()` that takes an `eventName` and an optional callback function that will be passed in by the component using this service. We simply use the `proxy` object that we created earlier and force an `$apply()` on `$rootScope` with the callback if available.

Figure 23.1 shows the process that the SignalR client library uses to set up a connection with the SignalR server, including the three HTTP requests made to the SignalR server.

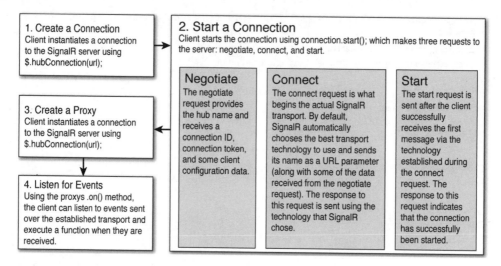

FIGURE 23.1
Request workflow for registering a SignalR client.

LISTING 23.7   SignalRHub Angular Factory

```
1:  (function() {
2:
3:  angular.module('app')
4:    .factory('SignalRHub', ['$rootScope', 'apiUrl',
5:    function ($rootScope, apiUrl) {
6:
7:      return function(hubName) {
8:        var connection = $.hubConnection(apiUrl);
9:        var proxy = connection.createHubProxy(hubName);
10:
11:       connection.start().done(function () {
12:         console.log("SignalR connection started");
13:       });
14:
15:       return {
16:         on: function (eventName, callback) {
17:           proxy.on(eventName, function (result) {
18:             console.log(eventName + " event received.");
19:             $rootScope.$apply(function () {
20:               if (callback) {
21:                 callback(result);
22:               }
23:             });
24:           });
```

```
25:              }
26:            };
27:          };
28:
29:   }]);
30:
31:   })();
```

DID YOU KNOW?

Autogenerated SignalR Proxy

If we weren't using Angular, we could replace our custom `SignalRHub` proxy component with one that is automatically generated by SignalR and served up as dynamic JavaScript. In your HTML, if you include a script reference to /signalr/hubs, the jQuery SignalR library will automatically create a proxy for you to work with (in a slightly different, but overall very similar fashion). For more on this, check out http://www.asp.net/signalr/overview/guide-to-the-api/hubs-api-guide-javascript-client#genproxy.

Finally, let's use this new component in our controller. We start out by injecting it. Then we execute the `factory` function and pass in the name of our hub (`'ArtistHub'`). We then set up the factory's `.on()` method to execute our `getArtists()` method whenever the `getArtists` event is received. Finally, because we are firing this event from the API whenever an artist is added, edited, or deleted, we no longer need to manually call `getArtists()` when these actions occur. Listing 23.8 shows the updated controller code.

LISTING 23.8   Updated ArtistsController with SignalR Interaction

```
1:    (function() {
2:
3:    angular.module('app')
4:    .controller('ArtistsController', ['$sce', 'SignalRHub', 'ArtistsManager',
                  'SpotifyService',
5:    function($sce, SignalRHub, ArtistsManager, SpotifyService) {
6:
7:      var vm = this;
8:      var artistHub = SignalRHub('ArtistHub');
9:      artistHub.on('getArtists', function () {
10:        getArtists();
11:      });
12:
13:      getArtists();
14:
15:      ////////////////
16:
17:      function getArtists() {
```

```
18:        ArtistsManager.getArtists().then(function(response) {
19:          vm.artists = response.data;
20:        });
21:      }
22:
23:      vm.add = function() {
24:        ArtistsManager.createArtist({
25:          name: vm.newArtist.name,
26:          rating: vm.newArtist.rating > 0
27:            ? vm.newArtist.rating
28:            : null
29:        }).then(function() {
30:          vm.newArtist = null;
31:        });
32:      };
33:
34:      vm.editMode = function(artist) {
35:        vm.editArtist = artist;
36:      };
37:
38:      vm.edit = function() {
39:        ArtistsManager.updateArtist(
40:        vm.editArtist.id,
41:        {
42:          name: vm.editArtist.name,
43:          rating: vm.editArtist.rating > 0
44:            ? vm.editArtist.rating
45:            : null
46:        }).then(function() {
47:          vm.editArtist = null;
48:        });
49:      };
50:
51:      vm.delete = function(id) {
52:        ArtistsManager.deleteArtist(id);
53:      };
54:
55:      vm.play = function(name) {
56:        SpotifyService.getSpotifyArtistIdByName(name).then(function(id) {
57:          SpotifyService.getTopTrackURLForArtist(id).then(function(url) {
58:            vm.playUrl = url;
59:          });
60:        });
61:      };
62:
63:      vm.closePlayer = function() {
64:        vm.playUrl = null;
65:      };
66:
```

```
67:    vm.getAudioUrl = function() {
68:      return $sce.trustAsResourceUrl(vm.playUrl);
69:    };
70:
71:  }]);
72:
73:  })();
```

Let's test it out! Open your app in two different browsers. Using the first browser, add an artist. Watch the second browser instantly update. Adding, editing, and deleting artists will trigger a refresh of the artist list on any browser windows you have open. Pretty cool!

Summary

This hour explained motivations behind SignalR and real-time programming in general. Then you learned about OWIN, Katana, and configuring SignalR in the OWIN pipeline. In this hour, we also created a SignalR hub and used it in our API. At the end of this hour, you learned about interacting with this hub from Angular.

Q&A

Q. I'm scaling my API out to multiple servers, and I'm using a load balancer to distribute requests. Because clients will randomly be connected to servers, each with its own SignalR instance, how can I make sure that messages get sent to all clients?

A. In this situation, you are looking for what is called a *backplane*. Instances of your application will send messages to this backplane component, which will in turn forward messages to all other application instances. Fortunately, the Microsoft product team behind SignalR has done much of the heavy lifting behind implementing backplanes for you. If you're running your app on Azure, you can easily configure an Azure Service Bus as the backplane. If you're running your app on-premises, you can configure either a Redis store or SQL Server as the backplane.

Q. I've heard of Socket.IO as a way to do real-time web apps. How is that related?

A. SignalR is a framework for doing real-time apps in the ASP.NET world, but Socket.IO is a framework for doing them in Node.JS. Although there are some Socket.IO clients for ASP.NET, the server must be written in Node.

Q. Why do we need to use `$rootScope.$apply()` when we receive a SignalR message in Angular?

A. Whenever you use other libraries in conjunction with Angular, Angular doesn't "know" about your interactions with these other libraries. You must kick off a digest cycle manually so that Angular knows to update the view. In this instance, we're using the Microsoft jQuery SignalR library.

Workshop

Quiz

1. What is a SignalR hub?

2. What is the difference between OWIN and Katana?

3. What code should you use to configure SignalR in the OWIN pipeline?

4. In your Web API, how do you get a reference to a configured SignalR hub?

5. Using Microsoft's jQuery SignalR library, how do you create a connection and proxy to your SignalR hub?

Answers

1. A SignalR hub is the component responsible for maintaining the state of all connected clients and proxying messages to them as required by your API.

2. OWIN is a specification, Katana is a framework.

3. `app.MapSignalR();`

4. `GlobalHost.ConnectionManager.GetHubContext<ArtistHub>();`

5. `$.hubConnection(locationOfURL)` for creating the connection and `connection.createHubProxy(hubName)` for creating the proxy.

Exercise

For the book management system mentioned in the Introduction, think about how real-time technologies like SignalR could enhance the functionality of the application. Perhaps you could write a component that displays the five most recently added books to any user's list in real time.

HOUR 24
Focus on the Future

What You'll Learn in This Hour:

- ▶ What the status of Angular is
- ▶ What's changing in Angular 2
- ▶ Steps to prepare for Angular 2
- ▶ What role ES6 plays in Angular 2
- ▶ How web components have shaped Angular 2
- ▶ Why Angular 1 is still relevant

Congratulations! You've made it through learning Angular and should now be able to build great applications using Angular with .NET! And now it's all going to change.

Wait, what? Yep, it's true. Angular 2 is coming at some point. And it's not just a complete rewrite of the framework, it's a different mindset and philosophy.

This final hour covers exactly what's changing in Angular 2 and how you can be prepared for its arrival. Don't stress too much about learning Angular 2 and start thinking you've wasted 23 hours of your life learning Angular 1. You'll learn why in this hour.

This hour also covers, at a high level, the latest in web technologies, including ES6, TypeScript, and web components.

You're almost at the finish line. Let's power through!

What's the Current Status of Angular?

At the time of this writing, Angular 2 is in developer preview mode. That means that if you're really daring, you can try to play with it. But it's going to break. There aren't just bugs; it's not even completely written yet. From each build release to the next, there are significant changes, and code you write in one build is likely going to work differently, if at all, in the next build.

There isn't even an anticipated release date yet. Some people are thinking by the end of 2015, some people are saying early 2016. The reality is that even the Angular 2 team doesn't know!

Our philosophy on new technology like this is that it's fun to play with and learn some new concepts, but it's not yet good for much else. Our advice is to use the best technology that's currently available and ready to use. And for now (and for the foreseeable future), that's Angular 1.

Speaking of Angular 1, 1.4 was just released with a number of bug fixes and performance improvements. However, the big piece of functionality that was originally expected to be available in 1.4 was pushed to 1.5: the component router (discussed a bit later this hour).

From this point onward, every point release of Angular 1 is meant to move the framework closer and closer to Angular 2 concepts and syntax to ease the transition to Angular 2. There is no anticipated release date for Angular 1.5 at this time.

So what we know at this point is that Angular 2 is coming, it's going to be drastically different, and it's not ready to do anything meaningful with yet.

What's Changing in Angular 2?

Everything! Just kidding. Kind of. Angular 2 really is almost a completely different framework. The creators of Angular learned a lot over the past couple of years and listened to all the criticisms of the framework: "It's slow." "There are too many concepts." "What's with all of these different services?"

Angular 2 is aiming to solve a lot of these criticisms. In initial tests, Angular 2 is up to five times faster than Angular 1. A lot of that is accomplished by utilizing native features of ES6, so browsers that support the new JavaScript standard will run Angular 2 apps significantly faster.

Although it's the next major release that uses native features of ES6, you can access those features in a couple of different ways. One is to write your Angular apps in ES6 and use a *transpiler* to convert your code to ES5 for browsers that don't support ES6. The most popular transpilers are Traceur and Babel. The other way to utilize ES6 features is to use TypeScript. Angular partnered with Microsoft to actually write Angular 2 using TypeScript. You'll learn a little more about ES6 and TypeScript later this hour.

Another goal the Angular team had was to make the framework much smaller and use simpler concepts. Any Angular 2 code samples you see are going to look much more complex, but it's just a different syntax that you likely aren't used to. A lot of the confusing Angular 1 concepts are being removed in Angular 2. The following is a list of what's being removed or significantly changed in Angular 2:

- ▶ `$scope` (removed)
- ▶ Controllers (removed)
- ▶ Templates (syntax changed)

- ▶ Services (removed)

- ▶ Different directive types (removed and changed)

- ▶ Event bindings (changed)

- ▶ Modules (removed)

That's a lengthy list, and it probably scares you. But trust us when we say that removing a lot of those concepts is going to make things easier. The Angular team is building the second version of the framework with a mindset of making it easy to learn and use.

They've also focused their efforts on making the framework the best it can be to address the criticisms mentioned earlier, even if that means that there isn't an easy migration path from Angular 1 to 2. The philosophy behind building Angular 2 was to create an amazing framework first and then worry about migrations later. So, as of now, there is no migration path.

When the Angular team announced this, there was understandable concern in the Angular community. There are a lot of apps written in Angular 1, including a lot of apps used internally at Google. Rewriting every Angular 1 app from scratch is going to be costly, so Google definitely has an incentive to make sure that there is a way to migrate to 2.

How Can You Prepare for Angular 2?

You can do a few things while the Angular 2 team is finishing up the next edition of the framework. Doing the following things will help you get ready to write apps in Angular 2 and start moving your existing apps to be a little more Angular 2ish.

Use the New Component Router (When It's Ready)

You might remember a few of the shortcomings in ngRoute (Angular's router for version 1) mentioned earlier in this book. As you learned earlier, the Angular team wrote a new router for Angular 2 and is back porting it for Angular 1. It was expected to be released in 1.4, but unfortunately, it wasn't quite ready for use, and so the Angular team pushed the new router to 1.5.

Let's not go into great detail about the new component router because it hasn't been released and is susceptible to change. Even so, this section covers a couple of concepts and provides a code example to give you an idea of what to expect.

The component router is named as such because Angular 2 is turning its focus from modules and controllers and services and moving to a component-based approach to web apps.

Table 24.1 lists some of updates for the new router.

TABLE 24.1   Component Router Versus ngRoute

ngRoute	Component Router
The views are inserted into `ng-view`.	Component templates are inserted into `ng-outlet`.
Only supports single views.	Supports nested views as well as sibling views.
Uses regular HTML links to navigate between views.	Uses `ng-link` to navigate between views.

The new router is convention based, and as long as you follow a few naming conventions, it takes care of some magic for you. Even though controllers and *ControllerAs* aren't core concepts of Angular 2, they are very much core to Angular 1. So instead of having to specify those in the component router, it takes care of it for you, as long as your files follow convention. Suppose you want to route to a books view with its controller. Take a look at Listing 24.1.

LISTING 24.1   Component Router

```
1:  //app.js
2:  $router.config([
3:    { path: '/books', component: 'books' }
4:  ]);
```

In this route, there's no mention of a controller, or ControllerAs. So, how does the router know what view and controller this route should use? The router looks in a folder called components, and inside of there should be a folder with the name of your component. That component then will need a template with the component name with an .html extension for the view. For the controller, the router looks for a controller with the component name and the suffix of Controller; the ControllerAs alias will simply be the component name. So for the earlier example, we need our template to be in the following path

```
/components/books/books.html
```

and to have a controller named `booksController`. The ControllerAs alias will just be `books`.

But what if your folder layout doesn't already use a components directory and that naming convention? The component router allows you to configure what path to look at and what controller to specify by using `$componentMapper` (see Listing 24.2).

LISTING 24.2   Configuring Component Router

```
1:  //custom template location
2:  $componentMapper.setTemplateMapping(function(name){
3:    //following the application organization mentioned in hour 13,
```

```
 4:    //we have our features separated by folder, so we want templates
 5:    //in a path like "./books/books.html"
 6:    return './' + name + '/' + name + '.html';
 7:  });
 8:
 9:  //custom controller mapping
10:  $componentMapper.setCtrlNameMapping(function(name){
11:    //following the same organization strategy,
12:    //we don't want anything appended to our controller names
13:    return name;
14:  });
```

Currently, there's another alternative to configure the router to use a different application organization structure: specify the view inside of your controller. However, this tightly couples that view to the controller in code, so we're not fans of this method.

Use ControllerAs Syntax

We strongly recommended using ControllerAs regardless of your plans for Angular 2; but with Angular 2 getting rid of $scope, now is as good a time as any for you to cut ties with it, too.

Learn TypeScript

You don't have to use TypeScript for Angular 2 applications, but the Angular developers wrote the framework itself using TypeScript. A lot of examples and resources you find will use TypeScript, as well. Angular 2 uses a lot of features of ES6 that you'll need to transpile anyway, and TypeScript will do that as well.

TypeScript is a superset of JavaScript that brings in features from ES6 and ES7. It also includes features that you're familiar with as a C# developer, such as classes, interfaces, type checking, and generics.

Again, we're not going to go into specifics of TypeScript here; that would take an entire book by itself. And you don't need to run straight out and learn TypeScript as soon as you set this book down. Your Angular 1 applications are just fine using plain old JavaScript. But when you're ready in several months to start playing with Angular 2, take a look at TypeScript.

ES6

The next version of JavaScript, ES6 (short for ECMAScript 6), introduced so many great new features that the next version of Angular will simply use those to replace features that were in the original version of Angular.

One of those is modules. ES6 introduced importing modules, as well as lazy loading modules. Angular's current modules and the current method of dependency injection will be going away.

Additionally, the built-in event system of ES6 has enabled Angular to get rid of some of the event binding directives from Angular 1. Now, instead of an ng-click, you can just use the native browser event handlers (see Listing 24.3). A word of warning, though, the syntax is different, but don't let it scare you.

LISTING 24.3   Native Event Binding with ES6

```
1:   //books.html
2:   <div>
3:     <div id="bookName" #bookName>AngularJS 2</div>
4:     <button (click)="addBook(bookName)">Add Book</button>
5:   </div>
```

Here we're using the native browser click handler, which is surrounded by parentheses. We told you it'd look funny. It's perfectly valid syntax for ES6, though, and soon many more browsers will begin supporting it.

You'll also notice #bookName in the div above the button. That associates the div with that DOM object, and allows the addBook function to actually access the DOM element, and not just an ID or DOM element wrapper.

Web Components

As you've read a number of times throughout this book, one of the most maintainable and extensible ways you can build an application is with small, reusable components. That's what web components aim to do, and that's the mindset the Angular team is following as well. You might be thinking that we already have something like this with element-style directives. And you're right. These types of directives will now be known as *components* in Angular 2, as shown in Figure 24.1. The attribute directives you learned about in Hour 9, "Using Built-In Directives," will just be known as *directives*.

What's so different, then? Well, Angular 2 is going all in with components. An Angular 2 application should be constructed as a tree of components, where every piece of functionality and logic in an application lives in a component that can easily be swapped out.

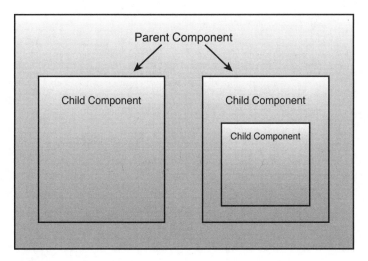

FIGURE 24.1
Angular 2 tree of components.

What's also different about this approach is the syntax. It's definitely different from what you're used to. If you're familiar with C# and using attributes to decorate methods and classes, however, you should feel right at home. Components are essentially a class that represents an element on the screen. Listing 24.4 shows an example in TypeScript.

LISTING 24.4   Angular 2 Component with TypeScript

```
 1:  //BookComponent
 2:  @Component({
 3:    selector: 'book'
 4:  })
 5:  @View({
 6:    template: `
 7:      <h1>{{ currentBook }}</h1>
 8:      <rating></rating>
 9:    `,
10:    directives: [PriceComponent]
11:  })
12:  class BookComponent {
13:    message: string;
14:
15:    constructor() {
16:      this.currentBook = "Teach Yourself AngularJS 2";
17:    }
18:  }
```

```
19:
20:  //RatingComponent
21:  @Component({
22:    selector: 'rating'
23:  })
24:  @View({
25:    template: `
26:      <h2>{{ averageRating }}</h2>
27:    `
28:  })
29:  class RatingComponent {
30:    averageRating: string;
31:
32:    constructor() {
33:      this.averageRating = "5 Stars";
34:    }
35:  }
36:
37:  <!-- view -->
38:  <book></book>
```

The first thing in this example that might jump out at you is the @ symbols. What on earth are they doing there? Those are the attributes that decorate the class and tell it that it's a component and has a view. That syntax is specific to TypeScript and Angular 2, but the concept behind it is almost exactly the same as if you were to add attributes to a C# class.

The next thing we need to talk about is that class sitting in those components. That's definitely different from the JavaScript we know and love. But classes are coming in ES6, and TypeScript makes liberal use of them. Essentially, though, the class in Angular 2 is just taking the place of the controller.

And finally, you can see how our book component has a child component called rating. This is how Angular 2 apps are constructed, as you saw in Figure 24.1. Although the syntax is quite a bit different, the concepts really are similar to constructing Angular 1 apps using lots of element directives, as shown in Figure 24.2.

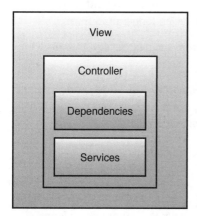
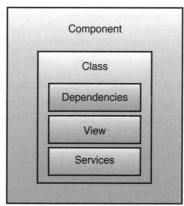

FIGURE 24.2
Angular 2 architecture versus Angular 1 architecture.

Our class is simply replacing the idea of a controller, and the class is decorated with "metadata annotations" such as the view and component attributes.

BY THE WAY

Syntax Is Subject to Change

Remember, Angular 2 is undergoing significant changes still. Even though this syntax is not in a final state, the concepts are fairly mature and shouldn't alter significantly from what you've learned here. It's still possible, though!

Why the First 23 Hours of This Book Are More Important Than This Last Hour

It's true that Angular is changing. But the web is changing, browsers are changing, and the machines we run them on are changing. To keep up with new technologies, the framework needed a complete rewrite. That rewrite is going to take some time.

The current state of Angular 2 is nowhere near ready to be used for a production application. And it won't be for months.

If you are starting a new project now, or in the next several months, you should use Angular 1. The latest version of Angular 1 is mature and reliable. Use the best technology and frameworks available to you now. Just because Angular 2 is on its way doesn't mean you don't have apps to write today.

Google is going to support Angular 1 for at least 2 years following the official release of Angular 2. And with the number of applications the Angular community has written with Angular 1, our guess is that community support is going to last even longer than that.

Regardless of when Angular 2 is ready, any app that you build in the next several months with Angular 1 is still going to work for years to come.

If you're the type of developer who really loves to use only the newest stuff, write your current apps with Angular 1 (it's still the newest stuff), and when Angular 2 is ready, you can use it to write any new components; Angular 2 can run concurrently with Angular 1.

Summary

This final hour took a very high-level overview of the status of Angular and what the future holds for Angular 2. There are a number of new concepts and technologies that Angular 2 is founded on, including TypeScript, ES6, and web components. Angular 2 is getting rid of a number of concepts, though, including controllers, modules, and `$scope`. In this hour, you also learned about the new component router, and how to make sure you're ready for the Angular 2 release at the end of 2015 or early 2016. This hour talked in more depth about components and Angular 2, and then wrapped up by covering why Angular 1 is still important for building solid web apps.

Q&A

Q. Do I have to use TypeScript for Angular 2?

A. Absolutely not. TypeScript is completely optional (but recommended) for Angular 2. It simply provides more features and more structure on top of JavaScript. JavaScript purists aren't the biggest fans of TypeScript, but most C# developers seem to like the features it provides around classes, interfaces, and generics. If learning both TypeScript and Angular 2 (when it's released) is too much, you can write an Angular 2 app in plain, good old JavaScript.

Q. I thought I heard something about AtScript. Is that another option besides TypeScript?

A. When the Angular team started working on Angular 2, they created AtScript to harness the power of ES6 while integrating Angular 2 features into it. After working with Microsoft, however, the two teams decided to merge the languages into TypeScript. AtScript is no more.

Workshop

Quiz

1. When is Angular 2 going to be released?

2. Which version of Angular should you use to write new apps in right now?

3. True or False: The component router is incompatible with Angular 1?

Answers

1. No one knows for sure, but its tentative release date is near the end of 2015 or early 2016.

2. The latest version of Angular 1. Angular 2 is definitely not ready to use for anything but experimentation.

3. False. Even though the Angular team pushed back the release of the component router, it was back ported to work with Angular 1 and should be useable in Angular 1 apps when it's released.

Exercise

Check out the Angular 2 documentation and examples at Angular.io. But don't spend too much time on it; you've got Angular 1 apps to write.

Index

Symbols

C

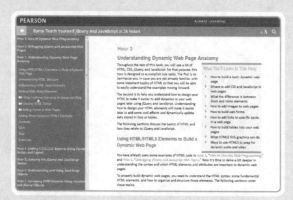
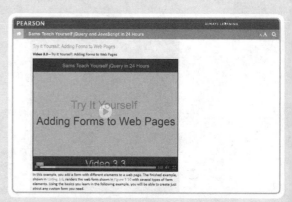
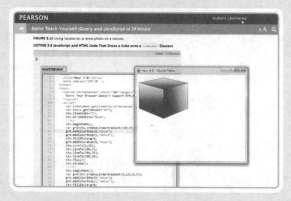
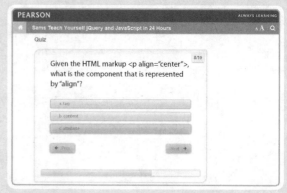